CHRISTIAN
POLITICAL
WITNESS

Edited by George Kalantzis
& Gregory W. Lee

IVP Academic

An imprint of InterVarsity Press
Downers Grove, Illinois

InterVarsity Press
P.O. Box 1400, Downers Grove, IL 60515-1426
World Wide Web: www.ivpress.com
Email: email@ivpress.com

InterVarsity Press® is the book-publishing division of InterVarsity Christian Fellowship/USA®, a movement of students and faculty active on campus at hundreds of universities, colleges and schools of nursing in the United States of America, and a member movement of the International Fellowship of Evangelical Students. For information about local and regional activities, write Public Relations Dept., InterVarsity Christian Fellowship/USA, 6400 Schroeder Rd., P.O. Box 7895, Madison, WI 53707-7895, or visit the IVCF website at www.intervarsity.org.

Cover design: Cindy Kiple
Interior design: Beth Hagenberg
Images: Pontius Pilate's Second Interrogation of Christ, by Duccio di Buoninsegna / De Agostini Picture Library / G.
Nimatallah / The Bridgeman Art Library
old paper: © peter zelei/iStockphoto
sari borders: © hpkalyani/iStockphoto

ISBN 978-0-8308-4051-9 (print)
ISBN 978-0-8308-9620-2 (digital)

Printed in the United States of America ∞

Library of Congress Cataloging-in-Publication Data
A catalog record for this book is available from the Library of Congress.

P 25 24 23 22 21 20 19 18 17 16 15 14 13 12 11 10 9 8 7 6 5 4 3 2 1

Y 35 34 33 32 31 30 29 28 27 26 25 24 23 22 21 20 19 18 17 16 15 14

Dedicated to the students of
Wheaton College
past, present and future

Beati pacifici,
quoniam filii Dei vocabuntur.
Beati qui persecutionem patiuntur propter iustitiam,
quoniam ipsorum est regnum caelorum.

Christo et regno eius.

CONTENTS

INTRODUCTION

George Kalantzis and Gregory W. Lee

On October 28, 312, Constantine won arguably the most fateful military victory in the history of Christianity. Having crossed the Alps during the spring of that year, Constantine had his eyes set on Rome, where his rival for the imperial throne ruled. Some time before the battle, as later authors would recount, Constantine experienced a vision of a cross in the sky, coupled with an inscription that read, "By this conquer." The Romans were used to signs and visions indicating the favor or disfavor of the gods, and Constantine knew immediately what to do. He had a copy of this sign made for his protection and a Christian symbol inscribed on his soldiers' shields, and prepared for war.

Constantine would proceed to defeat Maxentius and his troops decisively at the Milvian Bridge, an important entrance into Rome that crossed the Tiber River. But what exactly this victory meant would be debated even in Constantine's era. His greatest hagiographer, Eusebius of Caesarea, would compare the moment to the exodus. Like Moses, Constantine grew up in the household of a pagan ruler (not Pharaoh, but the emperor Diocletian) yet managed to remain faithful to the one true God. Moses' task was to deliver his people from tyrannical oppression; Constantine's was the same. And when Maxentius sank like a stone into the Tiber River, was that not like Pharaoh and his armies drowning in the Red Sea after Moses and the Israelites had crossed on dry ground?

Certainly, Eusebius had contemporary events on his side. Constantine would assume sole rule over the Roman West and soon issue with Licinius, his Eastern counterpart, a momentous decree of religious toleration. Promul-

gated in February 313, the "Edict of Milan" did not make Christianity the official religion of the Roman Empire, but it did legalize and promote Christianity throughout Rome's territories. Christians won the right to worship.
Seized territories were returned. Bishops received imperial powers. Enormous
churches were constructed. Scribes produced new copies of Scripture, some
of which remain our most important manuscripts today. Within a few generations, in 380, Christianity would complete the transition from suspicious "su-
perstition" to state religion when Emperor Theodosius I inscribed the faith
into law.

But what happens if circumstances change? In 410, fewer than two decades
after pagan religion was banned in 393, Rome was sacked for the first time in
hundreds of years. Romans who had never appreciated the Christian takeover
had a ready explanation: the gods were angry that Rome had abandoned its
traditional religion. This was divine retribution for converting to the God of
Jesus. In the massive *City of God*, Augustine took up his pen against such critics,
but his response posed as much of a challenge to the Christians of his day as to
the pagans. It was silly to blame Christ for Rome's recent calamity, when Rome
had suffered much worse long before the incarnation. God's mysterious will
cannot be read off the vagaries of temporal events in the first place. There is, at
bottom, no difference between the presumption of Christ's favor after some
military triumph and the attribution of some physical calamity to the wrath of
the gods. Each reduces worship to the attainment of earthly goods.

Moreover, God has not aligned himself with any one political community,
no matter its power or the duration of its reign—no community, that is, except
for the heavenly city, which is God's people. But this community lives a very
different existence from earthly orders. As Augustine argued, in a tradition of
Christian writers extending back to the second century, other peoples put
their hope in temporal reward, but the city of God looks for eternal blessing,
walking by faith and not by sight, as a pilgrim in a foreign land. During this
temporal existence, the heavenly city does need earthly goods, as does the
earthly city, but it will only pursue them for the sake of heavenly things. The
politics of God's people will therefore not conform to the politics of the world,
though there may be some room for cooperation and common ground. For
the goals of the two cities cannot finally be aligned.

Seventeen hundred years after the Edict of Milan, Christians continue to wrestle with the relation between church and state. What might a distinctively Christian witness mean in an increasingly polarized climate where the immensity of the challenges governments face seems matched only by the partisanship of the political system? What is the proper Christian response to unending wars, burgeoning debt, disregard for civil liberties, attacks on the sanctity of life, and economic injustice, not to mention ongoing challenges to traditional understandings of sexuality and marriage? Are Christians anything more than an interest group, open to manipulation by those who most enticingly promise to preserve a certain way of life? And how will Christians respond to their increasingly marginalized status in the West, where Christendom is at least on the wane, if not, as some have suggested, proceeding to its slow and final death?

The twenty-second Wheaton Theology Conference, held on the campus of Wheaton College in April 2013, furnished an opportunity to consider these questions afresh. Despite the variety of perspectives and approaches the presenters contributed, one may note in these essays a certain commonality of theme: Christians must remind themselves that the primary locus of Christian political activity is the church. We do not finally put our trust in military power, economic might or even the wisdom of founding fathers. Our faith is ultimately in Jesus Christ and his love for the community he founded. The shape of our corporate life should therefore reflect above all else fidelity to him, and not just identity politics or pragmatic concerns.

No one in contemporary theological discussion has insisted more persistently on the difference church makes than Stanley Hauerwas, so this volume begins with his defense of the church as a material culture defined by concrete practices and habits. The church's politics cannot accommodate the privatization of religion, as the Enlightenment would have us believe. The assertion that Jesus Christ is the Lord of the universe is no matter of personal opinion, and the church is indeed called to public witness. The great twentieth-century example of this vision is Karl Barth, whose rejection of any theology rooted primarily in human experience not only animated his assertion of God as God but also illuminated his perception of the threat Hitler posed. Yet, as Barth himself would learn, this God has embraced humanity in the person of Jesus Christ, and it is precisely Christ's materiality that grounds the church's politics and its hope before an uncertain future.

One way of reading Hauerwas's essay is that commitment to scriptural authority is critical to Christian fidelity but cannot secure moral discernment in the absence of the virtues that enable Scripture to be heard properly. Mark A. Noll's essay presents a more explicit warning in that regard, charting the ways preachers used the Bible both to oppose and affirm slavery during the era of the American Civil War. The Bible was very much the nation's book, and these preachers all shared a high reverence for Scripture. Yet their presumptive use of biblical rhetoric in support of partisan political agendas, their failure to recognize their own cultural presuppositions, and their heretical assumption of American exceptionalism combined in many cases to equate America's race-based slavery with the rather different institutions in view during the times of the Old and New Testaments. Thankfully, not all preachers fell into such traps, and Noll presents as a positive counterexample those more carefully attuned to the historical context of the biblical writings, the progressive character of revelation and the basis of biblical ethics in biblical theology.

So much for clearing the brush. The next three essays consider the witness of Scripture and early Christianity concerning the church's politics. Scot McKnight begins with Jesus' own example, focusing especially on Jesus' teaching about the kingdom of God. This term is best understood against Jesus' Jewish context as "the redeemed community under Jesus," and bears strong eschatological, ecclesial, christological and ethical valences. Indeed, the kingdom is essentially the church, whose politics are characterized by love, divine power and the cross. These dynamics can be seen most clearly in Jesus' responses to Pilate and Herod, his teachings on taxes and especially his entrance into Jerusalem, which marked Jesus' rejection of triumphalism as well as his public protest against the temple system.

Timothy G. Gombis turns his attention to Paul. Against common assumptions about Paul's theology, Gombis argues that Paul's gospel is thoroughly political, a quality best discerned against the narrative backdrop of Israel's hope for the restoration of *shalom*, the flourishing of creation and humanity under God. Preconversion Paul persecuted Christians because he considered them a threat to God's deliverance of Israel from her enemies. His experience on the road to Damascus helped him to see that God's work of salvation would take time, that God's politics must be shaped by the cross and that God's new *polis* embraced all nations under Christ. Gombis also addresses ongoing debates on how to interpret Paul's exhortation in Romans 13 to submit to earthly authorities, and whether Paul's political rhetoric was meant to encourage direct opposition to the Roman Empire.

George Kalantzis's essay switches gears from the Jewish context of the New Testament to the Roman context of the early church. Roman politics was intimately intertwined with Roman religion and a perpetual cycle of mutual exchange between humans and the gods. Christian refusal to participate in pagan sacrifice thus constituted a rejection of Rome's whole sacred world as well as a challenge to Roman identity itself. Christian martyrdom presented an alternate model of sacrifice in imitation of Christ that subverted Rome's power precisely through the embrace of nonviolent resistance. Because early Christians did not consider Christ's command to love one's enemies compatible with violent aggression, they instructed catechumens and believers in the military to refuse the order to kill others and to leave the military if possible.

Jana Marguerite Bennett's essay marks a transition into contemporary issues, presenting church and family as topics for political theology. These institutions are generally considered "private" space, in distinction from the "public" sphere of the nation-state, though it is often recognized that well-functioning families contribute to the public good. Despite their superficial political differences, conservatives and liberals both presume this distinction between private and public, along with the centrality of the individual and his or her rights. Bennett challenges this Enlightenment perspective by suggesting ways the new creation inaugurated by Christ reconfigures individual, family and state, as well as the distinction between private and public. The establishment of the church challenges especially the significance of family and state, though the New Testament authors do not entirely work out the implications.

William T. Cavanaugh's essay considers a next level of society, that of corporations. Cavanaugh takes his cue from the 2010 decision of the United States Supreme Court in *Citizens United v. Federal Election Commission* to grant corporations the same legal status as people. While Cavanaugh agrees with the dissent that this was a disastrous decision, he disagrees with the reason. Both classical and Christian traditions have stressed the individual's identity as part of a corporate body. In modernity, as political communities have come to be described by social contract theory, the body has become an image instead for the business corporation. The market economy has, in turn, become

a model for liberal democracy, where elections represent individual pref-
erence rather than sustained attention to the common good. Lost in this dynamic is a concern for social solidarity and equality, precisely the concerns the
church must address. What *Citizens United* got wrong was thus the emphasis
on business corporations and not the idea of corporate personhood itself.

The next two essays consider politics at the level of the nation-state, both
focusing on the question of violence. Peter J. Leithart asserts the Bible's absolute opposition to violence, defined as "unjust and sinful use of force." A
survey of the Old and New Testaments reveals that God's destruction of his
enemies does not constitute violence, while violence can encompass a wide
range of social sins not limited to physical harm. God's "war against violence"
reveals his refusal to overlook evil and serves as a paradigm for human
judgment. Contemporary theorists have valorized violence as an energizing
and creative force and as the necessary precondition for the state's power. The
church, by contrast, is a community of peace that absorbs violence in imitation of Christ. Leithart ends his essay by noting the failure of the church's
witness in its uncritical support for the military-industrial complex.

Daniel M. Bell Jr. considers the question of just war, which he presents in
two radically different forms: just war as Christian discipleship and just war
as public policy checklist. The latter primarily concerns nation-states and international law; the former concerns the church and the formation of virtues.
Bell brings this contrast to relief by considering the classic criteria of the just
war tradition: legitimate authority, just cause, right intention, last resort, reasonable chance of success, discrimination and proportionality. Should the
justice of a particular conflict be determined primarily by heads of states, or
by heads of state under the oversight of the church, with individual soldiers
given the right to exercise selective conscientious objection? Does proportionality permit overwhelming military force or only the minimum necessary
to advance a just and highly restricted goal? Bell then provides a series of reflections on the way worship shapes Christians in the virtues necessary to
conduct war justly.

These questions about violence naturally lead into the next essay, Jennifer M.
McBride's treatment of repentance as political witness. McBride highlights
the polarization of both society and churches on political controversies,
noting the contaminating effect of triumphalism in shutting down productive

conversation. She thus proposes a non-triumphalist witness that better pro-
motes the common good in imitation of the crucified Christ. McBride draws
particularly on the example of the Eleuthero Community, an evangelical congregation committed to ecological care that displays the value of confession
and repentance in working with other organizations. The theological foundation for such a witness is Christology, especially Bonhoeffer's emphasis on
Christ's solidarity with sinners. While Christ was indeed sinless, his assumption of human sin permits his public work to be understood as an act of
repentance. By imitating God's presence in public life, the church may also
participate in Christ's redemptive work—not by presenting itself as morally
superior to other communities, a temptation for Christians across the political
spectrum, but by acknowledging its own complicity in sin and thus directing
others to God.

The final two essays may be taken as a charge to action. David P. Gushee
notes the absence in evangelicalism of a social teaching tradition, which one
might find in Roman Catholicism or mainline Protestantism. His own work
has attempted to address this lacuna with a "social ethics of costly practical
solidarity with the oppressed." Gushee presents his reflections on ten contemporary issues that tend to attract much controversy: abortion, creation care,
the death penalty, economic justice, gay rights, gun control, immigration,
torture, US war making and women's rights. For some of these issues, the
proper approach involves some measure of balance: Christians should
promote the sanctity of life, but they must also foster environments where
children can be welcomed and women with crisis pregnancies will find community and financial support. On other issues, Gushee presents a more prophetic voice: there is no moral legitimation for America's post-9/11 use of
torture on suspected terrorists, and evangelicals should frankly be ashamed of
themselves for supporting torture more than people of other faiths or of no
faith do.

Archbishop David Gitari considers the implications of Jesus' teaching in
John 17 that Christians are in the world but not of it. Drawing on the 1976
Bossey Statement on church attitudes toward political powers, the 1974 Lau-
sanne Covenant edited by John Stott, and his own experiences in Kenya,
Gitari argues that Christian engagement with the world should involve social-
political action and not just evangelism. This position draws theological

support from the doctrines of creation, humanity and the incarnation, as well as reflection on the kingdom of God and the ministry of the prophets. As an Anglican bishop in Kenya, Gitari publicly challenged authorities for the assassination of powerful politicians and for rigging elections. This witness almost cost him his life in 1989 when thugs raided his home to murder him and his family, an incident that has still not received proper resolution. Gitari would advise Christian leaders against identifying too closely with any one politician or political party, but would support laypeople joining political life for the purpose of Christian witness. Still, he warns, Christian social-political action goes beyond humanitarian efforts to challenge the powers that be, and this will naturally invite resistance Christians must confront and not simply avoid.

▪ ▪ ▪

This volume has been made possible because of the longstanding partnership between Wheaton College's Department of Biblical and Theological Studies and InterVarsity Press. The 2013 Wheaton Theology Conference was also sponsored by The Wheaton Center for Early Christian Studies, whose mission to promote historical and theological engagement with the early church's witness complemented the vision for this year's conference particularly well. The editors are grateful to Bob Fryling, Gary Deddo and the whole IVP team for their unflagging support of the conference. David Congdon deserves special recognition for bringing this volume to completion. Jeffrey Greenman, Wheaton's outgoing associate dean of biblical and theological studies, provided leadership and encouragement at every phase of this project. Kristina Unzicker was the administrative guru who made the conference possible, Jillian Marcantonio played a critical role in the last stages of editing, and Shalon Park labored over the indices. Archbishop Gitari passed away before this volume could come to fruition. We are honored to include his call to sociopolitical involvement as final remarks from a life well lived. We dedicate this volume to the countless students of Wheaton College who engage in the very political act of bearing witness to the Lord Jesus Christ in all they do.

1

CHURCH MATTERS

Stanley Hauerwas

THE THEOLOGICAL POLITICS OF THE "AND"

I am a Christian.[1] I am even a Christian theologian. I observe in my memoir, *Hannah's Child*, that you do not need to be a theologian to be a Christian, but I probably did. Being a Christian has not and does not come naturally or easy for me. I take that to be a good thing because I am sure that to be a Christian requires training that lasts a lifetime. I am more than ready to acknowledge that some may find being a Christian comes more "naturally," but that can present its own difficulties. Just as an athlete with natural gifts may fail to develop the fundamental skills necessary to play their sport after their talent fades, so people naturally disposed to faith may fail to develop the skills necessary to sustain them for a lifetime.

By training I mean something very basic such as acquiring habits of speech necessary for prayer. The acquisition of such habits is crucial for the formation of our bodies if we are to acquire the virtues necessary to live life as Christians. For I take it to be crucial that Christians must live in such a manner that our lives are unintelligible if the God we worship in Jesus Christ does not exist. The training entailed in being a Christian can be called, if you are so disposed, culture. That is particularly the case if, as Raymond Williams reminds us in *Keywords, culture* is a term first used as a process noun to describe the tending or cultivation of a crop or animal.[2] One of the challenges Christians confront

---

[1]This chapter is in honor of Stan Grenz, who from an evangelical perspective helped us to see why the church matters.

[2]Raymond Williams, *Keywords: A Vocabulary of Culture and Society* (New York: Oxford University Press, 1976), pp. 77-78.

is how the politics we helped create has made it difficult to sustain the material practices constitutive of an ecclesial culture necessary to produce Christians.

The character of much of modern theology exemplifies this development. In the attempt to make Christianity intelligible within the epistemological conceits of modernity, theologians have been intent on showing that what we believe as Christians is not that different than what those who are not Christians believe. Thus MacIntyre's wry observation that the project of modern theology to distinguish the kernel of the Christian faith from the outmoded husk has resulted in offering atheists less and less in which to disbelieve.[3]

It should not be surprising, as David Yeago argues, that many secular people now assume that descriptions of reality Christians employ are a sort of varnish that can be scraped away to reveal a more basic account of what has always been the case. From a secular point of view it is assumed that we agree, or should agree, on fundamental naturalistic and secular descriptions of reality, whatever religious elaborations may lay over them. What I find so interesting is that many Christians accept these naturalistic assumptions about the way things are because they believe by doing so it is possible to transcend our diverse particularities that otherwise result in unwelcome conflict. From such a perspective it is only a short step to the key sociopolitical move crucial to the formation of modern societies, that is, the relegation of religion to the sphere of private inwardness and individual motivation.[4]

Societies that have relegated strong convictions to the private—a development I think appropriately identified as "secularization"—may assume a tolerant or intolerant attitude toward the church, but the crucial characteristic of such societies is that the church is understood to be no more than a voluntary association of like-minded individuals.[5] Even those who identify as "religious" assume their religious convictions should be submitted to a public

---

[3]Alasdair MacIntyre, *The Religious Significance of Atheism* (New York: Columbia University Press, 1966), p. 24.
[4]David Yeago, "Messiah's People: The Culture of the Church in the Midst of the Nations," in *Pro Ecclesia* VI/1, pp. 147-48.
[5]I have no intention to enter into the never-ending debates about secularization and the corresponding discussions concerning the demise of religion. Suffice it to say I am in general sympathetic with David Martin's contention that secularization is best understood in terms of social differentiation correlative of the division of labor with the result that discrete sectors of social life are assumed autonomous. See David Martin, *The Future of Christianity: Reflections on Violence and Democracy, Religion and Secularization* (Surrey: Ashgate, 2011), p. 124.

order governed by a secular rationality. I hope to challenge that assumption by calling into question the conceptual resources that now seem to be givens for how the church is understood. In particular I hope to convince Christians that the church is a material reality that must resist the domestication of our faith in the interest of societal peace.

There is a great deal going against such a project. For example, in his book *Civil Religion: A Dialogue in the History of Political Philosophy*, Ronald Beiner argues that in modernity the attempt to domesticate strong religious convictions in the interest of state control has assumed two primary and antithetical alternatives: civil religion or liberalism. Civil religion is the attempt to empower religion not for the good of religion but for the creation of the citizen. Indeed the very creation of "religion" as a concept more fundamental than a determinative tradition is a manifestation that, at least in Western societies, Christianity has become "civil."[6] Rousseau, according to Beiner, is the decisive figure who gave expression to this transformation because Rousseau saw clearly that the modern state could not risk having a church capable of challenging its political authority.[7] In the process the political concepts used to legitimize the modern state, at least if Carl Schmitt is right, have been secularized theological concepts.[8]

In contrast to civil religion, the liberal alternative rejects all attempts to use religion to produce citizens in service to the state. Liberalism in its many versions, according to Beiner, seeks to domesticate or neutralize the effect of religious commitment on political life.[9] Liberalism may well result in the production of a banal and flattened account of human existence, but such a form of life seems necessary if we are to be at peace with one another. In other words, liberalism as a way of life depends on the creation of people who think there is nothing for which it's worth dying. Such a way of life was exemplified by President Bush's suggestion that the duty of Americans after September 11, 2001, was to go shopping. Such a view of the world evoked Nietzsche's bitter

---

[6]Bill Cavanaugh provides an invaluable account of how the creation of "religion" was a correlative of the modern state. See his *The Myth of Religious Violence* (New York: Oxford University Press, 2009), pp. 60-71.
[7]Ronald Beiner, *Civil Religion: A Dialogue in the History of Political Philosophy* (Cambridge: Cambridge University Press, 2011), pp. 1-7.
[8]Carl Schmitt, *Political Theology: Four Chapters on the Concept of Sovereignty* (Chicago: University of Chicago Press, 2005), pp. 5, 35.
[9]Beiner, *Civil Religion*, pp. 301-5.

condemnation, ironically making Nietzsche an ally of a Christianity determined by martyrdom.[10]

An extraordinary claim to be sure, but as Paul Kahn has observed, the
Western state exists "under the very real threat of Christian martyrdom; a
threat to expose the state and its claim to power as nothing at all."[11] The martyr
does so, according to Kahn, because when everything is said and done sacrifice is always stronger than murder. The martyr wields a power that defeats
the murderer because the martyr can be remembered by a community more
enduring than the state. That is why the liberal state has such a stake in the
domestication of Christianity by making it but another lifestyle choice.

In contrast, the modern nation-state, Kahn argues, has been an extremely
effective sacrificial agent able to mobilize its populations to make sacrifices to
sustain its existence as an end in itself. The nation-state, therefore, has stepped
into the place of religious belief, offering the individual the possibility of transcending one's finitude. War becomes the act of sacrifice by which the state
sustains the assumption that though we die it can and will continue to exist
without end.[12]

I have earned the description of being "fideistic, sectarian, tribalist" because of my attempt to imagine an ecclesial alternative capable of resisting the
politics Beiner and Kahn describe.[13] For as Yeago observes, most churches in
the West, with the possible exception of the Roman Catholics, have acqui-
esced in this understanding of their social character and have therefore col-
laborated in the eclipse of their ecclesial reality.[14] As a result the church seems

---

[10]Ibid., pp. 374-94.

[11]Paul Kahn, *Putting Liberalism in Its Place* (Princeton: Princeton University Press, 2005), p. 82.

[12]Ibid., pp. 276-77. I am indebted to Sean Larsen for suggesting the importance of Kahn's understanding of
liberalism for the argument I am making in this chapter.

[13]Kahn argues that there is a liberalism of the will that can and does demand sacrifice. Liberalism of interest
and reason, however, cannot acknowledge the sacrifices required by the state. The result is what Kahn
calls the "paradox of democratic self-government," that is, "the more the nation believes itself to be a
product of the will of the popular sovereign, the less democratic it becomes—if by democratic, we mean
subject to control through broadly participatory electoral mechanisms." Kahn suggests this is the modern
form of Rousseau's distinction between the general will and the will of all; *Putting Liberalism in Its Place*,
p. 161.

[14]For an extremely informative comparison of the Catholic and Protestant responses to secularization, see
Martin, *The Future of Christianity*, pp. 25-44. Emile Perreau-Saussine's *Catholicism and Democracy: An
Essay in the History of Political Thought* (Princeton: Princeton University Press, 2011) is a fascinating account of how the rise of the political importance of the papacy after the French Revolution was at once
the manifestation as well as the result of the Catholic agreement with the liberal presumption that there
is "something irreducibly secular about the modern state"; p. 2.

caught in a "ceaseless crisis of legitimation" in which the church must find a justification for its existence in terms of the projects and aspirations of that larger order.[15]

In his extraordinary book *Atheist Delusions: The Christian Revolution and Its Fashionable Enemies*, David Bentley Hart observes that the relegation of Christian beliefs to the private sphere is legitimated by a story of human freedom in which humankind is liberated from the crushing weight of tradition and doctrine. Hart, whose prose begs for extensive quotation, says the story goes like this:

> Once upon a time Western humanity was the cosseted and incurious ward of Mother Church; during this, the age of faith, culture stagnated, science languished, wars of religion were routinely waged, witches were burned by inquisitors, and Western humanity labored in brutish subjugation to dogma, superstition, and the unholy alliance of church and state. Withering blasts of fanaticism and fideism had long since scorched away the last remnants of classical learning; inquiry was stifled; the literary remains of classical antiquity had long ago been consigned to the fires of faith, and even the great achievements of "Greek science" were forgotten until Islamic civilization restored them to the West. All was darkness. Then, in the wake of the "wars of religion" that had torn Christendom apart, came the full flowering of the Enlightenment and with it the reign of reason and progress, the riches of scientific achievement and political liberty, and a new and revolutionary sense of human dignity. The secular nation-state arose, reduced religion to an establishment of the state, and thereby rescued Western humanity from the blood-steeped intolerance of religion. Now, at last, Western humanity has left its nonage and attained its majority, in science, politics, and ethics. The story of the travails of Galileo almost invariably occupies an honored place in this narrative, as exemplary of the natural relation between "faith" and "reason" and as an exquisite epitome of scientific reason's mighty struggle during the early modern period to free itself from the tyranny of religion.[16]

This "simple and enchanting tale" is, Hart observes, captivating in its explanatory power. According to Hart, however, there is just one problem with this story. The problem is that every detail of the story, as well as the over-

---

[15]Yeago, "Messiah's People," pp. 148-49.
[16]David Bentley Hart, *Atheist Delusions: The Christian Revolution and Its Fashionable Enemies* (New Haven: Yale University Press, 2009), pp. 33-34.

arching plot, just happens to be false.[17] Hart's book provides the arguments and evidence to sustain that judgment. What I find so interesting, however, is that even if the narrative may be false in every detail it is nonetheless true that believer and unbeliever alike assume, though they may disagree about some of the details, that the main plot of the story is true.

That this story now has canonical status has deep significance for how Christians should understand the relation between faith and politics. Put even more strongly, in the interest of being good citizens, of being civil, Christians have lost the ability to say why what they believe is true. That loss is, I want to suggest, a correlative of the depolitization of the church as a community capable of challenging the imperial pretentions of the modern state. That the church matters is why I resist using the language of "belief" to indicate what allegedly makes Christians Christian.[18] Of course Christians "believe in God," but far more important for determining the character of Christian existence is that it is constituted by a politics that cannot avoid challenging what is normally identified as "the political." For what is normally identified as the political produces dualisms that invite questions such as, "What is the relation between faith and politics?" If I am right, that "and" prematurely ends any serious theological reflection from a Christian perspective.

As I have already indicated, to make this argument necessarily puts me at odds with the attempt to make Christian convictions compatible with the epistemological and moral presumptions of liberal social orders. That project presumed a story very much along the lines suggested by Hart. Theologians trimmed the sails of Christian convictions to show that even if the metaphysical commitments that seem intrinsic to Christian practice cannot be intellectually sustained it remains the case that Christianity can claim some credit for the creation of the culture and politics of modernity.

In particular, Christian theologians sought to justify Christian participation

---

[17]Ibid., p. 34.

[18]In his magisterial book *The Unintended Reformation: How a Religious Revolution Secularized Society* (Cambridge: Harvard University Press, 2012), Brad Gregory observes that the Reformation placed an unprecedented emphasis on doctrine for identifying what made Christians Christian. Such an emphasis led Protestant and Catholic alike to emphasize the importance of an "interior assent to the propositional content of doctrinal truth claims, whatever they were." Gregory observes this development "risked making Christianity seem more a matter of what one believed than how one lived—of making the faith a crypto-Cartesian matter of one's soul and mind, *rather than* a matter of what one does with one's body"; p. 155.

in the politics of democratic societies. The field of Christian ethics, the discipline with which I am identified, had as one of its primary agendas to convince Christians that their beliefs had political implications. The determinative representative who exemplified this mode of Christian ethical reflection was Reinhold Niebuhr. Thus his claim that "the real problem of a Christian social ethic is to derive from the Gospel a clear view of the realities with which we must deal in our common or social life, and also to preserve a sense of responsibility for achieving the highest measure of order, freedom and justice despite the hazards of man's collective life."[19] Niebuhr reminded Christians that we do not live in a world in which sin can be eliminated but we nonetheless must seek to establish the tentative harmonies and provisional equities possible in any historical situation.

Niebuhr, who prided himself for being a sober realist challenging what he took to be the unfounded optimism of liberal thinkers such as John Dewey, would have in like manner called into question the optimism of the story Hart associates with the celebration, if not the legitimization, of modernity. But Niebuhr's support of liberal democratic political arrangements drew on a narrative very much like the one Hart identifies as the story of modernity.[20] The result is ironic, a category Niebuhr loved, because Niebuhr's arguments for the political engagement by Christians presupposed a narrative that legitimates political arrangement that requires the privatization of Christian convictions. One of the consequences is the loss of any attempt to say what it might mean for the gospel of Jesus Christ to be true.

For instance, one of the curiosities associated with what have been popularly called "the new atheists" is their assumption that the most decisive challenges to the truthfulness of Christian convictions come from developments in the sciences, or perhaps more accurately put, the "method" of science. Such a view fails to appreciate that the most decisive challenge to the truthfulness of Christian convictions is political.[21] The politics of modernity has so suc-

---

[19]Reinhold Niebuhr, *Reinhold Niebuhr on Politics*, ed. Harry Davis and Robert Good (New York: Scribner's, 1960), p. 153.

[20]For a fuller defense of this account of Niebuhr see my *Wilderness Wanderings: Probing Twentieth-Century Theology and Philosophy* (Boulder: Westview Press, 1997), pp. 32-62, and *With the Grain of the Universe: The Church's Witness and Natural Theology* (Grand Rapids: Brazos Press, 2001), pp. 87-140.

[21]David Martin nicely shows that the assumption that science makes theological claims unintelligible is simply not sustainable. See his *The Future of Christianity*, pp. 119-31. Brad Gregory observes that "empirical investigation of the natural world has not falsified any theological claims." Much more troubling

cessfully made Christianity but another lifestyle option, it is a mystery why the new atheists think it is important to show what Christians believe to be false. Such a project hardly seems necessary given that Christians, in the name of being good democratic citizens, live lives of unacknowledged but desperate unbelief just to the extent that they believe what they believe as a Christian cannot be a matter of truth. As a result Christians no longer believe that the church is an alternative politics to the politics of the world, which means they have lost any way to account for why Christians in the past thought they had a faith worth dying for.

THE WITNESS OF KARL BARTH

I need an example of what the connection between the truthfulness of Christian speech and politics might look like. An example is necessary because I am not sure we know how Christianity so understood would look. I think, however, we have the beginnings in the work of Karl Barth. Barth, more than any theologian in modernity, recognized that the recovery of the language of the faith entailed a politics at odds with the world as we know it. For Barth there is no kernel of the Christian faith because it begins and ends with the extraordinary claim that what we mean when we say "God" is to be determined by Mary's willingness to be impregnated by the Holy Spirit.

That is not where Barth began. Barth began presuming the work of Protestant liberal theologians was a given. It was, however, a political event that called into question Barth's liberalism. On a day in early August of 1914, Barth read a proclamation in support of the war policy of Wilhelm II signed by ninety-three German intellectuals. To Barth's horror almost all his venerated theological teachers were among those who had signed in support of the war. Barth confessed he suddenly realized that he could no longer follow their theology or ethics. At that moment the theology of the nineteenth century, the theology of Protestant liberalism, came to an end for Barth.[22]

Barth characterized the theology he thought must be left behind, a theology identified with figures such as Schleiermacher and Troeltsch, as the at-

---

for the status of the truthfulness of Christian convictions, according to Gregory, were the unresolved disputes between Protestants and Catholics concerning the meaning of God's actions; *The Unintended Reformation*, p. 47.

[22]Karl Barth, *The Humanity of God* (Richmond, VA: John Knox Press, 1963), p. 14.

tempt to respond to the modern age by underwriting the assumption that Christianity is but an expression of the alleged innate human capacity for the infinite. From such a perspective Christianity is understood to be but one particular expression of religion. Such a view of the Christian faith presumed that the primary task of Christian theology is to assure the general acceptance of the Christian faith for the sustaining of the achievements of Western civilization. Barth observed that theology so conceived was more interested in man's relationship with God than God's dealings with man.[23]

For Barth, however, a theology understood as the realization in one form or another of human self-awareness could have no ground or content other than ourselves. "Faith as the Christian commerce with God could first and last be only the Christian commerce with himself."[24] The figure haunting such an account of Christianity is Feuerbach, whom Barth thought had powerfully reconfigured the Christian faith as a statement of profound human needs and desires.

Drawing on Kierkegaard, Dostoevsky and Overbeck, as well as his discovery of what he characterized as "the strange new world of the Bible," Barth proclaimed against the theology of his teachers: "God is God."[25] Barth did not think such a claim to be redundant, but rather to be the best expression of who God is; it is a response to the particularity of a God who has initiated an encounter with humankind. Barth says, "The stone wall we first ran up against was that the theme of the Bible is the deity of *God*, more exactly God's *deity*— God's independence and particular character, not only in relation to the natural but also to the spiritual cosmos; God's absolutely unique existence, might, and initiative, above all, in His relation to man."[26]

So Barth challenged what he characterized as the accommodated theology of Protestant liberalism, using expressions such as God is "wholly other" who breaks in upon us "perpendicularly from above." There is an "infinite qualitative distinction" between God and us, rendering any presumption that we can know God on our terms to be just that, namely, a presumption based on

---

[23]Ibid., p. 24. Barth noted, however, that theology so understood could be in continuity with Melanchthon's emphasis on the benefits of Christ. So there is no reason that an attempt should not be made to develop a Christian anthropocentrism in which theology is done, so to speak, from the bottom up.

[24]Ibid., p. 26.

[25]Timothy Gorringe suggests that Barth may well have seen *A Midsummer Night's Dream*, whose "Well roared Lion!" he liked to use to characterize his reaction against Protestant liberalism. See Gorringe, *Karl Barth: Against Hegemony* (Oxford: Oxford University Press, 1999), p. 25.

[26]Barth, *Humanity of God*, p. 41.

sinful pride. Thus Barth's sobering claim that God is God and we are not means that it can never be the case that we have the means to know God unless God first makes himself known to us.

Barth would later acknowledge that his initial reaction against Protestant liberal theology was exaggerated, but any theology committed to clearing the ground for a fresh expression of the Christian faith could not help but sound extreme. Barth acknowledged that his first salvos against Protestant liberalism seemed to be saying that God is everything and man nothing. Such a God, the God that is wholly other, isolated and set over against man, threatens to become the God of the philosophers rather than the God who called Abraham. The majesty of the God of the philosophers might have the contradictory results of confirming the hopelessness of all human activity while offering a new justification of the autonomy of man. Barth wanted neither of these results.

In retrospect Barth, however, confessed he was wrong exactly where he was right, but at the time he did not know how to carry through with sufficient care the discovery of God's deity.[27] For Barth the decisive breakthrough came with the recognition that "who God is and what He is in His deity He proves and reveals not in a vacuum as a divine being-for-Himself, but precisely and authentically in the fact that he exists, speaks, and acts as the *partner* of man, though of course as the absolute superior partner."[28] In short, Barth discovered that it is precisely God's deity that includes and constitutes God's humanity.

We are not dealing with an abstract God, that is, a God whose deity exists separated from man, because in Jesus Christ there can be no isolation of man from God or God from man. In Barth's language: "God's deity in Jesus Christ consists in the fact that God Himself in Him is the *subject* who speaks and acts with sovereignty. . . . In Jesus Christ man's freedom is wholly enclosed in the freedom of God. Without the condescension of God there would be no exaltation of man. . . . We have no universal deity capable of being reached conceptually, but this concrete deity—real and recognizable in the *descent* grounded in that sequence and peculiar to the existence of Jesus Christ."[29]

I am aware that this all-too-brief account of Barth's decisive theological turn

---

[27]Ibid., p. 44.
[28]Ibid., p. 46.
[29]Ibid., p. 48.

may seem but a report on esoteric methodological issues in Christian theology. But I ask you to remember that Barth's discovery of the otherness of God, an otherness intrinsic to God's humanity, was occasioned by his recognition of the failure of the politics and ethics of modern theology in the face of the First World War. I think it not accidental, moreover, that Barth was among the first to recognize the character of the politics represented by Hitler. Barth was a person of unusual insight, or as Timothy Gorringe describes him, he was a person of extraordinary vitality who was a profoundly political animal.[30] But his perception of the threat the Nazis represented cannot be separated from his theological turn occasioned by his reaction against his teachers who supported the war.

Timothy Gorringe rightly argues in his book *Karl Barth: Against Hegemony* that Barth never assumed his theology might have political implications, because his theology was a politics. That way of putting the matter, that is, "his theology was a politics," is crucial. The very structure of Barth's *Dogmatics*, Gorringe suggests, with its integration of theology and ethics displayed in his refusal to separate law from gospel, was Barth's way of refusing any distinction between theory and practice. Barth's Christocentrism meant that his "theology was never a predicate of his politics, but also . . . that politics is never simply a predicate of his theology."[31]

Gorringe's argument that Barth was a political theologian was confirmed in 1934, the same year Barth wrote the Barmen Declaration, by Barth's response to a challenge by some American and English critics that his theology was too abstract and unrelated to actual lives. Barth begins his defense by observing that he is after all "a modern man" who stands in the midst of this age. Like his questioners he too must live a life not merely in theory but in practice in what he characterizes as the "stormy present." Accordingly he tells his antagonists that "exactly because I was called to live in a modern world, did I reach the path of which you have heard me speak."[32]

In particular Barth calls attention to his years as a pastor in which he faced the task of preaching the gospel in the face of secularism. During this time he

---

[30]Gorringe, *Karl Barth*, p. 11.
[31]Ibid., p. 9.
[32]Karl Barth, *God in Action* (Eugene, OR: Wipf and Stock, 2005), p. 133. This little gem of a book contains lectures Barth gave in response to the Nazis in 1934.

was confronted with the modern world, but he was also confronted with the modern church. It was a church of great sincerity and zeal with fervid devotion to deeds of charity, yet one too closely related to the modern world. It was a church that no longer knew God's choice to love the world by what Christians have been given to do in the light of that love, that is, to be witnesses to the treasure that is the gospel. The problem, according to Barth, is that the church of the pious man, this church of the good man, this church of the moral man, became the church of man.[33] The result was the fusion of Christianity and nationalism.[34]

Consequently the modern church is a near relative to the godless modern world. That error, Barth suggests, began two hundred years before the present with Pietism's objections to orthodoxy. In the Reformation the church heard of God and of Christ, but love was not active.[35] The fatal error was the Christian response: they did not say, "Let God be even more God and Christ be even more the Christ," but instead they said, "Let us improve matters ourselves." Reverence for the pious man became reverence for the moral man, and finally, when it was found that man is of so large an importance, it became less important to speak of God, of Christ, of the Holy Spirit. Instead men began to speak of human reason.[36]

Barth then directly addresses his questioners, whom he identifies as "friends," to tell them he is well aware of what is happening and that is exactly why he insists that he must speak of God. He must speak of God because he must begin with the confession, "I am from Germany." Because he is from Germany he knows that he stands in a place that has reached the end of a road, a road that he acknowledges may be just beginning for social orders like America and England. Yet Barth claims he is sure that what has been experi-

---

[33]The role of Pietism in the development of Protestant liberal theology as well as the legitimating discourse for the subordination of the church to the state is a story in itself. It is not accidental that Barth was the great enemy of Pietism. David Martin suggests that Pietism was the ultimate working out of the implications of the Protestant Reformation for the development of the centralized sovereignty necessary to legitimate the formation of the nation-state. He observes, "German Pietism inculcated disciplines that helped ensure the smooth running of the state"; *The Future of Christianity*, p. 199.

[34]Barth, *God in Action*, pp. 134-35.

[35]In *The Unintended Reformation*, Brad Gregory convincingly argues "that the Western world today is an extraordinarily complex, tangled project of rejections, retentions, and transformations of medieval Western Christianity, in which the Reformation era constitutes the critical watershed"; p. 2. The secularization that was the result of the Reformation was, according to Gregory, unintended but no less a reality.

[36]Barth, *God in Action*, p. 137.

enced in Germany, that is, the remarkable apostasy of the church to nationalism, will also be the fate of those who think Barth's theology to be a retreat from political engagement. Thus Barth's challenge to his critics: "if you make a start with 'God *and . . .*' you are opening the doors to every demon."[37]

Barth early recognized such a demon had been let loose in the person of Hitler. He was able to do so because Hitler's attempt to make Christianity a state religion by creating the German Church meant the free preaching of the gospel was prohibited. Theological speech and politics were inseparable. It is, therefore, no accident that Barth in the Barmen Declaration challenged the "German Christians" on christological grounds.[38] Barth made this challenge because he assumed that Jesus' claim, "I am the way, and the truth, and the life. No one comes to the Father except through me" (Jn 14:6 NRSV), is the defining politics of Christianity. Barth writes:

> Jesus Christ, as he is attested for us in Holy Scripture, is the one word of God which we have to hear and which we have to trust and obey in life and in death. We reject the false doctrine, as though the Church could and would have to acknowledge as a source of its proclamation, apart from and beside this one word of God, still other events and powers, figures and truths, as God's revelation.[39]

The witness that is Karl Barth—that is, how such a life fits into the ongoing story we must tell as Christians of our faithful and unfaithful living out of the gospel—means there is no way we can avoid making clear to ourselves and the world that we believe a new world began in the belly of Mary.

WHERE ARE WE NOW? WHERE DO WE NEED TO GO?

You may be rightly wondering, if not worried, where all this has gotten us. I should like to be able to say more about where we are now and where we need to go, but I am unsure who the "we" or the "us" may be. I have assumed I should—or perhaps more truthfully, I can only—speak from a first-person perspective, but hopefully it is one shaped by my Christian identity. Yet just

---

[37]Ibid., p. 138.

[38]The Barmen Declaration was the statement of protest by the Confessing Church, that is, the church in opposition to Hitler's formation of the German Christian Church. The synod met in Barmen on January 4, 1934. Though the Barmen Declaration was a joint effort of several theologians, Barth was the primary author.

[39]I am quoting from Arthur Cochrane, *The Church's Confession Under Hitler* (Philadelphia: Westminster Press, 1962), pp. 172-78.

as Barth confessed that he was German, so I must acknowledge that I am American. Indeed it may be I am more American than Christian, and thus tempted to confuse the Christian "we" and the American "we." That confusion tempts Americans to assume we represent what any right-thinking person should say because our "we" is the universal "we."

American presumption is always a problem, but the problem is deeper than my American identity. For I think none of us can assume an agreed upon "we" or "us" to be a manifestation of the cultural and political challenges that are the subject of this conference. Given the difficulty of locating the "we," some may worry that directing attention to Barth in order to show the political character of Christian convictions is morally and politically the exemplification of a profoundly reactionary position. In Nazi Germany a Barmen Declaration may have seemed prophetic, but after Hitler a Barmen-like account of the politics of Christian convictions suggests theocracy.[40]

I confess I often enjoy making liberal friends, particularly American liberal friends, nervous by acknowledging that I am, of course, a theocrat. "Jesus is Lord" is not my personal opinion; I take it to be a determinative political claim. So I am ready to rule. The difficulty is that following a crucified Lord entails embodying a politic that cannot resort to coercion and violence; it is a politic of persuasion all the way down. It is tiring business, slow and time consuming; but then we, that is, Christians, believe that by redeeming time Christ has given us all the time we need to pursue peace. Christ, through the Holy Spirit, bestows on his disciples the long-suffering patience necessary to resist any politic whose impatience makes coercion and violence the only and inevitable response to conflict.

For fifteen hundred years Christians thought Jesus' lordship meant they should rule the world. That rule assumed diverse forms, some beneficial and some quite destructive. *Constantinianism* or *Christendom* are descriptions of the various ways that Christians sought to determine the cultural and political life of the worlds in which they found themselves. Some Christians look with nostalgia on that past, seeking ways to recapture Christian domi-

---

[40]During a visit to the Holocaust Museum in Washington, D.C., my wife and I encountered school children wearing shirts emblazoned with the slogan "Celebrate Diversity." There is much good, no doubt, in training the young to enjoy difference, but I worry for those who think the celebration of diversity an adequate response to a movement like National Socialism.

nance of the world. That is obviously not my perspective.

For as David Hart observes, Christianity's greatest historical triumph was also its most calamitous defeat. The conversion of the Roman Empire, in which it was thought that the faith overthrew the powers of "this age," found that the faith itself had become subordinate to those very powers. Like Hart I have no reason to deny the many achievements of Christendom. I think he is right to suggest that the church was a revolution, a slow and persistent revolution, a cosmic sedition, in which the human person was "invested with an intrinsic and inviolable dignity" by being recognized as God's own.[41] But this revolution, exactly because it was so radical, was absorbed and subdued by a society in which nominal baptism became the expression of a church that was reduced to an instrument of temporal power, and the gospel was made captive to the mechanism of the state.[42]

In *The Stillborn God: Religion, Politics, and the Modern West*, Mark Lilla has written in defense of what he calls "the great separation" of politics and religion represented by Thomas Hobbes. He observes that though Christianity is inescapably political it has proved incapable of integrating this fact into Christian theology.[43] The problem, according to Lilla, is that to be a Christian means being in the world, including the political world, but somehow not being of it. Such a way of being, Lilla argues, cannot help but produce a false consciousness. Christendom is the institutionalization of this consciousness just to the extent the church thought reconciliation could be expressed politically.[44] Politics so constituted cannot help but suffer from permanent instability.

Lilla, I think, is right that the eschatological character of the Christian faith will challenge the politics of the worlds in which it finds itself. But that is why, even at times when the church fails to be true to its calling to be a political alternative, God raises up a Karl Barth. For as Barth insisted, this really is all

---

[41] Hart, *Atheist Delusions*, p. 167.

[42] Ibid., p. 194. It is true, nonetheless, as Brad Gregory argues in *The Unintended Reformation*, that the church was never coextensive with or absorbed by any secular political entity. A thousand years after Constantine, from the papacy to the parishes into which Christendom was parceled, the church remained distinct from secular political entities such as medieval kingdoms, principalities, duchies, and cities and city states; pp. 136-37. One of the great virtues of Gregory's book is his treatment of the often-ignored Anabaptists. He rightly understands the Anabaptist alternative to represent a political alternative to the magisterial Reformers just to the extent the latter led to the increasing control of the church by the state.

[43] Mark Lilla, *The Stillborn God: Religion, Politics, and the Modern West* (New York: Knopf, 2007), p. 85.

[44] Ibid., p. 169.

about God, the particular God of Jesus Christ. The humanity of that God, Christians believe, has made it possible for a people to exist who do in fact, as Nietzsche suggested, exemplify a slave morality. It is a morality Hart describes as a "strange, impractical, altogether unworldly tenderness"—expressed in the ability to see as our sisters and brothers the autistic or Down syndrome or disabled child, a child who is a perpetual perplexity for the world, a child who can cause pain and only fleetingly charm or delight; or the derelict or broken man or woman who has wasted their life; or the homeless, the diseased, the mentally ill, criminals and reprobates.[45]

Such a morality is the matter that is the church. It is the matter that made even a church in Christendom uneasy. From the church's standpoint today, Christendom may be a lamentable world now lost, but it is not clear what will replace it or shape the resulting culture or politics. Hart observes that when Christianity passes from a culture the resulting remainder may be worse than if Christianity had never existed. Christians took the gods away and no one will ever believe in them again. Christians demystified the world, robbing good pagans of their reverence and hard-won wisdom derived from the study of human and nonhuman nature. So once again Nietzsche was right that the Christians shaped a world that meant that those who would come after Christianity could not avoid nihilism.[46]

Why this is the case is perhaps best exemplified by how time is understood. Christians, drawing as they must on God's calling of Israel to be the promised people, cannot help but believe that time has a plot; that is to say, Christians believe in history. A strange phrase to be sure, but one to remind us of how extraordinary it is for Christians to believe we come from a past that will find its fulfillment in the future. Accordingly we believe that time has a narrative logic, which means time is not just one damn thing after another. The story of creation is meant to remind us that all that exists lends witness to the glory of God, giving history a significance otherwise unavailable. *Creation, redemption, reconciliation* are names Christians believe constitute the basic plotline that makes history more than a tale told by an idiot.[47]

Yet the very assumption that history has a direction is the necessary con-

---

[45]Hart, *Atheist Delusions*, pp. 213-14.
[46]Ibid., pp. 229-30.
[47]Ibid., pp. 201-2.

dition that underwrites the story of modernity earlier characterized by Hart. This story has underwritten the new atheists' presumption that if history is finally rid of Christianity we will discover through unconstrained reason how our politics can be made more just and humane. Thus Hart speculates that the violence done in the name of humanity, a violence that is now unconstrained, might never have been unleashed if Christianity had not introduced its "peculiar variant of apocalyptic yearning into Western culture."[48] Hart rightly observes that such a judgment is purely speculative given the reality that great empires prior to Christianity claimed divine warrants for murder. Yet Hart thinks that the secularization of Christian eschatological grammar is the "chief cause of the modern state's curious talent for mass murder."[49] An exaggerated claim, perhaps, but it is at least a reminder that it is by no means clear why the killing called war is distinguishable from mass murder.[50]

This last observation, I hope, draws us back to Karl Barth's theological work. I suggested Barth exemplifies the politics of speech that is at the heart of Christian convictions. At the heart of Christian convictions is the belief in "the humanity of God," a humanity made unavoidable by our faith in Jesus Christ as the second person of the Trinity. Christ's humanity means no account of the church is possible that does not require material expression that is rightly understood as a politic. Church matters matter not only for the church, but we believe what is a necessity for the church is a possibility for all that is not the church.

I suspect humans always live in times of transition; what is time if not transition? But I believe we are living in a time when Christendom is actually

---

[48]Ibid., pp. 222-23.

[49]Ibid., pp. 223-24.

[50]In a recent blog post Noah Berlatsky defends my arguments for pacifism against Eric Cohen's critique of my book *War and the American Difference* that appeared in the conservative magazine *First Things*. Cohen described my views as "a form of eschatological madness"—a description that Berlatsky quite rightly suggests I would happily accept. Berlatsky suggests that Cohen missed my argument that war produces its own logic and morality. In fact, according to Berlatsky, Cohen's defense of war as a heroic story exemplifies the view of war I was criticizing: when war becomes a "heroic story" it becomes idolatry. Berlatsky observes that though I would like to get rid of war, what I really want to get rid of is a church of war. What Cohen missed is that my argument is aimed at Christians. Berlatsky then makes what was for me the surprising claim that he finds this to be a relief for someone like him because he is an atheist, so he can cheerfully continue to support Caesar. Yet he observes there is a bit of discomfort, because if Christians began to take up nonviolence—he hates to have to say it—"it would be hard to escape the suspicion that that might actually be the work of God." Berlatsky, "Bend Your Knee," *The Hooded Utilitarian* (blog), April 18, 2012, http://hoodedutilitarian.com/2012/04/bend-your-knee.

coming to an end. That is an extraordinary transition whose significance for Christian and non-Christian has yet to be understood. But in the very least it means the church is finally free to be a politic. If I may summarize what I take to be one appropriate response to this observation, it is quite simply this: let Christians make the most of it.

2

The Peril and Potential of Scripture in Christian Political Witness

Mark A. Noll

The Rwenzuru kingdom lies north of Lake Edward and northwest of Lake Victoria in far western Uganda.[1] It experienced postcolonial political independence not as a blessing but as an occasion for guerilla warfare. The Rwenzuru felt particularly oppressed by the larger Toro kingdom, under whose authority they were placed by the new Ugandan government of President Milton Obote. In 1962, leaders of Rwenzuru issued a declaration of independence; acts of violence against Toro kings and armed resistance to the Ugandan government followed. Then in early October 1970 appeared a charismatic prophet, Timosewo Bawalana, who made a dramatic public appeal for the violence to stop. On October 3 he preached from Isaiah 1:10 ("Hear the word of the Lord, you rulers of Sodom! Listen to the law of our God, you people of Gomorrah!"). On October 15 he wrote to the District Commissioner that the Rwenzuru soldiers had laid down their weapons unilaterally in a desire to follow the teaching of Revelation 19:11-16 with its apocalyptic depiction of "the King of Kings and Lord of Lords." Later that month, and after the prophet had crowned a new king in Rwenzuru, he turned to Isaiah 2:4-6 as his text to guide the now-pacified kingdom ("They shall beat their swords into plowshares, and their spears into pruning hooks. Nation shall not lift up sword against nation, neither shall they learn war any more").[2] Significantly, because the prophet

---

[1]The first two paragraphs rely exclusively on Derek R. Peterson, *Ethnic Patriotism and the East African Revival: A History of Dissent* (New York: Cambridge University Press, 2013), pp. 262-80.
[2]For these specific texts, see ibid., pp. 274-75.

Bawalana had ties to the East African Revival, which since the 1930s had exerted such a great influence in the region and around the world, he made effective use of public confession as a means to establish this peace.

The end of this episode is, however, complicated. In early 1972, resurgent nationalists drove Timosewo Bawalana out of Rwenzuru, but negotiations with agents from Kampala eventually allowed the Rwenzuru kingdom to establish a peaceful, quasi-independent state under Ugandan government oversight. The Bible that the prophet Bawalana had brought directly into political conflict faded from view. Although its striking immediate influence may actually have contributed to the region's eventual peace, larger political forces and more obviously secular interests were, in the end, the primary elements shaping Rwenzuru political life.

I have taken the Rwenzuru incident from Derek Peterson's fine new book titled *Ethnic Patriotism and the East African Revival*. Its pages offer much to contemplate for Christian believers who seek a political witness that matches the integrity of Christian faith itself. Prominent in Peterson's account is the role of Scripture. The Bible inspired practices that made revival into the effective established religion of the Toro kingdom. But the Bible also was much contested when, besides its prominence for revivalists, it was also used by African critics to denounce the revival and by missionaries who expounded the Scriptures both to promote and to restrain revival practices.[3] Likewise in the political sphere, although revivalist-inspired preachers like the prophet Bawalana used Scripture to promote peace, in other parts of East Africa Bible-faithful converts did little to stop horrific violence.[4] The recent experience of African Christians, in other words, repeats the history of Western Christianity in putting the Scriptures to use for political witness. Sometimes it has helped, other times not. More generally, in newly Christianized parts of the world the same appeal to Scripture is appearing that has characterized Christian political efforts throughout Western Christian history. And there is the same mixed record of Scripture functioning to sanction violence and oppression as well as to promote peace and justice.

---

[3]Ibid., p. 119.

[4]In Rwanda during 1993 and 1994, the people most closely associated with the East African Revival sometimes did resist the genocidal slaughter because of their strong disdain for politics of any kind; see Timothy Longman, *Christianity and Genocide in Rwanda* (New York: Cambridge University Press, 2010), pp. 113-14, 160 and especially p. 196.

This chapter examines the Bible and political life primarily through one extended American example. It is a distinctly Protestant chapter because of my belief that without the Scriptures there can never be Christian political witness, and also because of my conviction that Scripture should be the ultimate authority for Christian political witness as for every other Christian activity. The chapter, however, is also trying to show that political use of Scripture, even extensive use of Scripture, is no guarantee that any given political appeal will be meaningfully Christian. Many more examples would be necessary to suggest how Scripture might function in politics for good instead of for ill. But even this one example should be enough to indicate that the application of Scripture to politics has been a persistent problem. If my example from American history is more extensively documented than the Rwenzuru example, it does not by any means imply that American Bible-believers have done any better in political use of Scripture than our East African brothers and sisters. In particular, this American example of Scripture deployed for Christian political witness illustrates a number of specific problems that have recurred throughout much of Western biblical usage, especially since the Reformation: (1) the covert complications of biblical rhetoric, (2) the persistent problem of Protestant biblicism, (3) the heretical hubris of American exceptionalism, (4) the subtle seduction of fallen human nature and (5) the complicated question of biblical revelation itself.

FAST DAY SERMONS: OR, THE PULPIT ON THE STATE OF THE COUNTRY
The American example concerns the use of Scripture as found in only one book, an unusually comprehensive volume published at an unusually intense political moment. The book, titled *Fast Day Sermons: or, The Pulpit on the State of the Country*, appeared in early 1861, after the election of Abraham Lincoln and the secession of South Carolina from the Union but before the firing on Fort Sumter in April 1861 that began the Civil War.[5] This book contains eleven chapters: ten sermons or discourses delivered on fast days proclaimed either by state governments or by President James Buchanan, and one paper responding to two of the sermons. Three sermons came from states that would

---

[5]Anonymous, ed., *Fast Day Sermons: or, The Pulpit on the State of the Country* (New York: Rudd & Carleton, 1861). There is also some discussion of this collection in Mark A. Noll, *The Civil War as a Theological Crisis* (Chapel Hill: University of North Carolina Press, 2006), pp. 2-4 and passim.

join the Confederacy, one from a border slave state that stayed in the Union, and seven from the North. Six addressed slavery extensively, and the others at some length, with a common conviction—which historians long refused to acknowledge—that this issue was the key to the national crisis. Nine of the sermons took the form of a biblical text followed by exposition and application; one "discourse," though delivered on the national fast day proclaimed by President Buchanan, lacked a text and was almost entirely political; the one rebuttal article was given over entirely to biblical interpretation. Although Presbyterians, as well as ministers from New York, were overrepresented in this volume, the anonymous editor nonetheless chose well, since several of the contributors were widely recognized as religious leaders. Alongside six Presbyterians, the authors included one Episcopalian, one Congregationalist, one Unitarian, one Dutch Reformed college professor and one Jewish rabbi. Two of the contributors, James Henley Thornwell, a Presbyterian professor of theology in South Carolina, and Henry Ward Beecher, pastor of the Plymouth Congregational Church in Brooklyn, were among the best-known national figures of any kind at that time.[6]

With this particular collection of sermons, it is easier to show problems in how the Scripture was put to use than to glean positive wisdom. Yet the ministers deserve considerable sympathy. They were all recognized as elite members of their communities, widely respected as public intellectuals as well as simply pastors. Moreover, their role as expounders of Scripture meant a very great deal in a nation where—with no national communications media, no national advertising, no national business firms, no nationally recognized sports or entertainments, and a very light federal government—deference to the Bible came as close to a unifying national possession as anything else. In these circumstances, the ministers who in November 1860 and January 1861 were asked to address congregations with a biblical word from the Lord faced a very great challenge. Several of them accurately predicted the immense cost in lives, family heartache and material destruction that did in fact ensue. They were placed in a very difficult situation, and they did their best.

In the crisis of that parlous hour, the ministers had to rely on previously formed theological principles, previously practiced exegetical strategies and previously entrenched interpretive conventions as they opened the Scrip-

---

[6]See the Roster of Fast Day Sermons at the end of this chapter for a full list of contributors, texts and summaries of the sermons. Parenthetical numbers in the text refer to pages in *Fast Day Sermons*.

tures. On a few particular matters, these previous constructs served the ministers well as they selected texts and crafted expositions of, or taking off from, those texts.

So it was that two of the speakers who stood at polar extremes on the question of slavery said virtually the same thing about the true character of repentance. Robert Dabney, who after brief service with General Stonewall Jackson during the war would become one of the most embittered defenders of the South's Lost Cause, and Henry Ward Beecher, the nation's best-known clerical opponent of the slave system, both reflected biblical wisdom in how they defined the duty of repentance. Beecher observed perceptively, "it has been found not difficult for men to repent of other people's sins; but it is found somewhat difficult and onerous to men to repent of their own sins" (270). Dabney was more succinct: "It will do our hearts no good to confess to God the sins of our fellow-men" (89). Both were following scriptural wisdom in trying to treat the beam in their own eyes before worrying about the speck in the neighbor's eye.

In light of Dabney's later stance as a die-hard Confederate, it is also noteworthy that he recognized how often civil conflicts had damaged the church by "dividing brother against brother in Zion" (82). In addition, he commented accurately concerning the many past instances in which armed conflict had hamstrung Christian life: "there are few things which can affect the interests of Zion so disastrously as political convulsions and war" (82). The northern New School Presbyterian William Adams joined Dabney, the southern Old School Presbyterian, by teaching that once "vituperation and angry reproaches" (331) came to dominate public discourse, "fanaticism" could be the only result, "and fanaticism is a fire which, once kindled, burns you know not where or what" (327). Dabney's denunciation of the partisan "*trick* of imputing odious and malignant motives to all adversaries" was even more extensive (94). Adams and Dabney both took pains to describe for their congregations the evils arising from "the chains of party" (Adams, 324), particularly how "the unrighteous behests of party" (Dabney, 92) replaced fidelity to Scripture with fidelity to faction. These sermonic warnings about the perils of political partisanship resonated well with Dabney's text from Psalm 122 ("I will seek thy good") and Adams's text from 1 Timothy 2 ("that we may lead a quiet and peaceable life in all godliness and honesty").

By far the most positive aspect of these sermons was their supreme respect for the Scriptures as providing a standard of divine truth for the orientation of human life as a whole. That respect was implied in all eleven chapters and explicit in the great majority. It was also striking that the preacher who expatiated at greatest length on the supreme authority of the Bible was Rabbi Morris Raphall of New York City's Jewish synagogue. To him, Scripture defined "the highest Law of all, the revealed Law of the Word of God" (230). He paused to explain how the history of the world's diverse people offered "a most convincing and durable proof that the Word of God is true, and that the prophecies of the Bible were dictated by the Spirit of the Most High" (233). And he insisted especially about the Ten Commandments, that they were "the word of God, and as such, of the very highest authority" (238).

Others, however, were almost as fulsome. Henry Van Dyke, a northern Old School Presbyterian who devoted his long sermon to attacking abolitionism and defending slavery as biblically legitimate, began by spelling out what it meant that "we are Christians here"; this fact indicated above all that "we acknowledge . . . but one standard of morals—but one authoritative and infallible rule of faith and practice" (127, and similar expressions passim). As it happens, Van Dyke's definition of biblical supremacy was matched by Tayler Lewis, the college professor who devoted his lengthy chapter to rebutting Van Dyke and arguing that the American slave system was everywhere condemned in Scripture. To Professor Lewis, the many New Testament passages aimed at moderating the Roman system of slavery of the first century constituted "the richest internal evidence of the super-human origin of the Scriptures" (225). Lewis in his arguments many times cited the evidence found, or not found, in every "line or word of Scripture" (187, with similar expressions 195, 222). In sum, one of the most striking features of these sermons from late 1860 and early 1861 was the confidence that the speakers expressed in the truthfulness and the authority of the Bible.[7]

THE COVERT COMPLICATIONS OF BIBLICAL RHETORIC

Yet, as indicated by the contrary conclusions on slavery that Henry Van Dyke

---

[7]For some of the other such expressions, see statements by Thornwell, pp. 19, 21, 51; Dabney, p. 92; Van Dyke, pp. 139-40, 164, 165; Lewis, pp. 197-98; Francis Vinton, p. 259; Beecher, pp. 286-87, 289; and Adams, pp. 315, 333.

and Tayler Lewis drew from the Bible they both revered, incompatible conclusions about the day's political controversies were an even more striking feature of these sermons. A first problem was the covert complications of biblical rhetoric. Alongside the frequent appeal to scriptural warrants in support of their political conclusions, all the authors quoted or paraphrased the Scriptures as constituent parts of their own discourse. That is, the preachers used the words of the Bible as their own words even when the quotations or paraphrases had nothing to do with the substance of their teaching. Three examples, out of scores, illustrate the practice.[8] Benjamin Palmer, a renowned Old School Presbyterian from New Orleans, enlisted Hebrews 8:13 when he commented on "the bonds that were ruptured in the late election" when the Republican Lincoln emerged victorious: "We may possibly entertain the project of reconstructing it; but it will be another union, resting upon other than past guarantees. 'In that we say a new covenant, we have made the first old, and that which decayeth and waxeth old is ready to vanish away'" (73). Henry Van Dyke did the same with Genesis 2:24 when he spoke of how recent controversies were dividing the United States: "What evil spirit has put enmity between the seed of those whom God, by his blessing on the wisdom and sacrifices of our fathers, made one flesh?" (170). Henry Ward Beecher was, characteristically, even more flamboyant in his use of John 11:43. As he described the depths of evil perpetrated by slave owners, he claimed that Jesus himself opposed those evils: "Be sure of one thing: He that would not come when the sisters sent, but tarried, has come, and the stone is rolled away, and he stands by the side of the sepulchre. He has called, 'Liberty, come forth!' and bound yet hand and foot, it has come forth" (291).

Two realities made this rhetorical use of Scripture all but inevitable. First was the extraordinary degree of attention that Americans of all educational levels and from all positions on the social scale paid to Scripture. The prevalence in public speech of biblical words, phrases and cadences is now difficult to fathom. But this was the Holy Book from which Americans learned to read, which was distributed in immense quantities by the American Bible Society,

---

[8]For a very incomplete roster of other instances, see Thornwell, pp. 34, 40; Palmer, pp. 48-49, 62, 74, 78, 80; Dabney, pp. 82-83, 88, 96; Robert J. Breckinridge, pp. 122, 125; Van Dyke, pp. 136, 153, 165-66, 169-70, 174-76; Lewis, pp. 197, 203, 209; Raphall, pp. 231, 236; Vinton, pp. 249, 254, 257, 259; Beecher, pp. 266, 288; Bellows, pp. 299, 310; Adams, pp. 312, 322, 332, 335-36.

which was sold in dozens of formats and editions by the nation's leading publishers, which was read constantly in private, in homes and in churches, which
frequently appeared as the only book in inventoried estates, and which constituted (with Shakespeare as the only far-distant competition) the literary
coin of the realm. But second was the fact that the vast majority of public Bible
references came from a single translation. Although American publishers provided many Bibles not in English and although the Douay-Rheims translation
was the official English version for Catholics, the ubiquity of the King James
Version meant that for all practical purposes, that translation simply was *the*
national book.

Yet if constant rhetorical employment of the national book was inevitable,
it was also a problem for Christian political witness. Not only did such rhetorical use lend a sacred aura to the speaker's own thoughts, it also implied
that those who opposed the speaker's *rhetoric* were somehow opposing the
Word of God. This usage was dangerously presumptive, because it communicated implicitly that the speaker's purposes shared the divine purposes that
inspired the Scriptures. In our day the scope of this problem has diminished.
National spokespersons do not channel Scripture easily, and the King James
Version has faded. Now it is by no means certain that audiences would even
recognize biblical phrases in a public address. Thus, when considering national political rhetoric, the modern decline of the Bible certainly reflects a
regrettably lessened consciousness of God, but it may also speak to a welcome
decline in offensive public speech.

THE PERSISTENT PROBLEM OF PROTESTANT BIBLICISM

A second issue arising in many of the fast day sermons was the persistent
problem of Protestant biblicism. Biblicism is a loose concept, but I am using
the word to designate not simply traditional Protestant belief in the divine
character and supreme authority of Scripture, but that traditional belief
treated as sufficient unto itself for proclaiming the word of God.[9] Phrases referring to the Bible as "the great moral charter by which our laws must be

---

[9]For *biblicism* as a neutral term for anthropological investigation, see James S. Bielo, ed., *The Social Life of
Scriptures: Cross-Cultural Perspectives on Biblicism* (New Brunswick, NJ: Rutgers University Press, 2009);
for *biblicism* as an evaluative term with negative connotations, see Christian Smith, *The Bible Made Impossible: Why Biblicism Is Not a Truly Evangelical Reading of Scripture* (Grand Rapids: Brazos, 2011).

measured" (Thornwell, 19), "God's written words" (Episcopalian Francis Vinton, 259), and "dictated by the Spirit" (Raphall, 233) appeared regularly in these sermons. Such sermons evinced biblicism not in the phrases themselves, but when the speakers proceeded to treat what they brought to their texts with the same authority ascribed to the Bible itself.

The problem of biblicism arises when a dogmatic profession to follow the Bible alone morphs into an inability to recognize, acknowledge or address the other influences that come to bear when interpreting individual texts of the biblical witness as a whole. The example that fairly leaps from the page when reading the fast day sermons now, but that most Bible expositors circa 1860 seemed oblivious to, was the confusion of slavery as such and black-only slavery. Seven of the eleven authors either defended slavery as a biblically justified institution or simply took that justification for granted. Most of them explicitly proclaimed their desire to follow only the Bible. But when they spelled out what this Protestant profession of ultimate biblical authority meant, they imported a great unexamined truth claim that had nothing to do with scriptural teaching. Thus, in the very same paragraph James Henley Thornwell slid from discussing "our duty to our slaves" to describing "the Africans" (49). Benjamin Palmer similarly slid without apparent awareness from describing southern whites as "the constituted guardians of the slaves" to decrying opponents whom he called "the worst foes of the black race" (65). Other apparently unthinking elisions of the same sort occurred regularly.[10]

The problem was not the obvious fact that in the United States slaves were of African descent. The problem was rather that preachers expended great effort in defining their faithfulness to Scripture as the infallible guide for adjudicating the question of slavery, but then immediately went beyond Scripture when talking as if slavery simply equated to the enslavement of only African Americans. Biblical application would have looked quite different if white preachers had considered the possibility that their own children might one day be sold as slaves. But when expounding scriptural revelation on slavery, the possibility of Caucasians being enslaved was an exegetical conclusion more faithful to the text than one applying biblical words only to Africans.

---

[10]For only some examples, see Breckinridge, pp. 111, 114, 120-21; Van Dyke, pp. 151-52; and Adams, pp. 325, 332.

One of the sermons in the book, the defense of slavery by Rabbi Raphall, did teach that Scripture itself ordained Africans for slavery (231-35). But, as the college professor Tayler Lewis pointed out, this interpretation had long been thoroughly overturned by impeccable scholarly research (209). For most of the speakers, the threat of biblicism arose as the temptation unself-consciously to cloak conventional wisdom of the day with the divine aura of biblical authority.

This biblicistic temptation did even more damage when it was linked to hermeneutical naiveté. Invariably, when a preacher spoke of the Bible's plain and obvious meaning, it meant that serious disagreements existed with preachers who came to opposite conclusions respecting the same or other texts. The two contributors who clashed most directly also illustrated the un-reflectiveness of this hermeneutical ploy most directly.

For Henry Van Dyke's defense of slavery as biblical, hermeneutical questions could not be simpler. As he saw it, "the Divine Law [was] plainly written" (139), he relied on "plain passages" (140) and "the obvious meaning of plain Scriptural texts" (166), in Scripture there existed "not one distinct and explicit denunciation of slaveholding" (145), and those who contradicted these views were utterly lacking in "the proof texts" (140). Tayler Lewis's long rebuttal to Van Dyke featured more attention to the history of ancient Israel and to the New Testament. But once that history was filled in, he concluded that proslavery arguments gave "a wrong direction . . . to the more truthful exegesis" (180); as he put it, "a careful critic" would see that ancient Israel was very different from the United States and so would regard comparisons between the two as "far-fetched" (193); he argued that in ancient Israel the permission to sell slaves was "not in the writing," and that "there is not a word in the New Testament about buying and selling slaves" (222).

As illustrated by this clash, "clear," "obvious" and "plain" interpretations of Scripture almost never appeared the same to opponents who interpreted the Bible differently. Protestant trust in the divine authority of Scripture need not spill over into naiveté about the ease of applying the Bible to political issues. But it certainly did so in debates over the most important political crisis of that day, as it threatens to do when Christians apply the Scriptures to the political contentions of our day.

THE HERETICAL HUBRIS OF AMERICAN EXCEPTIONALISM

A third difficulty for Christian political action as illustrated from the fast day sermons was the heretical hubris of American exceptionalism. Part of this problem came from simple enthusiasm; preachers fell over themselves expressing the conviction that in the whole history of the world there had never been a nation so uniquely successful in achieving liberty, so unambiguously righteous in its political history, and so singularly blessed of God as the United States of America. Maybe my sense of a problem at this point is a product of postmodern cynicism, but at least a few of the preachers seemed also to see the difficulty. Henry Ward Beecher, for one, took considerable pains to explain why all Americans needed to repent of national sins before he turned to denounce the sin of slaveholding. If, asked Beecher, the United States was so good and so blessed by God, why had it acted with such brutal malice toward its Native American inhabitants and its Mexican neighbors? "It is a sorry commentary upon a Christian nation, and indeed, upon religion itself, that the freest and most boastfully religious people on the globe are absolutely fatal to any weaker people that they touch" (275).

The extent of Beecher's self-criticism was, however, unusual. While many other preachers extensively detailed personal and social causes for repentance, they nevertheless regularly spoke of the United States as unique among the nations. Thus, the Kentucky Presbyterian Robert Breckinridge specified a number of sins in need of repentance, especially the crime of tearing the nation into fragments (100). Yet he also went on to laud "the blessing of our glorious example to all nations and to all ages . . . the blessing of irresistible power to do good to all peoples . . . and possessing the widest and the noblest inheritance ever given to any people" (101). Others were just as full of praise for the moral uniqueness of the United States.[11] Sober realism, in other words, about the character of the United States was in short supply.

A more serious source of questionable American exceptionalism was frequent reference to the United States as fulfilling in the modern world biblical promises made to ancient Israel. The trope of America as the new Israel was deeply rooted in Puritan conventions, even as it had been embraced by many outside of New England during the War for Independence. The five sermons

---

[11]See also Thornwell, p. 33, "we were a city set upon a hill"; Dabney, p. 86; Beecher, p. 267; the Unitarian Henry Bellows, p. 310; and Adams, pp. 321, 334-35.

with Old Testament texts lent themselves especially to this usage, but they were not the only ones to make the identification.

Again, however, it is noteworthy that at least one of the speakers paused deliberately to scotch the Israel-America parallel. James Henley Thornwell began his sermon by disavowing any intention "to intimate that there is a parallel between Jerusalem and our own Commonwealth in relation to the Covenant of God" (9). But many others were far less cautious. As an example, the northern Episcopalian Francis Vinton bemoaned the prevalence of political corruption, then referenced the account in 1 Samuel of the bribe-taking sons of the prophet Samuel, and concluded: "In this short history is not the portrait of our country sketched?" (253, also 248, 263).[12]

The identification of Israel's history with the history of the United States was, moreover, assumed rather than argued. No serious biblical exegesis supported the notion that any modern nation, much less the United States, deserved to be understood in relationship with God as ancient Israel stood in relationship with God. It was an assumption rooted in national pride, and hence heretical. It was a mistake that hamstrung that Bible's universal gospel message then, and to the extent that the same mistake is made today about American exceptionalism, it exerts the same crippling effect on the gospel message.

THE SUBTLE SEDUCTION OF FALLEN HUMAN NATURE

A fourth problem that disfigured the fast day sermons was the subtle seduction of fallen human nature. This difficulty appeared when preachers presumed that their assessments of developments were as infallible as God's assessments. The faulty lines of reasoning that supported this mistake all had the same shape. They began with a proper sense of God's perfection: God inspired Scripture perfectly, God providentially ruled over all events perfectly, God provided perfect guidelines for repentance of sin and reconciliation with himself. The next step was to believe, again properly, that God had graciously allowed humans to grasp the truth of divinely inspired Scripture, to understand something of God's providential control of all things and to be in reality reconciled to God. The difficulty came in the next step, when the proper belief

---

[12]Others who drew Israel-US parallels included Palmer, pp. 67-68, and Adams, pp. 335-36.

in God's gracious power fed the improper conclusion that humans enjoyed capacities for knowledge and control that equaled God's capacities for knowledge and control. The line could be very fine between justified trust in God's self-revelation and unjustified idolatry concerning one's own infallible grasp of that revelation.

The most serious example of this difficulty was confusion between recognizing God's all-embracing providence and treating one's own reading of events as divinely sanctioned. Benjamin Palmer's sermon defending "slavery as a divine trust" was particularly full of references to "the dispensations of Providence" (57), "a universal and ruling Providence" (58) and the like (also 63, 69, 76). But Palmer's conception of providence meant little more than the assumption that because something existed, it existed because God not only ordained but actively approved it. In his view, African Americans "providentially [owed] me service, which, providentially, I am bound to exert" (66). Once slavery was seen as a necessity, so also was established in his mind "our present trust to preserve and transmit our existing system of domestic servitude, with the right, unchanged by man, to go and root itself wherever Providence and nature may carry it" (70).

Indeed, God certainly is the author of nature who providentially controls all that occurs, but for Palmer to view his own understanding of nature as infallible and his own reading of history as providential was to mistake the creature's imperfection for the Creator's perfection. This sacrilegious idolatry, moreover, paralleled the blithe confidence that what was clear in the Bible to oneself had to be clear for everyone else. It expressed the persistent human tendency to place oneself at the center of the moral universe, an error compounded by treating the results of actions undertaken from this mistaken self-conception as though from God. Palmer was joined by many others who also presumed a Godlike ability to tell God what he was about.[13]

A particularly sensitive manifestation of this misplaced trust in the capacities of fallen human nature was the attitude expressed toward repentance and political well-being. The very existence of the fast days combined a good thing with a questionable thing. It is always good for humans humbly to acknowledge their sins before God; it is questionable to think that any one particular act of

---

[13]See also Thornwell, pp. 37, 48; Dabney, p. 90; Van Dyke, pp. 152, 173; Raphall, pp. 235, 245; Beecher, p. 269; Bellows, pp. 294-95, 300, 309-10; and Adams, pp. 314, 328.

repentance will lead to one completely predictable consequence.

The jeremiad tradition, which stretched back far before the founding of the United States, featured that combination. The term *jeremiad* came from the prophet Jeremiah's stern warnings to the people of Judah: repent or suffer the consequences, which turned out to be captivity by Babylon. The jeremiad, which colonial Puritans had perfected, took for granted the identity between national Israel and modern nation-states. It took for granted almost as easily the belief that human actions could compel divine reactions. So in late 1860, the government officials who called for fast days and the congregations that gathered to observe them together expressed the conviction that if Americans repented of their personal and corporate sins, the nation could be spared a bloodbath. The conclusion of the sermon from the Unitarian pastor Henry Bellows was especially noteworthy in this respect. Bellows began by denying that he and his New York congregation had any special reason to repent, since the nation's sin at that hour lay entirely with the slave system (294). His solution to what he called this "national disease" (293) was to let the southern states go (304). Yet as he came to the end of his sermon, he combined Scripture, American exceptionalism, his own reading of providence, and the standard quid pro quo of jeremiad reasoning into a rousing finale:

> The Union is strong enough to bear even this tremendous strain now trying its hoops. We want only faith in the Constitution as it is; faith in the right of political majorities to exercise their legitimate power; faith in the original wisdom of our fathers; faith in humanity; faith in Christ and in God, to carry us triumphantly through this glorious but awful hour, when the grandest political structure the providence of God ever allowed to be erected is to be finally tested by earthquake, and to prove, I doubt not, that it rests on the rock of ages, and will endure while time shall last. (310)

In their great self-confidence about the ability to read providence as if they were God, Americans North and South, and of all political opinions, fell prey to the weakness of fallen human nature. They had lost the deeper biblical wisdom that William Cowper, the intermittently mad poet of the previous century, had caught so powerfully in a memorable hymn. That hymn was printed in more than a third of the hymnals published in the United States during the 1850s. It began, "God moves in a mysterious way / His wonders to perform"; it ended, "God is his own interpreter / And he will make it plain."[14] They sang it, but they did not believe it.

THE COMPLICATED QUESTION OF BIBLICAL REVELATION ITSELF

The last, and most serious, difficulty for Christian political witness as illustrated in these fast day sermons touched the complicated question of biblical revelation itself. This question of course extends far beyond the particular concerns of politics to all efforts that believers make to heed the word of the Lord. How should Scripture inform the Christian's life? How does the Bible, which believers universally regard as bringing the message of redemption in Christ to humankind, speak to the manifold spheres of human existence? In late 1860 and early 1861, the specific questions flew thick and fast: What does Scripture teach about the status of modern nation-states? When is political revolution justified? When is force justified to put down a revolution? How should well-known passages—like the injunctions about "rulers" in Romans 13, or Christ's differentiation between what to give to Caesar and what is owing to God, which several contributors cited—be applied to the American situation on the verge of civil war?[15]

But above all, what does Scripture teach about human slavery? That question lay at the foundation of appeals to use the Bible for Christian political witness. From the antithetical statements that answered this question peremptorily, it should have been obvious that much greater care was required to move from heeding the Scripture's message of salvation in Christ to applying biblical faith in Christ to the American crisis. The chasm separating rock-solid contradictory interpretations was, in fact, immense. For James Henley Thornwell, "That the relation betwixt the slave and his master is not inconsistent with the Word of God, we have long since settled. Our consciences are not troubled, and have no reason to be troubled, on this score" (45). Rabbi Raphall spoke with the same assurance to the same end: "'Is slaveholding condemned as a sin in sacred Scripture?' How this question can at all arise in the mind of any man that has received a religious education, and is acquainted with the history of the Bible, is a phenomenon I cannot explain to

---

[14]Text and information on frequency of publication are found at www.hymnary.org/text/god_moves _in_a_mysterious_way.

[15]On Romans 13, see Thornwell, p. 14; Lewis, p. 222; and Adams, p. 319; and on Caesar, see Adams, p. 330.

myself, and which fifty years ago no man dreamed of" (235-36). Henry Ward
Beecher was also completely confident in his understanding of the Bible, but
with a diametrically opposing conviction: "I should like no better amusement
than to answer the sermons of men who attempt to establish the right of
slavery out of the Bible. It would be simple butchery!" (289).

Unlike Thornwell, Raphall and Beecher, Henry Van Dyke and Tayler Lewis
dove back into the exegetical trenches to fight over what the others considered
too obvious to contest. Their struggle over competing biblical interpretations
is particularly instructive since both believed in what we would today call the
inerrancy of Scripture, both felt that infallible Scripture delivered a definite
message about slavery, and both held that to distrust this message on slavery
was to distrust the Bible as a whole.

Leaving aside the admittedly much more important issue of what a properly
biblical understanding of slavery should look like, the way their debate un-
folded in 1861 reveals several cruxes of interpretation for any attempt to use
Scripture for Christian political witness. Although my sentiments lie overwhelmingly with Tayler Lewis on these substantive questions, I believe it is
possible to state the cruxes objectively with fairness to both debaters.

Van Dyke, whose uncomplicated defense of slavery is all but impossible to
accept today, nonetheless approached the issue with a commendably self-
conscious protocol. As he stated the issue, if the Old Testament contains a
positive command that the New Testament does not abrogate, that command
must continue in force. In fact, as Van Dyke showed, it does stand "plainly
written" (139) in Leviticus 25:46 that from "the heathen that are around you"
Israelites could purchase "bondmen and bondmaids" whom their children
could inherit "for a possession," and that "they shall be your bondmen forever"
(138-39). Moreover, concerning his sermon's New Testament text from
1 Timothy 6, Van Dyke could quote several notable interpreters to prove that
there was "no room for dispute" (128): when the apostle told "as many ser-
vants as are under the yoke" to obey their masters and to reject as an enemy of
Christ anyone who counseled differently, Bible believers had to recognize a
New Testament reaffirmation of the Old Testament command. Van Dyke was
also at pains to show that while the New Testament denounced the polygamy
that the Old Testament allowed, no New Testament witness ever made the
same move against slavery. Although Tayler Lewis would strenuously contest

the application of Van Dyke's conclusion to the American situation, Van Dyke was laudably explicit in his biblical claim for the legitimacy of slavery.

Tayler Lewis responded with the most sophisticated biblical wrestling in the collection. My judgment that he was using Scripture appropriately should not obscure the more general value of his article in highlighting crucial questions for anyone who turns to Scripture for Christian political witness. It will be obvious how Lewis answered these questions, but implications of the questions go far beyond the specifics of the dispute in which he was engaged.

First, how much in-depth understanding of biblical cultures is necessary in order to apply Scripture properly to contemporary cultures? Lewis's answer was, Much in every way. Key to his interpretation of relevant biblical texts were his claims about "the vastly changed condition of the world" (180), especially his extensively developed contention that slavery in both the Hebrew and Roman worlds was fundamentally different from slavery in the modern United States. In particular, the American restriction of slavery to one race confirmed that difference.[16] His principle in this approach to Scripture was that "whilst truth is fixed, eternal, immutable as God himself, its application to distant ages, and differing circumstances, is so varying continually that a wrong direction given to the more truthful exegesis may convert it into the more malignant falsehood, making it, in fact, 'the letter that killeth instead of the spirit that giveth life'" (180). To demonstrate this principle, Lewis argued at length that since Hebrew slavery did not permit a slave trade—that is, the Old Testament spoke of the Jews buying slaves, but never selling them (181, 183-85, 187-88)—and since Roman slavery denoted absolute governance but not absolute ownership of the slave (182-85, 211-20), the biblical permissions of slavery did not address the American situation at all. He was, in other words, asserting that the only true interpretations of Scripture were those that took culture fully into account.

Lewis's response to Van Dyke posed and then answered a second question: Is biblical revelation static or progressive? In his view, it was definitely progressive. To support this conclusion, he attacked the defenders of slavery who claimed that the institution had been a providential means for bringing Christianity to Africans. His withering response affirmed a principle of progressive

---

[16]Lewis used the term *caste* for race, pp. 181, 189-90, 215, 217.

revelation: "What a commentary . . . on the world's ethical progress, that the enslaving of those called heathen should be justified by going back to this old Jewish 'statute,' and perverting it to an end historically so remote from any-thing intended by the ancient law-giver" (208). But Lewis's claim that biblical revelation progressed rested on deeper theological ground. His exegesis of the Leviticus passage focused on the Hebrew permission to purchase "heathen" slaves. But, he argued, "Israel, with all its imperfections, was the type of the better humanity to come" (203). Specifically, what Leviticus called "the na-tions that are round about you" must now be viewed differently, because "God has given them to Christ" (206). Surely, Lewis went on, this truth must dictate a missionary strategy like David Livingstone's, which aimed at bringing the gospel and civilization to Africans where they were, not kidnapping them and treating them like material objects. It was biblical, Lewis insisted, to say that biblical revelation progressed.

A third question that Lewis's antislavery arguments answered was the most substantial: Were biblical ethics and biblical theology both drawn directly from Scripture or did biblical ethics spring from biblical theology? Lewis answered that while the ethical directions of specific texts must not be discounted, it was far more important to root Christian ethics in the biblical story as a whole. For Lewis, the Christology of that story was crucial. The brutalization that Lewis held slavery to entail "reaches the deep spot where we are all one in Adam, and hope to be one in Christ. May we not say with all reverence, He feels it too, that Ineffable One who took our sin-degraded nature and now bears it in the highest heavens?" (186). Further, proper contemplation of the incarnation, of "Christ's taking our one common, universal humanity," demonstrated "how unchris-tianlike when worldliness and selfishness lead us to degrade ourselves by casting out of the bound of human brotherhood any whose nature Christ as-sumed, and for whose salvation He gave his own human life" (187). Lewis carried this theological principle into his reading of the much-contested book of Philemon, when he concluded that the Christian slave-owner "could rule [his slaves, but] he could no longer own them, because they were his kind, Adamically and Christianly" (219-20, italics omitted).

Tayler Lewis was able to rebut Henry Van Dyke's conclusion concerning what, in Van Dyke's view, the Bible taught clearly about slavery because he foregrounded broad interpretive considerations: cultural context was imperative, biblical revelation progressed and properly biblical ethics sprang from biblical theology as a whole. Significantly, however, this strategy still allowed Lewis to agree with several of the conclusions that Van Dyke drew from specific biblical texts. Thus, he agreed up to a point with Van Dyke's application of 1 Timothy 6: if abolitionists attacked slavery on "the ground of mere natural right" and in so doing rejected "the authority of Scripture," Van Dyke was correct to call them out as "poor interpreters of Scripture" (180). Again, he held that Van Dyke was correct to chastise any abolitionists who denied the force of 1 Timothy 6 and urged slaves to disobey believing masters (219).

These concessions by Lewis, the contextual interpreter, to Van Dyke, the proof-texting interpreter, are instructive. Fruitful use of Scripture for Christian political witness can never be a simple matter of choosing to follow either the spirit or the letter of the Bible; it means, instead, comprehensive discernment in which individual texts will sometimes carry great weight when at other times contextual, cultural, progressive and broadly theological reasoning should carry the day.

Conclusion

Bible believers today would do well to examine how Scripture was being used in the political crisis that led to the American Civil War. The array of contemporary political issues demanding careful Christian attention is daunting. On the home front there is gun control, immigration reform, health care, same-sex marriage, abortion, foreign policy decisions and the nature of political participation itself. Globally, Christian believers face many political dilemmas: What programs are appropriate for people taking advantage of new democratic opportunities? What tactics should be followed to survive under hostile regimes? Should Christians join revolutionary movements against despotic regimes? Is economic liberalization always the best government policy? And many more.

In the modern United States since the end of the civil rights era, the Bible has faded in public life. Public officials may occasionally deploy Scripture to bring comfort at times of public tragedy, as when President Bush quoted words from "the prophet Isaiah" (Is 40:26) in his address after the Columbia disaster in February 2002,[17] or when President Obama quoted "the words of

---

[17]"Bush to Families: 'Entire Nation Grieves with You,'" Cable News Network LP, February 1, 2003, www .cnn.com/2003/US/02/01/shuttle.bush.statement/index.html.

Scripture" (from Ps 147) to memorialize the Newtown shooting victims in December 2012.[18] And partisans occasionally enlist Scripture to promote expanded health care, oppose gun control restriction, or chart a course on right-to-life issues. But for the most part, debates over the Bible and politics take place within the churches.

In other places throughout the world, however, the public use of the Bible appears more like that in the mid-nineteenth-century United States: as in Uganda with the prophet Bawalana, in Brazil because of the political efforts of the Universal Church of the Kingdom of God, recently in Zambia where proponents and opponents of President Frederick Chiluba hurled scriptural texts at each other, or in still other regions where recent church growth has pushed believing communities into the center of a nation's political life.

Especially in these regions where believers now confront political opportunities similar to those faced by American Christians at the time of the Civil War, heirs of those earlier Americans can only hope that the prophet Bawalanas of the world will learn from what has gone before in our own history. Put positively, the lessons can be stated like this: Biblical rhetoric can strengthen political speech, but there are great dangers in using such rhetoric. Reliance on Scripture is imperative, but naive biblicism is dangerous. It is a Christian injunction to love one's country, but an evil to treat any modern nation as if it were Israel of old. Christians in political life must guard against the lingering effects of fallen human nature as diligently as believers in every other sphere of life. And the Bible's revelation will work most propitiously for the healing of nations when that revelation is appropriated contextually, culturally and theologically. The lessons from American experience are sobering. May the God who rules the destinies of all nations make his children, as they seek the good of their various cities, as politically wise as serpents and innocent as doves.

ROSTER OF FAST DAY SERMONS

William Adams (Madison Square Presbyterian [New School] Church, NY, Jan. 4, 1861). "Prayer for Rulers; or Duty of Christian Patriots." 1 Timothy 2:1-2.

---

[18]"Statement by the President on the School Shooting in Newtown, CT," The White House, December 14, 2012, www.whitehouse.gov/the-press-office/2012/12/14/statement-president-school-shooting-new town-ct.

Slavery not justified by Scripture, but most important need is to moderate fanaticism and to pray for leaders.

Henry Ward Beecher (Plymouth Congregational Church, NY, Jan. 4, 1861). "Peace, Be Still." Mark 4:37-39. Repentance, especially for northern complicity in the great evil of slavery.

Henry W. Bellows (All Souls Unitarian Church, NY, Jan. 4, 1861). "The Crisis of Our National Disease." Revelation 17:14. Repentance appropriate only for those who have perpetuated the barbarous system of slavery in a free republic.

Robert J. Breckinridge (Danville Theological Seminary, KY, Jan. 4, 1861). "The Union to Be Preserved." [No text.] Slavery only protected by a nation part free and part slave.

Robert L. Dabney (Union Theological Seminary, VA, Nov. 1, 1860). "The Christian's Best Motive for Patriotism." Psalm 122:9. Repentance, especially for extreme public speech and political factionalism.

Tayler Lewis (Professor of Oriental Languages, Union College, Schenectady, NY). "Patriarchal and Jewish Servitude No Argument for American Slavery." An extensive biblical rebuttal of Van Dyke (and Raphall).

Benjamin M. Palmer (First Presbyterian Church, New Orleans, Nov. 29, 1860). "Slavery a Divine Trust." Psalm 94:20; Obadiah 5. Slavery the solution to labor-capital contentions, to be perpetuated.

Rabbi Morris J. Raphall (Jewish Synagogue, NY, Jan. 4, 1861). "Bible View of Slavery." Jonah 3:5-10. Biblical warrant for slavery, but appeal for slave owners to moderate treatment of slaves.

James Henley Thornwell (Columbia Theological Seminary, SC, Nov. 21, 1860). "Our National Sins." Isaiah 37:1. Repentance, including repentance for abusing master-slave relationship.

Henry J. Van Dyke (First Presbyterian [Old School] Church, Brooklyn, Dec. 9, 1860). "The Character and Influence of Abolitionism." 1 Timothy 6:1-5. An extensive biblical explanation for why abolitionism equals infidelity.

Francis Vinton (Trinity Episcopal Church, NY, Jan. 4, 1861). "Fanaticism Rebuked." Judges 21:2-3. Slavery permitted by Scripture, but slaves to be treated as humans.

3

EXTRA ECCLESIAM NULLUM REGNUM

The Politics of Jesus

Scot McKnight

One commonly begins a discussion of the politics of Jesus by reconstructing his political world and locating his place in the options. Explain from right to left the Maccabees and the Zealots, the Essenes and the Pharisees, and then the Herodians and Sadducees. Or one could sketch the various Herods themselves and, in particular for Jesus, Herod Antipas. Admittedly, what one often observes is that the reconstruction rules the conversation. Less benignly, the problem is that the reconstructer rules the conversation. Even more, one starts to plot the first-century groups as analogies to political parties and theories today. Studies of the politics of Jesus spread across the spectrum, including American social-gospel proposals, a vast array of liberation theologies as well as classic Anabaptist studies, especially John Howard Yoder's *The Politics of Jesus*, not to ignore sketches of how Jesus might speak into the options for political involvement today.[1] But more directly about Jesus in his world, one thinks of Alan Storkey and Morten Hørning Jensen, then on to the more radical Obery Hendricks Jr. and Richard Horsley, or to others like Seán Freyne, Warren Carter, Walter Wink and John Dominic Crossan. Such studies sometimes get ramped up into Manichean or Malthusian alarms as they tell different stories about Jesus. To be blunt, some of them reveal much about the

---

[1]The font of liberation studies is Gustavo Gutiérrez, *A Theology of Liberation: History, Politics, and Salvation*, rev. ed. (Maryknoll, NY: Orbis Books, 1988). See also John Howard Yoder, *The Politics of Jesus: Vicit Agnus Noster*, 2nd ed. (Grand Rapids: Eerdmans, 1994). For a sketch of how Christians participate, see Mark A. Noll, *One Nation Under God? Christian Faith and Political Action in America* (San Francisco: Harper & Row, 1988).

author's politics and little about Jesus.[2] One typical logic is simple: the New Testament talks about kingdom; the ruling kingdom is Rome; therefore, when the New Testament talks about kingdom it is anti-Rome; in fact, Rome is just like the United States of America. What Jesus says about Rome is what he says about the United States. This antiempire approach has mushroomed in the last two decades, but one is at least entitled to ask if perhaps "kingdom" could be set into Israel's history and not so much over against Rome.[3] That kind of logic would be different: the New Testament talks about kingdom; the ruling kingdom is hoped to be Davidic; therefore the New Testament kingdom talk is speaking of fulfillment in Israel and not of Rome.[4] The difference between the two logics could hardly be more stark.

My methodological proposal is only that we begin with Jesus, with his words and his claims in his location in Israel's story, and only then can we find our way to ponder the politics of Jesus and their significance today. Unlike Paul or Peter, both of whom have observations to be used in our politics, Jesus stood within the majority. So first Jesus.

What Is the Kingdom?

Jesus declared the kingdom's inauguration and summoned his hearers to decide if they would follow him into the kingdom or walk away. Declaring the kingdom led Jesus into public discourse—that is, to label Herod Antipas a "fox" (Lk 13:32), to deconstruct taxation (Mt 17:24-27; Mk 12:13-17 pars.), and to declare at the beginning of his ministry on the mountain of temptation (Mt

---

[2]Alan Storkey, *Jesus and Politics: Confronting the Powers* (Grand Rapids: Baker Academic, 2005); Obery M. Hendricks Jr., *The Politics of Jesus: Redicovering the True Revolutionary Nature of the Teachings of Jesus and How They Have Been Corrupted* (New York: Doubleday, 2006); Richard A. Horsley, *Jesus and Empire: The Kingdom of God and the New World Disorder* (Philadelphia: Fortress, 2003); Seán Freyne, *Galilee from Alexander the Great to Hadrian, 323 BCE to 135 CE: A Study of Second Temple Judaism* (Edinburgh: T & T Clark, 1998); idem, *Galilee and Gospel: Collected Essays* (Boston/Leiden: Brill, 2002); Morten Hørning Jensen, *Herod Antipas in Galilee* (Tübingen: Mohr Siebeck, 2006); Warren Carter, *The Roman Empire and the New Testament: An Essential Guide* (Nashville: Abingdon, 2006); Walter Wink, *The Powers That Be: Theology for a New Millennium* (New York: Doubleday, 1998), a condensation of his three-volume series on the Powers; John Dominic Crossan, *God and Empire: Jesus Against Rome, Then and Now* (San Francisco: HarperSanFrancisco, 2007).

[3]By way of clarification, this relocating of Jesus more into a Jewish history is not to depoliticize Jesus. On which see Horsley, *Jesus and Empire*, pp. 6-9.

[4]It is a pity so many of these studies about Jesus ignore the brilliant Vatican document called *Compendium of the Social Doctrine of the Church*. See www.vatican.va/roman_curia/pontifical_councils/justpeace/documents/rc_pc_justpeace_doc_20060526_compendio-dott-soc_en.html.

4:8-10 par.) and at the end of his ministry in a trial before Pilate (Jn 18:36) that his kingdom was at odds with the kingdoms of this world. The politics of Jesus is a kingdom politics. Everything Jesus says is politics, kingdom politics.

This word *kingdom* is a very happy word today. It is used for a variety of deeds, including voting for Obama, building water wells in Africa, striving against drug and sex trafficking, as well as working in local soup kitchens. *Kingdom* has been set hard against *church*, which is now a bad word and connotes institutional and organized religion, legalism, hierarchy, pastors who preach dogmatic sermons, and traditional beliefs like the Nicene Creed. Kingdom folks gag on the word *church*. For many *kingdom work* refers to good deeds good Christian people do in the public sector, while church is about religion. And sometimes this is all tied into the *missio Dei*, rarely defined with precision, so that the *missio Dei* becomes much wider than the church and begins to look like doing good, establishing justice and working for peace. In some of these sketches, *missio Dei* begins to look like a blend of the older social gospel and versions of liberation theology.

Three streams have shaped this good word versus bad word stalemate. Protestant liberalism slid kingdom into culture in either a Reformed or Lutheran mode of activism so that one can say, in America at least, the liberal Protestant ethos and the liberal American ethos are more or less the same. The Roman Catholic–inspired liberation theology focuses on economic justice and power while it extends some of what is found in the Protestant liberal tradition. The other stream, rather oddly, is the evangelical reduction of kingdom to one's personal surrender to God or to God's powerful act in a healing or miracle.[5] So, kingdom has come to mean either the common good or personal conversion.

Redeemed community under Jesus. In spite of these trends in churchspeak about kingdom, in church history *kingdom* has had other emphases; that is, the kingdom is the *redemption* of God in Christ or the *community* of God in Christ. Which comes first: redemption or community? Again, while many evangelicals today prefer personal redemption and Protestant liberals social redemption, the church's history, dominated as it was for fifteen hundred

---

[5]This is not just recent evangelicalism, as it is the chief emphasis in Calvin's exposition of the third petition of the Lord's Prayer. See John Calvin, *A Harmony of the Gospels: Matthew, Mark and Luke*, Calvin's Commentaries, ed. D. W. Torrance and T. F. Torrance, trans. A. W. Morrison (Grand Rapids: Eerdmans, 1972), 1.207-8.

years by Catholicism and Orthodoxy, has preferred the word *community*. More pointedly, the church sees in the word *kingdom* another word for the church. Contemporary uses of the term *kingdom* tend either to diminish *community* as church or reduce *redemption* to peace and justice activism. These two terms, *redemption* and *community*, need to be reinserted into the center of this discussion.

The danger here is the false dichotomy. So let me propose that we enter into a discussion of the politics of Jesus by defining kingdom as the *redeemed community under Jesus.* The substantive here is "community," not "redeemed." When we make the substantive "redemption" we turn toward the cultural captivity of kingdom or toward an overindividualized sense of conversion; when we make "community" the substantive we turn our faces beyond the church toward the biblical sense of the term. The kingdom is the redeemed community and only the redeemed community. If this understanding of kingdom begins to sound like "church," then I'm saying what I want to say. I want to defend this in what follows.

Geopolitical social reality. The word *kingdom*—*malkut* and *basileia*—in the Bible denotes a geopolitical reality. If you are a cheerleader and shout to the crowd "kingdom" in a first-century Jewish gymnasium they don't shout back "salvation" or "redemption." They say "God" or "Israel" or "land" or "Jerusalem," and instead of "redemption" they may well say "liberation." Zechariah clearly understood kingdom in Luke 1:67-79 this way. To say "kingdom" then was to speak of a geopolitical reality. Hence, in 1 Samuel 15:28 we have the "kingdom of Israel" and in 2 Chronicles 11:17 we have the "kingdom of Judah" and in 1 Kings 2:12 we have the "kingdom of Solomon." This geopolitical sense of kingdom comes to the surface in texts like 1 Chronicles 28:5: "Of all my sons," David declares, "and YHWH has given me many—he has chosen my son Solomon to sit on the throne of the kingdom of YHWH over Israel" (author's translation). Abijah, king of Judah, facing a battle with Jeroboam, will say a bit later, "And now you plan to resist the kingdom of YHWH, which is in the hands of David's descendants" (2 Chron 13:8).

God as king. Because kingdom requires a king on a throne, the term will always have a sense of "rule" or "reign." The one who rules in the kingdom vision of Jesus is *God and not any human ruler, including Rome.* There is something a little on the side of anarchism here that needs to be appreciated, though we can but mention it. I point directly at 1 Samuel 8 where it is abundantly clear that God sees a human king on the throne over Israel to be a rejection of God as king, and it is worth noting here that some see Deuteronomy along the same line (Deut 16:18–18:22). The implication here is colossal. When Jesus announces the kingdom of *God* one must at least consider that he's just erased human kings and that now Jesus, the incarnate one, is God on the throne.

The issue is not whether the sense of "rule" is at work in "kingdom" language. The issue is that for a Jew to say what Jesus did—as in "The time has been fulfilled and the kingdom *of God* has drawn near" (see Mk 1:15)—the first thought of the Jewish listener was not of redemption in a personal sense but of God and community, society, Israel, land, temple and government from Jerusalem. In other words, a geopolitical reality. The redemption will be the eschatologically anticipated liberation of Israel from the hand of her enemies and the restoration of Israel to the land to live in holiness, wisdom, love and justice under Israel's God. Let us not forget that in Jesus' world Rome was a cuckoo ruling in Israel's nest, and getting the cuckoo out was the aim of Jewish politics and theology. When the cuckoo flew from the nest there would be salvation.

Liberation as historical context. Kingdom language excited precisely that "kick the cuckoo out" kind of hope and expectation and a belief that the promises of Israel's story were about to be fulfilled. In one of the most famous noncanonical texts quoted and cited for understanding first-century messianism, *Psalms of Solomon* 17–18, one finds what a typical first-century Jew would think of kingdom. We read lines like these:

> Lord, you chose David to be king over Israel,
> and swore to him about his descendants forever, that his kingdom should
> not fail before you. (*Pss Sol* 17:4)[6]

But a Gentile overpowered the kingdom of God housed in Jerusalem, and Israel took on Gentile immorality and idolatry. So the psalmist pleads,

> See, Lord, and raise up for them their king, the son of David,
> to rule over your servant Israel in the time known to you, O God.

> Undergird him with the strength to destroy the unrighteous rulers,
> to purge Jerusalem from gentiles. (*Pss Sol* 17:21-22)

---

[6]Translation from James H. Charlesworth, *The Old Testament Pseudepigrapha* (London: Darton, Longman & Todd, 1983).

God will act, the psalmist says, and he will deliver through judgment and will send them their Messiah.

> And he will purge Jerusalem and make it holy as it was even from the beginning. (17:30)

> And he [Messiah] will be a righteous king over them, taught by God. There will be no unrighteousness among them in his days, for all shall be holy, and their king shall be the Lord Messiah. (17:32)

This Messiah will be compassionate, Torah observant and a blessing to Israel and the Gentiles. He will pastor the people and lead them into holiness.

I have quoted from this text both because it is not as familiar and because it is typical of what a first-century Jew thought when the word *kingdom* was used. Kingdom was about the redeemed community, living under the Messiah, in the land and observing Torah. When Jesus said "the kingdom has drawn near," then this is what he had to mean at some level or no one would have known what he meant.

Summary: *The meaning of* kingdom. Kingdom was *eschatological* because it was about the story of Israel coming to fulfillment in the story of Jesus. It was *ecclesial* because it was for the people of Israel, now winnowed to those who confessed allegiance to King Jesus. It was *christological* because Jesus revealed it, Jesus created it, Jesus ruled in it, and anyone who chose to submit to him was in the kingdom; those who didn't weren't kingdom people and were outside the kingdom. It was *ethical* because those who submitted to Jesus lived as Jesus taught them within the boundaries of a kingdom ethic.

My claim, then, is that this eschatological, ecclesial, christological, ethical set of lines gives birth to a *redeemed community under Jesus*. This redeemed community under Jesus *is the politics of Jesus*. Take any one element from this set of lines—be it eschatological hope, ecclesial institution, christological formulation or ethical vision—and strip it from the others and you diminish the politics of Jesus. His politics is a robust politics, aimed at creating entire communities from the ground up, which means that when we talk about the politics of Jesus we have to talk about the church.

THE POLITICS OF JESUS IS THE CHURCH

For centuries Catholics and Protestants battled it out over one set of verses, namely, Matthew 16:17-19, where Peter confesses Jesus as Messiah and where Jesus informs his listeners about the church. This is no place to settle debates. Instead, I want to draw your attention to something sometimes ignored. There is an indissoluble connection here between "church," what Jesus came to build, and "kingdom of heaven," where "heaven" means the divine over-againstness with respect to worldly kings. The kingdom is the future for those who are now in the church. Church people are kingdom people. The church is the present reality, the present embodiment, of the future kingdom. There is no kingdom outside church people, the community of Jesus gathered under him. To Peter is given the keys to the kingdom; that is, to Peter, through the declaration and implementation of the gospel, is given authority about entrance to and exclusion from the kingdom, and the church is the "on earth" expression of that kingdom.

Even more can be said. Jesus reveals the kingdom; Jesus is the Messiah, or the King, of that kingdom. And Jesus is the foundation of the church; there is no church outside Jesus. Therefore we can conclude that while it would not be wise to equate kingdom with church or church with kingdom, they are the same in our world today. There is no kingdom outside the church—*extra ecclesiam nullum regnum*. Why? Because the only kingdom is one where people live under Jesus, and the church is the redeemed community of Jesus. The kingdom is not an ethic that can be flattened into a secular social ethic and then announced that wherever we find that secular ethic we've got kingdom. The kingdom is fellowship and discipleship under Jesus, and only there.

Which means we need to look at three marks of the politics of Jesus, the marks of life under King Jesus as we form a fellowship under him.

Love. One element of the politics of Jesus is an ethic, and the ethic of Jesus is reduced on two occasions to love. I begin with the big one, namely, Mark 12:28-32, when the scribe asks Jesus to weigh in on one of the debates of the day: When discerning how best to know the will of God, do we multiply the *mitzvot* into a myriad of *halakhot*—that is, do we multiply the 613 Torah commandments into interpretations, or do we reduce the 613 to their essence? The scribe's question of Jesus belongs to the second hermeneutical tradition, so he asks, "What is the greatest commandment?" Jesus' response is what I call the Jesus Creed. He swipes the heart of Jewish piety, the daily recitation of the *Shema*, from Deuteronomy 6:4-9 and welds to it Leviticus 19:18, forming a reduction of Torah to two: love God and love your neighbor as yourself. The second instance of this is what we call the Golden Rule, now found at Matthew 7:12 (par. Lk 6:31), where Jesus reduces the Torah and the Prophets to doing to others what you want done to you. The use of a self-ethic to frame an other-ethic unites the Golden Rule to the Jesus Creed. We can but mention the important uses of love in John's Gospel (Jn 13:34; 15:12), where Jesus' own self-sacrificing love is the template for the disciples.

But this raises an important question: What is love?[7] Until love is defined its import for the politics of Jesus will be ignored. A biblical theology of love begins by observing God's love in relation to creation and to God's people, Israel-kingdom-church. What one discovers, and here I must make a long discussion quite short, is that God's love is a rugged covenant commitment shaped by three prepositions: *with, for* and *unto*. God's rugged commitment is to be *with* Israel and the church, to be *for* Israel and the church as its covenant maker and protector and warrior, and this sense of being with and for is shaped by an eschatology of *unto*: God's love is about forming God's people into people of holiness, purity, love, wisdom and justice. The politics of Jesus is all about this sense of love.

Briefly a defense of each element: the fundamental relationship of God with humans, most notably with Israel and the church, is as a covenant or a rugged commitment to someone. From Genesis 12 onward covenant forms the core of God's relation with humans. That covenant is formed first as divine presence: God is *with* his people in entering vulnerably into the covenant with Abraham in Genesis 15, in the tabernacle, in the temple, in the dwelling of the glory (*kabod*) in that temple, then radically in the incarnation, where God is Immanuel in the flesh (Mt 1:23; Jn 1:14), and finally when God dwells with his people in the new heavens and the new earth (Rev 21:3). God's covenant is to be *for* his people, which is precisely what "I will be your God and you will be my people" means as a covenant formula in the Bible (Gen 17:7-8; Ex 6:2-8; Rev 21:7).[8] With and for are designed for the eschatological *unto*: God forms a covenant with Israel to make it a people for his own possession, God liberates Israel from the clutches of Pharaoh to lead them to the Torah for life in

---

[7]Thomas Jay Oord, *Defining Love: A Philosophical, Scientific, and Theological Engagement* (Grand Rapids: Brazos, 2010). Oord's definition is noteworthy: "To love is to act intentionally, in sympathetic response to others (including God), to promote overall well-being" (p. 15).

[8]Rolf Rendtorff, *The Covenant Formula: An Exegetical and Theological Investigation*, trans. M. Kohl (Edinburgh: T & T Clark, 1998).

the land, and God saves Israel and the church in order to make his people holy and loving and pure.

This apologetic for defining love by God's love leads to a radical conclusion: the politic of Jesus subverted the kingdoms of this world because instead of conquering one's enemies, instead of killing one's foes and instead of dominating others Jesus urged his followers to love enemies. Love has content because it means a covenant commitment to be with enemies, to be for enemies, and to dwell with them as God works through them for the eschatological unto. Love, in other words, incorporates themes like justice and liberation and peace.

Power unleashed. On occasions Jesus' kingdom vision is connected to the unleashing of liberating, redeeming power. If the kingdom is the "redeemed community," redemption marks the politics of Jesus. What kind of redemption? Holistic. Three texts will get this point established. First, at Jesus' inaugural sermon in Nazareth we hear the guiding themes of Jesus' entire kingdom ministry when Jesus quotes from Isaiah 61:1-2 and announces the text is about himself:

> The Spirit of the Lord is on me,
>   because he has anointed me
>   to proclaim good news to the poor.
> He has sent me to proclaim freedom for the prisoners
>   and recovery of sight for the blind,
> to set the oppressed free,
>   to proclaim the year of the Lord's favor. (Lk 4:18-19)[9]

Jesus redeems the poor, the prisoners, the blind and the oppressed by liberating them. The text originally was about the exiles, so we would be foolish not to recall that this is clearly an end-of-exile passage and Jesus is the one who redeems by ending exile. Many properly see a social-justice kind of kingdom vision. After all, both the Magnificat and Benedictus in Luke 1 lead us to see a radical social rearrangement under King Jesus, and John the Baptist's concrete demands for repentance—economic distribution to the core—lead us to the same ideas (Lk 3:10-14). Yet I want to urge that we not reduce these words to social ethics but recall that these words quoted by Jesus were about the exiles in Babylon, and the terms "poor" and "prisoners" and "blind" and "oppressed"

---

[9]Unless otherwise noted, Scripture quotations in this chapter are from the NIV.

were metaphors for Israel's disciplined condition. Perhaps then we are wise to see in these terms liberated Israel, the new people around Jesus, and not spread our net too widely or at least too quickly.

In Matthew 12:28 (par. Lk 11:20), we learn that Jesus' exorcisms are kingdom redemptions and liberations: "If it is by the Spirit of God that I drive out demons, then the kingdom of God has come upon you." Here the redemptive powers of Jesus derive from the Spirit. Thus, the politic of Jesus is a power politic, a liberating, Spirit-driven redemption. Finally, when Jesus sent out the seventy-two he told them, "Heal the sick who are there and tell them, 'The kingdom of God has come near to you'" (Lk 10:9).

Kingdom and unleashing the redemptive, liberating power of God for those trapped in sin, systemic injustice and satanic oppression are tied together for Jesus. But this liberating power is the work of God in Jesus and in the Spirit, so that a kingdom politic is a politic that is christological and pneumatological at the core. These two elements cannot be stripped from the politic of Jesus without stripping the politic of its essence. We can press this harder: the *only* place where kingdom is a reality is where the redeeming, liberating reality has already occurred. In Latin, *extra salutem nullum regnum.*

Cross. The distinguishing feature of the politics of Jesus is the cross. Earlier we cited texts from the Psalms of Solomon, considered by some to be the *Purpose Driven Life* book of its day, in which kingdom, Messiah and conquering are all brought into a potent mixture. The same kind of mixture is found in the Dead Sea Scrolls, especially in the famous scrolls called *The War Scroll.* Kingdom, Messiah and war belong together: no battle, no conquering of the enemies, no kingdom, no Messiah. (Some of us may now be singing a Bob Marley song.) Kings and military victories belong together in Judaism as much as they do in *The Chronicles of Narnia.* But not with Jesus' kingdom vision.

Jesus utterly deconstructed king and kingdom, the Messiah and his kingdom, by draping a cross over their necks. Peter confesses that Jesus is the Messiah, Jesus reveals his cross; Peter rejects Jesus' suggestions of a death, Jesus must rebuke Peter for not comprehending that exaltation and victory will occur through the cross and the resurrection. Peter can enter into that kingdom if he, too, embraces the way of the cross (Mt 16:13-28 pars.). The Last Supper both reveals and embodies the way of the cross. We think of Jesus washing his disciples' feet in John 13:1-17. When, according to Luke, the disciples want to know who will rule in the kingdom (Lk 22:24-30), and Simon boldly announces that he would never deny Jesus in utter confusion of what's actually occurring (22:31-38), Jesus leaves them and heads to Gethsemane— and so the Last Supper becomes the Lord's Supper, and the temple sacrificial system finds its fulfillment in the death of Jesus, and powers of death are cracked when Jesus rises from among the dead.

The cross is the way of following Jesus, and a politic of Jesus is a politic that embraces the cross. As the Son of Man did not come to be served but to serve (cf. Mk 10:45 with Lk 22:27), so disciples are to serve one another by embracing the cross of Jesus. As Jesus once said it, "Whoever wants to be my disciple must deny themselves and take up their cross and follow me" (Mk 8:34). Yoder long ago noted four typical uses of "cross" language: to encourage those who are suffering, to point to the inner experience of humility before God, to affirm the renunciation of pride and to identify imitation with renunciation.[10] Yoder interprets imitation singularly as the cross. "Servanthood replaces dominion, forgiveness absorbs hostility."[11]

So what is the cross? The cross evokes humiliating rejection as the way of love: it is the ultimate form of with-ness, for-ness and unto-ness. Jesus identifies so fully with his followers, with God's people, that he enters Jerusalem for them, he enters into their humiliation, their sinfulness and their death unto a new creation resurrection. He takes on himself the Roman curse against Jerusalem's powers and evacuates it of its deathly powers. Instead of overturning violence with violence, Jesus' path was the way of suffering that overcomes violence. The politic of Jesus, then, is a politic of self-denial, co-crucifixion and exaltation through the path of sacrifice for others. *Extra crucem nullum regnum.*

What does this look like when it comes to the state? I suggest we get four hints from Jesus of what a kingdom politic looks like when it faces the state, four hints rising to the surface in four of Jesus' interactions with the state.

KINGDOM POLITICS AT WORK IN JESUS

God's time, God's way. When the devil took Jesus to "a very high mountain" to offer Jesus his rightful assumption of the universal throne on the condition

---

[10]Yoder, *The Politics of Jesus*, pp. 129-31.
[11]Ibid., p. 130.

of worshiping Satan, Jesus said, "Away from me!" and "Worship the Lord your God, and serve him only" (Mt 4:8-10; cf. Lk 4:5-8). Satan claimed to have this world in his grip. Jesus wanted it. It was why he came. But Jesus will not have it Satan's way.

We can wed this text to the famous line before Pilate in John 18:33-37. We would do well to hear the brief passage:

> Pilate then went back inside the palace, summoned Jesus and asked him, "Are you the king of the Jews?"
>
> "Is that your own idea," Jesus asked, "or did others talk to you about me?"
>
> "Am I a Jew?" Pilate replied. "Your own people and chief priests handed you over to me. What is it you have done?"
>
> Jesus said, "My kingdom is not of this world. If it were, my servants would fight to prevent my arrest by the Jewish leaders. But now my kingdom is from another place."
>
> "You are a king, then!" said Pilate.

John 18 adds something not seen or perhaps seen only in inchoate form in the temptation. That is, here Jesus says the kingdom way is not the way of violent domination. His kingdom is "not of this world" and is "from another place" because the kingdom is nonviolent and because, unlike Caesar's rule, his kingdom is about service (Mk 10:35-45) and erasing human hierarchies (Mt 23:8-12). There is an inscription in Rome in the temple of Minerva recounting the victories of Pompey that included over 2.1 million subjects surrendering, nearly 900 ships sunk or taken, and over 1500 towns and forts acquired.[12] As Dom Crossan frames Jesus' posture so well, "Your Roman Empire, Pilate, is based on the injustice of violence, but my divine kingdom is based on the justice of nonviolence."[13] This is part of the politics of Jesus.

"Tell that fox!" Jesus' cruciform kingdom politics, shaped as it is in a redeemed community under the servant king, can surprise in its boldness. Antipas is the tetrarch of Galilee and, perhaps in reprisal of the crowd's attempt to make Jesus king (see Jn 6:15) or perhaps because he thinks Jesus opposes his unlawful marriage as much as John did (cf. Mk 6:18; 10:11-12),

---

[12]Pliny, *Natural History* 7.96-98.

[13]Crossan, *God and Empire*, p. 4.

Antipas wants to kill Jesus (Lk 13:31). The Pharisees inform Jesus of Antipas's designs on Jesus. Here's Jesus' response:

> He replied, "Go tell that fox, 'I will keep on driving out demons and healing people today and tomorrow, and on the third day I will reach my goal.' In any case, I must press on today and tomorrow and the next day—for surely no prophet can die outside Jerusalem!" (Lk 13:32-33)

Prophets do not fear rulers. Jesus knows Antipas is devious, manipulative and dishonest. Regardless of what Antipas wants, Jesus declares he will continue in his redemptive, liberating work of the kingdom and it will end, as did John's prophetic life, in death. But Jesus' death will be in the center of power, in Jerusalem. Like John's death, Jesus' will take place in conjunction with a festive meal. The politic of Jesus entails words for devious earthly kings, words that will kill Jesus.

Taxes. Taxes embody the state and empire and at the same time embody one's relation to the state and the empire. Once his disciples are asked if Jesus pays the "temple tax" (Mt 17:24-27), and once he is asked if it is right to pay taxes to Caesar (Mk 12:13-17 pars.). These are not simple texts to examine, and it would not be hard to exhaust the space for this study on each of these texts.[14] The tax revolt of Judas (not the biblical character) in the days of Coponius was perhaps still simmering in the Jews' memories. Josephus said Jesus upbraided "them as cowards for consenting to pay tribute to the Romans and tolerating mortal masters, after having God for their Lord."[15]

Tax collectors ask Peter if Jesus pays the "two-drachma" or two-shekel tax, a quasi-voluntary tax for every Jewish male that was about atonement and loyalty (Ex 30:11-16),[16] even though this tax tended toward enormous bounties for the temple and its personnel. Not all paid the tax, and the Essenes at Qumran offered their passive-aggressive protest by paying it only once per lifetime.[17] Pharisees paid the tax but priests did not (*m. Sheqalim* 1:3).[18] They

---

[14]See Richard Bauckham, *The Bible in Politics: How to Read the Bible Politically*, 2nd ed. (Louisville: Westminster John Knox, 2011), pp. 73-84. Strangely, Yoder was silent on the tax statements in *The Politics of Jesus*.

[15]Josephus, *Jewish War* 2.117; see also *Antiquities* 18:4-5, 23.

[16]William Horbury, "The Temple Tax," in *Jesus and the Politics of His Day*, ed. Ernst Bammel and C. F. D. Moule (New York: Cambridge University Press, 1984), pp. 277-82.

[17]4QOrdinances.

[18]The Mishnah's text reads as follows: "From whom do they exact a pledge? Levites, Israelites, proselytes,

ask Jesus because they think he sits loose on such issues. Peter informs them Jesus does pay. Then three moves are made in the text. Jesus opens the discussion when Peter enters the house by asking, "From whom do the [Gentile] kings of the earth collect duty and taxes—from their own children or from others?" They exact revenue from *others*, Peter answers. What Jesus says next is not anarchic or radical; it is boilerplate, at first. "Then the children are exempt." But the boilerplate is about to get hot: "So that we may not cause offense," pay the taxes, Jesus responds. But then he provides, miraculously, revenue for the taxes in the mouth of a tilapia, the fish now known in the Holy Land as "St. Peter's fish."

Jesus claims the status of citizens for Peter and himself, which means they are exempt. But in order not to offend Jesus pays the taxes. Jesus' logic is from the lesser to the greater: if kings of the earth don't tax their own citizens, then God, who is surely more fatherly, doesn't tax his citizens. Richard Bauckham draws this conclusion: "Thus Jesus' objection is to theocratic taxation, taxing God's people in God's name, because it is inconsistent with the way Jesus understands the rule of God."[19] The story substantiates this fatherly love for his children by providing the revenue for Jesus and Peter. What we see here is probably a subtle form of deconstruction: we won't pay taxes as duty, but we will pay taxes voluntarily in order not to offend, even if it offends Anabaptist idealisms.

The logic of this passage in part hangs on one word: *we*. Jesus identifies himself and Peter with the children of the Father, and we can rightly spy here an ecclesiology at work. In this "we" Jesus distanced himself from both Roman and Galilean/Judean citizens by claiming that he and his followers are citizens of the Father's kingdom and, as such, are free from taxation as a duty. They are no longer worldly citizens but kingdom citizens and, as such, operate on a different basis in that they pay taxes as loving acts of voluntary charity, which is closer to Anabaptist idealisms.

Jesus has now spoken about a Jewish tax. What about taxes to Rome? The temple establishment sends some Pharisees and Herodians to trap Jesus, and

---

and freed slaves, but not from women, slaves, and minors. . . . And they do not exact a pledge from priests for the sake of peace." Debate ensues about whether or not priests should pay; Gentiles and Samaritans who offered to pay were to be refused.

[19]Bauckham, *The Bible in Politics*, p. 75.

they ask, "Is it right to pay the imperial tax[20] to Caesar or not?" Jesus perceives their hypocrisy, asks for a denarius and asks them a question in return: "Whose image is this? And whose inscription?" "Caesar's," they say. Jesus' final riddle-like word: "Give back to Caesar what is Caesar's and to God what is God's" (Mk 12:13-17). Is this diplomacy[21] or intentional ambiguity?[22] The Zealots hated this tax and saw it as idolatrous, and some have set the question and Jesus' response in a Zealot context. The spectrum then shifts toward those who thought complicity with Rome might be the way forward and opposition the way to war. The priestly establishment ambassadors seem then to have expected Jesus to side with the Zealots and implicate himself in the resistance movement. Whether they did or not, he does not. How then to read the riddle?

Richard Bauckham moves this in a kind of subordinationist direction where the rule of God permits taxation by Caesar. His conclusion is that "God's claim on his people does not conflict with Caesar's right to receive taxation."[23] N. T. Wright points us in a different direction.[24] Wright sums up the context with this: "Zeal for YHWH and Torah meant revolution." That is, Jesus was heard as saying "Pay Caesar back what he is owed!" So Wright asks more: "Had [Jesus] told them to revolt? Had he told them to pay the tax? He had done neither. He had done both."[25] That is, Jesus came to bring a revolution against all would-be gods, including Caesar, but it will not come by violence. He takes both sides and at the same time neither. Richard Horsley, in an extended and wide-ranging discussion of this saying, argues the tax question is about a thriving controversy of resistance. Jesus asserts that all belongs to God, God's kingdom is now present. Jesus is calling people to the kingdom of God, and Jesus' riddle expresses his antiestablishment posture against the taxation system of the empire.[26]

I believe the traditional, more subtle ironic view has much to commend it

---

[20]A non-Roman, subjected peoples tax that led to a revolt in 6 C.E.

[21]Joel Marcus, *Mark 8-16*, Anchor Bible 27A (New Haven: Yale University Press, 2009), pp. 825-26.

[22]Adela Yarbro Collins, *Mark: A Commentary*, Hermeneia (Minneapolis: Fortress, 2007), p. 557.

[23]Bauckham, *The Bible in Politics*, p. 80.

[24]N. T. Wright, *Jesus and the Victory of God*, Christian Origins and the Question of God 2 (Minneapolis: Fortress, 1996), pp. 502-7.

[25]Ibid., pp. 504-5.

[26]Richard A. Horsley, *Jesus and the Spiral of Violence: Popular Jewish Resistance in Roman Palestine* (San Francisco: Harper & Row, 1987), pp. 306-17.

and can be tightened up a bit in the direction of Horsley if one considers Luke 23:2—words that will appear in the trial of Jesus not long after this encounter, words (to be sure) that could be misrepresenting Jesus: "We have found this man subverting our nation. He opposes payment of taxes to Caesar and claims to be Messiah, a king." I suggest then that Luke 23:2, like the temple tax statement, requires a Jesus who opposes the tax, and I infer, in light of what Jesus said about the temple tax, that he permits it for pragmatic reasons. That is, because he is forming a redeemed community, a kingdom *ecclesia*, this community resists the temple establishment and Caesar because it listens now to Jesus as its king. And, in light of listening to him, it will pay taxes to the temple and to Caesar *so as not to create offense* but only for that reason. "Give to Caesar" describes, then, the nonoffensive, actively nonviolent but seditious act of paying taxes because one "gives to God what is God's," and what is God's is that Jesus is the king and his followers are the kingdom's redeemed community.

In both of these tax episodes then we have a similar logic: kingdom people, because they live under a new allegiance to Jesus, are exempt but pay taxes for pragmatic reasons.

Temple entry. Of all the events in the life of Jesus nothing was any more political than his street theater–like staged but daring entry into Jerusalem on a colt (or an "ass," according to Matthew) that began what we now call Holy Week (Mt 21:1-9; Mk 11:1-10; Lk 19:28-40; Jn 12:12-15). Luke alone attaches to this narrative a description of Jesus' weeping over Jerusalem, predicting its demise and explaining its fall because Jerusalem did not recognize when God came to it (Lk 19:41-44). I offer four brief observations.

First, the entry is about messianic mockery. Military victories were celebrated with massive parades designed to display domination. We have records of such military entries into cities, including Jerusalem, in both Jewish and Greco-Roman contexts. One can trace this back as far as Solomon in 1 Kings 1:32-40, and one thinks also of how Jaddus, high priest, met and escorted Alexander from Joppa to Jerusalem into the temple courts where a sacrifice was offered on the king's behalf.[27] The pattern of these two and others is rather clear: a victory, a formal parade into the city, acclamations, entry into the

---

[27]Josephus, *Antiquities* 11:325-39; David R. Catchpole, "The 'Triumphal' Entry," in *Jesus and the Politics of His Day*, ed. Ernst Bammel and C. F. D. Moule (New York: Cambridge University Press, 1984), pp. 319-21.

temple with various kinds of cultic activity. The distinguishing features of
Jesus' "triumphal" entry are that he has won no military victory, his entry is
staged by more or less his friends, he is acclaimed as king by nobodies, and
most notably he enters on a new/young colt draped with cloaks. In other
words, this is a grand mockery of the sorts of entries one finds with military
victors. Divine victory, Jesus seems to be saying, cannot be achieved by the
sword. It is not exaggeration to see subversion of the powers in this act of Jesus.

Second, the entry is simultaneously the paradoxical entry of God and a new
stage in the dawning of the Davidic kingdom. Matthew alone attaches Zechariah 9:9, a text evoking a number of themes in Israel's eschatological hopes:

> See, your king comes to you,
> gentle and riding on a donkey,
>   and on a colt, the foal of a donkey. (Mt 21:5)

Matthew's use of this text only makes explicit what is already implicitly at
work: Jesus is evoking the Zecharian vision of the return of God, in the form
of God's appointed messianic king, to Zion. But God presents himself not
in terms of a battle warrior but offers a king to the city on peaceful terms, for
as Zechariah will say one verse later, "He [that king] will proclaim peace to
the nations" (Zech 9:10). The passage evokes the return of God to Zion to
restore her fortunes. Now we have two themes: humility and the return of
God for peace.

Third, the acclamations are from Psalm 118, part of the *hallel* hymns sung at
Passover, and the targumic tradition, perhaps alive at the time of Jesus, tied
the words used here even more to the Davidic king. Either way, Psalm 118 is
about God's redemption of Israel and Jerusalem and the parade of acclamation
to the very center of the temple. It ought now to be observed that hope for
redemption in words like this, at Passover, by Jewish peasants, is more than a
"Kumbaya, Lord, Kumbaya" or "It Only Takes a Spark." Passover evoked the
exodus in literal detail, the exodus was about liberation, and Passover remembered Passover into a hope for its present and future, so Rome was nervous
about this feast. That Jesus is acclaimed here threatens the fragile stability of
Jerusalem.

Fourth, and very briefly, the messianic mockery leads to the entry into the
temple, where Jesus creates a public scene through a public protest and even-

tually clarifies that the temple's sacrificial system is being fulfilled in his own self-offering as a Passover-like liberating death. This offering is demonstrated at the Last Supper and indicates that the sword is overcome by the cross. Jesus' kingdom politics are not the politics of a sword but instead the politics of a cross, a cross where it was self-sacrificial love and death that would lead to resurrection and victory. The entry and cleansing events evoke then four themes in the politic of Jesus: humility, God's return for peace, liberation and all these through the cross.

CONCLUSION

Like a magnet hidden under the table that attracts all metal bits to its power, so there is a hidden element in all of these themes when it comes to the politics of Jesus: Jesus himself. Jesus may have preached the kingdom of *God*, but it was Jesus who revealed and declared that kingdom. He is the one through whom God will rule. He exhibits the kingdom's love, he unleashes its power, and it is his cross and resurrection that take the powers of death and darkness under to drown them. Time after time in these sketches the magnet of Christology pulls us into its orbit and we realize that kingdom is very close to what Origen once said it was: Jesus is the *autobasileia*, Jesus is the kingdom itself. There is, then, no kingdom outside of Christ. The first word in the politics of Jesus, then, is a word about Jesus.

Extra Christum nullum regnum.

4

THE POLITICAL VISION OF THE APOSTLE TO THE NATIONS

Timothy G. Gombis

The prospect of bringing the apostle Paul fruitfully into this conversation to gain wisdom for Christian political witness may seem, at first glance, like an utterly hopeless task. According to the overwhelming consensus of New Testament scholarship over the last two centuries, Jesus had much to say about politics, but Paul was silent. Jesus taught openly and at length about the kingdom of God. This teaching involved public repentance, a redeemed use of money, care for the poor, justice for the oppressed, inclusion of the marginalized and transformed economic and political practices. Paul, according to many biblical scholars, had a different orientation altogether. He didn't have much to say about the kingdom of God and wasn't terribly interested in relationships with outsiders. He was a theologian of the heart set free, giving counsel on sustaining the inner spiritual life and maintaining one's affections for the things of God. He called for minds set on heavenly things and hearts fixed on eternal realities. Engaging politically with the gritty realities of the here and now was of little interest to him. If Paul had anything at all to say about such things, he said it in Romans 13:1-7, where he briefly exhorts the Roman Christians to be supportive of governing authorities and leave politics to the world.

While this consensus no longer predominates in New Testament scholarship, it has profoundly affected the way many Christians imagine Paul regarded political involvement on the part of the church. This conception, however, dislocates Paul from his historical context and disconnects him from the narrative that shaped his thought.

I hope to offer an alternative and compelling case that Paul's gospel is first and foremost a political proclamation. Paul's gospel is fundamentally and thoroughly political. It is political from beginning to end, both in its central convictions and its endless implications. Paul could have seen things only in political terms. To depoliticize Paul's vision is to tear out its very heart, turn it into something completely different, and to end up with a so-called gospel that Paul would hardly recognize.

That may strike modern evangelical ears as highly unusual, if not impossible. But I wonder if we need to reconsider how we regard the term *politics*. It may be that our assumptions of what politics means have been corrupted, shaped as they are by culture wars, national power politics of a two-party system, and various media outlets that seem to survive on stoking cultural anger, fear and anxiety. We will gain a far clearer vision of Paul and politics by setting the apostle in a new narrative context, reading him no longer in a post-Enlightenment narrative determined by individualism and talk about liberties and pursuits of happiness.

In order to demonstrate the political character of Paul's vision, I will take a narrative approach to Paul, situating him within the scriptural story that shapes his thought.[1] This approach allows us to see aspects of his life and hear notes in his letters that may be far more politically oriented than we have previously recognized. I hope to demonstrate that, for Paul, Israel's identity and mission shaped the church's identity and mission. I will then consider briefly two important issues in current discussions of Paul and politics: his instruction in Romans 13, and the notion that Paul's letters contain rhetoric that critiqued or subverted the Roman empire and the claims of Caesar's lordship. Finally, I'll offer a few brief reflections on how we may faithfully embody Paul's political vision today.

Before I proceed, I'd like to define a few terms. First, I'll be referring quite a bit to "politics" and that which is "political." By *politics*, I'm speaking about that which has to do with rulership—who is in charge and what right do they have to order our lives? Politics involves the proper ordering of social practices and relationships, and patterns of economic exchange within a social group.

Politics has to do with all sorts of behaviors in the *polis*. That term—*polis*—

---

[1]For an introduction to a narrative reading of Paul, see J. R. Daniel Kirk, *Jesus Have I Loved, but Paul? A Narrative Approach to the Problem of Pauline Christianity* (Grand Rapids: Baker Academic, 2012).

is the Greek term that denoted ancient cities and all that held them together as cohesive social and cultural units. The *polis* is the body politic, a gathered people regarded as a political body under an organized government. Politics, then, has to do with ruling and socially ordering a *polis*.

Simply by defining our terms we can already discern that Paul was politically oriented. He proclaimed the lordship of Jesus Christ and established communities that enjoyed his gracious reign. His letters of instruction to these bodies politic involved their social ordering, the transformation of their community practices, their economic exchanges with one another and their treating one another according to radically alternative social rules. They were to relate to one another, in fact, according to the realities of a coming political order—the kingdom of God. Paul imagined each church as a *polis* functioning and flourishing in the midst of the wider *polis*. When Paul talks about the church, then, he is elaborating a political vision.

Let's turn to Paul and his scriptural heritage—the biblical narrative that shaped his thinking.

PAUL'S STORIED POLITICAL HERITAGE

Paul's thought was most fundamentally shaped by the scriptural narrative of the Creator God and his call of Israel to be his special possession. The God of Israel spoke a creative word, ordered the world and placed humanity within the Garden of Eden. God charged Adam and Eve to rule over creation as vice regents on God's behalf in such a way that reflected his ultimate rule and brought forth the earth's fruitfulness. They were to cultivate *shalom*, the flourishing of humanity and creation together. God's original intentions, therefore, were political, having to do with the reign of God and the right ordering of humanity's social behaviors.

Humanity rebelled, however, and no longer ruled creation in the name of the one true God, and they no longer sought to cultivate *shalom*, looking after God's good world in harmony with others. They exploited the creation for short-term and selfish pleasures, spoiling it and dishonoring one another. The fall into sin introduced the disordered politics of chaos and destruction.

In response to this, God made promises to redeem, and began to fulfill these by calling Abraham, vowing to make of his descendants a great nation and through it to redeem the nations of the world (Gen 12:1-3). The dominant subject of the Abrahamic promises—certainly as Paul understands them—is international relations.

God called Israel out from Egypt to make them a "holy nation" (Ex 19:5-6; Lev 20:26), his own unique possession. Through Israel God intended to fulfill his promises to Abraham, making them a blessing to the nations. Israel was a "kingdom of priests" in that they were to represent God to the nations, leading the nations in the worship of the one true God. The Mosaic law laid out a political vision for God's people and involved both domestic and international relations. Domestically, they were to be holy, having an internal life that was completely different from the nations. They were to be a nation of justice and compassion, looking after the poor, the orphan and the widow. There was to be no one needy among them, since they were all brothers and sisters, and the one true God whose world is one of plenty was to dwell among them uniquely.

And they had a very unique foreign policy. While maintaining their distinct identity, they were to develop relationships of mutual sharing in order to disciple the nations in the way of the God of Israel, who was also the great King over all the earth. Israel's foreign policy as a kingdom of priests was a seriously risky mission! It involved, after all, a military policy of vulnerability and weakness. According to God's original design, however, if Israel was faithful to God regarding its domestic practices and international relations, God himself would be their security.

As we know, the Scriptures tell the story of tragic unfaithfulness. Rather than being a light to the nations, Israel wanted to be like the nations. Rather than cultivating a politics of holiness, they mimicked the corrupted political, economic and social practices found among their idolatrous neighbors. They practiced injustice, exploited the weak and defenseless, and adopted the worship of the gods of the nations. They did not trust God to protect them or their national interests, so they made treaties with the nations in order to guarantee their security.

Israel further perverted their foreign policy of holiness, distorting God's law. They turned its practices into a set of distinctives that they then held over against their neighbors, adopting an arrogant and judgmental posture toward the nations God wanted to redeem. Rather than being agents of the life of God to the peoples of the world, they grew to fear and despise the nations, longing for their destruction. And they imagined that God regarded outsiders with the same attitude of contempt. Because of the vast range of their corruptions as a body politic, God sent Israel into exile.

Even in exile, however, God wanted his people to maintain a political vocation of holiness. They were to remain cohesive and distinct, becoming a wandering people among the nations—a *polis* among the *poleis*. They were to cultivate internal practices of mutual care, love, servanthood, humility and economic sharing. And they were to seek the blessing of the surrounding *polis*—the wider culture within which they were now situated.

Jeremiah, in a letter sent from Jerusalem to Babylon, relayed this vision to the exiles in a prophetic word:

> Thus says the LORD of hosts, the God of Israel, to all the exiles whom I have sent into exile from Jerusalem to Babylon: Build houses and live in them; plant gardens and eat what they produce. Take wives and have sons and daughters; take wives for your sons, and give your daughters in marriage, that they may bear sons and daughters; multiply there, and do not decrease. But seek the welfare of the city where I have sent you into exile, and pray to the LORD on its behalf, for in its welfare you will find your welfare. (Jer 29:4-7)[2]

While they were in exile, the God of Israel insisted that this was not the end of the story. He promised that he would return to gather them back to the land and establish his kingdom among them once again. He would restore his people, sending his Spirit to breathe new life into dead bones and reconstitute Israel as a nation that would truly "know God" (Jer 31:31-34). They would practice justice and look out for the poor, the orphan and the widow, and they would lead the nations in the worship of the one true God, enjoying along with them his magnanimous blessing.

These promises of a restored body politic shaped Jewish expectations of salvation in the centuries preceding the turn of the eras. First-century Jews lived under the oppressive domination of Rome and called out ever more passionately to the God of Israel for political redemption—freedom from oppression, the installation of righteous leaders, a restored society of political and economic justice and compassion where everyone was looked after. They longed for *shalom*, the political order of flourishing that comes from God's very presence among them.

---

[2]Unless otherwise noted, Scripture quotations in this chapter are from the NRSV.

PAUL'S PRECONVERSION POLITICS OF COERCION

Saul the Pharisee would have shared this vision of salvation. The Pharisaic hope was in the God of Israel fulfilling his promises to set Israel free from oppression and to restore the nation to its rightful place as God's chief agent of salvation and of rule over creation.

Because he was passionate about this hope, Saul found Israel's current domination and oppression at the hands of Rome intolerable. As Saul read the Scriptures of Israel, he understood that the nation had been sent into exile for unfaithfulness to God, for idolatry, for neglecting the Mosaic law and its practices. If unfaithfulness to the Mosaic law led to exile, then renewed faithfulness to the law at the national level would surely move God to act on behalf of Israel to deliver the nation from its enemies and bring about salvation.

Before his conversion, then, Saul was involved in a national campaign for the honor of the God of Israel, advocating for faithfulness to the Mosaic law. His zeal for a righteous nation explains his persecution of the early Christians. That a movement would have sprung up around a man whom the law had cursed was blasphemous and intolerable, since it could only be characterized as a defiant rejection of God's own verdict on Jesus and his claims. Saul could not afford to ignore this movement or maintain any kind of neutral posture toward it. The early Christians were standing in the way of the God of Israel redeeming his people!

This set Saul on a religiopolitical mission of coercion and violence. If you were to ask Saul the Pharisee, "What is keeping God from coming in power to save his people and to judge the nations?" he might answer, "It's the presence of sinners in Israel, their unfaithfulness to the law and lack of conformity to the traditions of the fathers—*they* are preventing God from saving Israel and bringing about the resurrection from the dead."

It is instructive for us to remember that Saul's political vision was indeed largely shaped by Scripture. But there were several elements that had become perverted and distorted. Saul had become captive to an us-versus-them mentality. He longed for God's vengeance against foreign nations rather than their redemption. And his political mode had become corrupted because of his zeal. He was violently coercive toward others, seeing others as the problem he needed to solve on God's behalf. Only once people got on board with the Pharisaic agenda of a righteous *polis* would Israel experience God's blessing.

Saul was not only coercing other Jews, he was also trying to force God's hand. He truly believed that he could get God to send salvation based on works of righteousness.

THE CONVERSION OF PAUL'S POLITICAL IMAGINATION

To say that Saul's perspective changed on the Damascus road would be a fairly dramatic understatement. Of course it did. But just *how* did it change, and *what aspects* of it were transformed? First, when Saul saw the resurrected and ascended Jesus on his heavenly throne, he realized that God had initiated his resurrection-oriented salvation program, involving political, economic and social aspects of life, including the transformation of the entire cosmos.

Second, Saul realized that God had begun his resurrection agenda with the crucified Jesus—*the crucified Jesus*. We're so used to this central component of our faith that we have difficulty realizing how shockingly scandalous it was— and how shockingly scandalous it should remain. God accomplished salvation through Jesus' death on the most potent political symbol of imperial domination and shameful political defeat. Jesus died on a cross along with political agitators, violent criminals and others that Rome simply wanted to be rid of. Far from being cursed by the God of Israel, this Jesus had been vindicated, shown to be in the right, revealed to be God's chief agent of salvation, resurrected, exalted and installed as cosmic Lord, ruler of all things. God does not accomplish his saving purposes through power, domination or coercion, but through self-giving love, servanthood and giving himself fully for the life of the world and the flourishing of his enemies. That is, God initiates and executes his redemptive mission *only* by his grace, and *not* based on works of righteousness.

Third, because of this Saul realized that God's politics must be shaped by the cross. According to the ideology of ancient kingship, the character of the king dominates, fills and orients the life of the realm over which he rules.[3] If Jesus triumphs by means of the cross, then all those loyal to him must be *cruciform*—that is, cross-shaped. The *polis* of Jesus has its political, economic and social life holistically determined by the cross—not by power, not by coercion, not by violence in any form. For Saul this was a breathtakingly radical reversal; indeed, it is so profound we can hardly grasp it.

---

[3]Julien Smith, *Christ the Ideal King: Cultural Context, Rhetorical Strategy, and the Power of Divine Monarchy in Ephesians*, WUNT II, vol. 313 (Tubingen: Mohr Siebeck, 2011), pp. 221-35.

A fourth transformation of Saul's political vision is that resurrection doesn't work like Saul had anticipated. He expected one singular end-time event. On the Day of the Lord, God would judge the wicked, save his people, raise the righteous dead and bring in the fullness of God's new creation political order. But Saul came to understand this mystery: that God had *begun* his work of salvation, *but will complete it over time*. Christ was raised as the firstfruits, after which God will raise from the dead all those who are loyal to Jesus in another future end-time event—the day of Christ. In the meantime, God is building his church—the *polis* of Jesus set among the *poleis* of the world.

Fifth, Saul underwent a radical reversal regarding Israel's relationship to the nations. Saul now sees that the God of Israel loves the nations and Jesus died so that they might truly live. God is building a new people—a new *polis*—and the singular defining identity marker of the people of God is "Jesus-follower," and not Jew, or non-Jew, Greek, Scythian, European, Italian, Irish, white American, African American, Hispanic, Arab, whatever. *All* are united in the one new *polis* of Jesus in which all other identities are subordinated to our membership in the body of Christ.

Saul of Tarsus, therefore, had a radical political conversion. His conversion wasn't merely "spiritual," involving a profound change of heart. Saul came to see that God had installed a new ruler of all things, seen and unseen, things in heaven and things on earth—the Lord Jesus Christ. Saul's conversion, then, is a thoroughly political one, and his politics are transformed thoroughly.

PAUL'S POLITICAL PROCLAMATION

I've claimed thus far that Paul's gospel is political, and I've already given some hints about the basic shape of his outlook. But what are the more specific political contours of his thought? Just how does this work out when we turn to the sorts of things he actually wrote to churches?

First, the heart of Paul's gospel is the announcement of a new ruler—Jesus Christ as cosmic Lord. This is a political title. Jesus is not only the Messiah of Israel, but Lord over all things, highly exalted over all powers and authorities (Eph 1:20-22). Jesus Christ is the political ruler of a newly gathered people—the new-creation *polis* of God.

Second, Paul's gospel is the announcement of the arrival of the long-awaited kingdom of God. This political reality is the emergence of a God-empowered, Spirit-animated realm that manifests the reign of the Lord Jesus through a radically new social order—the *polis* of Jesus.

Third, the church as a body politic takes its orientation from Israel as a political entity. Israel's identity and mission shape the church's identity and mission. This is signaled by Paul's language for the church, which he borrows from Scripture's language about Israel. Paul uses holiness language quite often to speak of his churches' identity with reference to God, referring to believers as "holy ones." This does not merely point to a moral purity before God, though it may include this. It points to Israel's politically oriented vocation. God called them as a radically different sort of people who were to embody a radically different domestic set of social practices and a completely unique set of relationships with the surrounding nations. When Paul uses holiness language for the church, he's getting at how the *polis* of Jesus is supposed to be this sort of people among the various peoples of the world.

In several of his letters, Paul refers to readers as "chosen," or "elect" (1 Cor 1:26-31; Eph 1:3-14). Rather than providing material for the development of a doctrine of predestination in these places, Paul is referring to Israel's election. God chose Abraham and Israel, not because he loved them more than the nations, but precisely *because* he loved the nations. His chosen ones are those who are special recipients of God's love *so that* they can be agents of that love to others. When Paul uses election language with reference to the church, he's thinking of the identity of Israel as agents of God's pursuit of the nations and of the missional character of Israel. This vision of a political unit that embodies God's relentless love for the nations shapes how Paul conceives of the church.

Fourth, the church, for Paul, is God's new temple (1 Cor 3:16; Eph 2:19-22). God now resides *among* his people—God inhabits the church. Beyond a mere religious notion, this is a profoundly political reality. In the ancient world, the existence of a deity's temple indicated the existence of that deity. And the establishment of temples with cultic worship of that deity in far-flung places indicated the expanding rule of that deity. The events of Christ's exaltation, the sending of his Spirit and the growth of the church follow this pattern. The establishment of the church in Jerusalem indicates that in the heavenly sphere Christ has been seated on his throne as Lord. And the growth of the church—even into the heart of the Roman Empire—is the story of the Lord Jesus establishing his universal and cosmic lordship, extending his life-giving reign as he carries out God's mission to reclaim creation for the glory of his name.

Finally, Paul begins nearly every letter with a greeting of "grace and peace." Peace, of course, is one way of translating the Hebrew term *shalom*. Beyond merely indicating the mental or spiritual state of his readers, Paul wishes for them an experience of the political order of universal flourishing that was to characterize God's world from the beginning.

Much more could be said about each of these, but my main contention is that the political identity and political mission of Israel determined how Paul conceived of the church. He did not envision the church as the weekly gathering of all the individuals who are each conducting their own private relationship with Jesus. The church is a body politic, and Paul's vision is thoroughly political, though in a way that may require a conversion of the imagination on our part when it comes to conceiving of and speaking about politics.

Paul's Counsel to the Roman Churches

Let us now consider Paul's instruction in Romans 13:1-7, historically regarded as the main passage in which Paul speaks about the church's relation to worldly powers. How can a narrative approach provide help in understanding Paul's political word of exhortation to the Roman church? I offer here a few brief suggestions.

First, we must keep in mind the character of Paul's letter to the Romans. The Roman church (or network of house churches) was a community struggling to stay together. Paul wrote them a pastoral letter with exhortation and counsel on how to restore and maintain their unity. Romans is not a work of abstract theology or systematic reflection on a series of topics beginning with soteriology, moving to election and God's plan for Israel, and touching briefly on a theology of the secular state.

Second, Paul's pastoral purpose shapes his exhortations in Romans 13:1-7 and his comments about "governing authorities." He meant to give them wisdom to navigate their situation fruitfully as a vulnerable community in need of resolving internal disputes and maintaining community cohesion. His aim here is not primarily to shape the church's conception of the state so that they have a well-rounded understanding of secular governments. This is a highly situational text, and we must keep in mind *why* Paul says what he says in helping them negotiate life together as a *polis* of Christ within a wider *polis*.

Third, a narrative method is especially helpful here in that the trajectories of Israel's Scriptures shape Paul's thought and provide a wider context within which to understand Paul's instruction. Paul's exhortations to the Roman church have the same narrative shape as Jeremiah's instruction to the Israelites taken to Babylon. The exiles in Jeremiah's day needed to grapple with their identity as the people of God in an unfamiliar situation, embracing the role of a wandering community in a threatening and hostile environment. Paul's exhortations to the Roman church are in continuity with Jeremiah's instruction to the exiles.

Along this line, we must keep in mind the direction and intention of Jeremiah's and Paul's instruction. Jeremiah's exhortation to seek the peace of Babylon is intended to shape the character and outlook of the exiled community as it considers how to make a way forward. It is not an endorsement of the goodness of the Babylonian empire or the rightness of its actions. If the prophet intended to speak of the Babylonian empire in itself, he would reflect prophetic critiques found elsewhere, referring to beasts with voracious appetites heading for destruction. In the same way, Paul's instruction to the Roman church is intended to shape its character and outlook as it considers its future. Paul is not validating Rome's conduct in any way, affirming neither the empire's goodness nor the rightness of its actions. If he were to speak of the character of the empire in itself, he would also likely take up the prophetic critique (as John does in Revelation) and make reference to beasts that devour and are headed for destruction.[4]

Fourth, the pressing issue giving rise to Paul's words here is most likely the burden of taxation. It may have been that a heavy tax load on the Jewish Christians was exacerbating the developing divisions in the Roman church. Robert Jewett notes that Nero's administration was wary of people fleeing localities to avoid paying taxes.[5] Jewish Christians who were banished from Rome in 49 and who returned in 54 may have been susceptible to an unusually burdensome series of taxes.

In light of a temptation to join the tax-revolt movement, Paul commands the Roman Christians to be in subjection (Rom 13:1, 5) and to continue to pay

---

[4]Because Paul's intention is not to address the character of the secular state per se, it is likely an overstatement to claim that this passage is a "primary" text in "teaching about the responsibilities of civil government"; Wayne A. Grudem, *Politics According to the Bible: A Comprehensive Resource for Understanding Modern Political Issues* (Grand Rapids: Zondervan, 2010), pp. 188, 196.

[5]Robert Jewett, *Romans: A Commentary,* Hermeneia (Philadelphia: Fortress, 2007), p. 799.

the taxes owed (vv. 6-7). Because God is a God of order, and the governing authorities in some way are "ministers of God" (Rom 13:6 ESV), the Roman Christians are to order themselves rightly, taking their place in subjection to authorities. Paul does not exhort his readers to endorse—or even to be supportive of—the governing authorities. But they must not oppose the authorities, for they would be opposing God, resisting his rule.

One troubling aspect of this text is Paul's designation of tax farmers and other corrupt rulers as "ministers of God." This is no less troubling, however, than Isaiah referring to Cyrus as God's messiah (Is 45:1).[6] The prophet interprets current events so that his audience can discern the ways of God and understand how God means for his people to walk faithfully before him. Such a title does not endorse Cyrus, the Babylonian empire or its mode of operation. In the same way, Paul's description does not imply that the church owes governing authorities unquestioning support. If anything, it indicates that ruling authorities and other public officials are not ultimate—contrary to their own claims—or beyond judgment. They are accountable to the one true God, and the church can rest in confidence that the Judge of all the earth misses nothing and will judge rightly.[7]

Though much more can be said about Romans 13:1-7, Paul's instruction functions to remind the Roman church to resist temptations to retaliate or take vengeance to achieve what it perceives to be justice. They are to leave justice and judgment to God alone, lest they enter the realm of wrath.

The resonance of this passage with Jeremiah's instruction to the exiles in Jeremiah 29 indicates that the period of the exile may be the most fruitful narrative moment against which to interpret Romans 13:1-7. The people of God are, in the time of the Gentiles, a wandering people among the nations. This notion has received little attention in evangelical discussions of politics—perhaps because it runs counter to desires to influence policy, control the levers of power and determine the course of national history. We'll have more to say about this in conclusion.

PAUL AND ANTI-IMPERIAL RHETORIC

A recent trend in the interpretation of Paul claims that his letters contain anti-

---

[6]Most English versions translate the Hebrew *mashiach* as "anointed" rather than "messiah."
[7]N. T. Wright, *Paul: In Fresh Perspective* (Philadelphia: Fortress, 2005), p. 78.

imperial rhetoric. That is, Paul sets the church as a political entity over against the Roman Empire, proclaiming the lordship of Jesus Christ to counter the claims of Caesar as lord. After all, similar claims are made about Caesar as are made about Jesus Christ. The following is from an inscription dating to about 9 B.C.E, celebrating the birthday of Augustus:

> The providence which has ordered the whole of our life, showing concern and zeal, has ordained the most perfect consummation for human life by giving to it Augustus, by filling him with virtue for doing the work of a benefactor among men, and by sending in him, as it were, a savior for us and those who come after us, to make war to cease, to create order everywhere. . . . The birthday of the god [Augustus] was the beginning for the world of the glad tidings that have come to men through him.[8]

The term translated "glad tidings" in the final line of this inscription is the same term translated "gospel" in the New Testament. This is very similar language to that used by Paul of Jesus Christ in Colossians 1. He refers to the "gospel that has come to you" (Col 1:5-6) before speaking in exalted terms of Jesus Christ, emphasizing his cosmic lordship over all competing cosmic powers:

> He is the image of the invisible God, the firstborn of all creation; for in him all things in heaven and on earth were created, things visible and invisible, whether thrones or dominions or rulers or powers—all things have been created through him and for him. He himself is before all things, and in him all things hold together. He is the head of the body, the church; he is the beginning, the firstborn from the dead, so that he might come to have first place in everything. For in him all the fullness of God was pleased to dwell, and through him God was pleased to reconcile to himself all things, whether on earth or in heaven, by making peace through the blood of his cross. (Col 1:15-20)

Some scholars argue that Paul is deliberately subverting the notion that Caesar was the embodiment of the gods and was himself divine. Caesar received worship in the well-established emperor cult, and was seen as the guarantor of the *Pax Romana*—the peace of Rome. According to this view, Paul's rhetoric flies deliberately in the face of such idolatrous claims.

This quite recent trend reminds interpreters of the political dimensions of

---

[8]Arthur Darby Nock, *Early Gentile Christianity and Its Hellenistic Background* (New York: Harper & Row, 1964), p. 37.

Paul's letters. It is clear that Paul speaks of the church as the kingdom of God, a redemptively alternative political body that orients its social patterns in ways that resist the corrupted practices of any surrounding culture. We must note that Paul never mentions Caesar, nor is there definitive anti-imperial rhetoric in his letters. In the absence of explicit statements, those who advocate this approach will continue to emphasize broader patterns and hidden scripts within Paul's letters.

Paul's rhetoric is clearly directed toward explicating the reign of God. It is less oriented toward fostering in his hearers a posture of opposition to the Roman Empire. It may be that this is because he doesn't want his churches directly opposing the empire. He wants them, rather, to resist its idolatries, its social corruptions and its perverted economic practices. It may be that Paul does not speak explicitly about opposition to or subversion of the empire because he doesn't want to fuel anti-imperial passion leading to outright insurrection. Certainly the Lord Jesus is an alternative ruler to Caesar. But, as Kavin Rowe points out in his brilliant book *World Upside Down*, the Christian movement isn't meant to oppose Rome, but Rome's corruptions.[9]

The positive mission of Paul was to shape kingdom-of-God communities in the heart of the empire. The kingdom rule of God in Christ is not embodied through violent insurrection; such a strategy surrenders to the powers of the present evil age and enters into the unending cycle of violence that can never be redemptive. Paul's rhetoric is directed toward churches cultivating alternative communities oriented by life-giving patterns of behavior. They are to embody the reign of the Lord Jesus, who didn't raise an insurrection or seek violent overthrow. Rather than using rhetoric to fuel antagonism toward the empire, Paul wants Christians' hearts, passions and community dynamics to embody the empire of God while not conforming to social patterns of conduct determined by the corrupted rulers of this present evil age. This is just to suggest, then, that Paul is less explicitly anti-imperial rhetorically, for the reason that he wants his communities to forge a radically different style of life. To join in political insurrection is to capitulate to the corrupted forms of politics inherent to the present evil age.

---

[9]C. Kavin Rowe, *World Upside Down: Reading Acts in the Graeco-Roman Age* (Oxford: Oxford University Press, 2009).

CONTEMPORARY POLITICAL IMPLICATIONS

Paul's gospel, then, is a political proclamation, but not political according to the corrupted status quo of what we call politics in twenty-first-century America. God's creation purposes and the identity and mission of Israel shaped Paul's gospel and his vision of the church. For Paul, God is making all things new in Jesus Christ and in and through the *polis* of Jesus. How might the contemporary church embody Paul's political vision?

First, a lesson from Saul the Pharisee. Saul had a mind and heart more thoroughly saturated by Scripture than anyone currently alive. His aims and ambitions were completely oriented by God's agenda! Or so he thought. It's all too easy, once our passions are aroused, for us to distort Scripture, to see in the Bible what we want to see, and to have our notions of the ideal society determined by cultural prejudices rather than by God's agenda. And it's all too easy, driven by growing anger, to adopt a cultural mode of rhetorical violence and coercion. We can deceive ourselves into thinking that we're advocates for God's agenda but instead be in serious need of political repentance.

Second, American evangelicals would do well to consider how Israel's exile shaped Paul's conception of the church—his vision of a weak and vulnerable wandering people among the nations. We feel that we're losing power, influence, access, our former position of political leverage and cultural dominance. We grow worrisome, anxious, nervous about the sort of future our churches will face and the conditions our children will encounter. I'll just suggest to you that this might be a strategic moment for us to embrace our identity as God's wandering people among the nations. It just may be that this emerging moment of cultural weakness is God's gift to his church. What if it's an opportunity for the God revealed in the crucified Jesus to press his people into the shape of the cross? What if the Lord of the church is grieved when we strive for power and agitate to control the course of history? Do we risk being blind to Paul's vision for the *polis* of Jesus because we're overcome by cultural resentment fueled by memories of former days when our opinions held sway?

Third, the politics of Paul are thoroughly and holistically shaped by the cross. The wisdom of God, according to Paul, is the cross. That is, God's way of working is through weakness, self-giving love, love for enemies and fearless embrace of the other. The God revealed in the crucified Jesus strategizes politically to bless, to pour out his political order of flourishing on his enemies.

Whatever their goals, political behaviors that do not reflect the character of the God revealed in the crucified Jesus can make no claim to be Christian.

Fourth, when it comes to politics, Christian people ought to think first of their church, its internal networks of relationships and its postures toward outsiders. For Christians, politics has to do with how we conduct ourselves in our churches and how our churches relate redemptively toward outsiders. Christians churches, therefore, ought to be intensely politically involved. But let's think first about the efforts of our local bodies of Jesus followers acting among our wider communities and neighborhoods. How can we get involved in practical ways to bless our local communities in the name of Jesus? We are to be communities of *shalom* and justice and self-giving love, rather than of coercion and quests for power and influence, making demands that others meet our standards or become like us.

Fifth, our Christian identity, our loyalty to Jesus and to those in our church, far outstrips any earthly affiliation and especially national political party identification. While Christians differ over policies and political ideologies, we ought to celebrate our common participation in the life of God in Christ by the Spirit.

And finally, we must reconsider what is shaping our imaginations. Through whose eyes are we seeing the world and our national situation? Cable news? Newspapers? Talk radio? Politically charged websites? Are they so stirring us up with anger that we speak of this or that political figure derisively, dismissively and in angry terms? Do our stirred-up passions drive us to think, act and speak as non-Christians? Let's have minds and hearts shaped by Scripture, oriented by hope in the coming kingdom of God. Let's reconsider our words and treat people as if we truly are followers of Jesus. And let's set our hearts and minds on eternal things, on that kingdom that is to come and that is already here in power.

5

A WITNESS TO THE NATIONS

Early Christianity and Narratives of Power

George Kalantzis

In a famous sermon on Paul's categorically contra-cultural proclamation, "I will boast all the more gladly of my weaknesses, so that the power of Christ may dwell in me" (2 Cor 12:9b),[1] Dietrich Bonhoeffer declared,

> Against the new meaning which Christianity gave the weak, against [the Christian] glorification of weakness, there has always been the strong and indignant protest of an aristocratic philosophy of life which glorified strength and power and violence as the ultimate ideals of humanity. . . . Christianity stands or falls with its revolutionary protest against violence, arbitrariness, and pride of power, and with its plea for the weak. Christians are doing too little to make these points clear rather than too much. Christendom adjusts itself far too easily to the worship of power. Christians should give more offense, shock the world far more, than they are doing now. Christians should take a stronger stand in favor of the weak rather than considering first the possible right of the strong.[2]

What Bonhoeffer identified in this sermon is the relationship between the competing narratives of power and weakness that form the irreducible dialectic between those who claim the name of Christ and the structures of

---

[1]Paul's statement, of course, is predicated on Christ's own promise, immediately preceding: "My grace is sufficient for you, for my power is made perfect in weakness" (2 Cor 12:9a). Unless otherwise noted, Scripture quotations in this chapter are from the NRSV.

[2]Dietrich Bonhoeffer, *My Strength Is Made Perfect in Weakness* (Sermon for the Evening Worship Service on 2 Corinthians 12:9, London, 1934), in *The Collected Sermons of Dietrich Bonhoeffer*, ed. Isabel Best (Minneapolis: Augsburg Fortress, 2012), p. 169; also DBW 13, pp. 401-4.

domination that surround them. And though one might argue that Bonhoeffer's admonition was hued by the German experience of the 1930s, his hermeneutical premise is neither localized nor idiosyncratic. It stands as a diachronic *first principle* that stems from the seemingly oxymoronic Christian claim that the Savior of the world hung on a cross—the ultimate glorification of weakness against the omnipotent state. For at the core of the Christian message is not power, but love.

This is not an ordinary kind of love, as one has for one's kin. It is God's love for God's enemies. And it is this love of God for the world, expressed in the divine self-giving through the incarnation of the Son, that reconciles God's enemies with the triune God, Father, Son and Holy Spirit (see Jn 3:16; Jn 1:14; Rom 5:10). The result of that reconciliation is peace: God's peace. A peace unlike any other. A peace the world cannot recognize. A peace not based simply on the absence of conflict, but rather a peace based on the proactive love of one's enemies as the *sine qua non* of the community that claims to have been born of this gospel of peace (see Jn 14:27; Mt 5:43-44; Eph 6:15).

Even from the earliest times of the church's story, the twin commandments to not kill (Ex 20:13; Mk 10:19) and to love one's enemies (Mt 5:43-44; Lk 6:27) were not simple gnomic sayings but formed a commanding moral topography for the communities of The Way, so much so that even in the third century the Christian writer Tertullian presented this distinctive *love of enemy and persecutor* as unique among all peoples and as a sign of divine grace: "Here lies the perfection and distinctiveness of Christian goodness," Tertullian declared. "Ordinary goodness is different; for all men love their friends but only Christians love their enemies."[3]

In order for us to evaluate Bonhoeffer's proclamation and, for that matter, understand more fully the evangelical admonition to love one's enemies and pray *for* (not *against*) those who persecute us (Mt 5:44; Lk 6:27), we need to venture into a bit of cultural anthropology and history, and understand the world into which Christianity was birthed and took root. This, however, is not simple antiquarian curiosity. Rather, since Christians claim to stand in historical continuity with the work of God through time and space, we also claim

---

[3]Tertullian, *To Scapula* 1.4.

that even though the everyday reality of the earliest Christians may be somewhat different from ours, it is still part of us.

To read the history of the earliest communities of Christ well we must place them within their own cultural context and the power narratives of their time, while resisting the temptation to make a tidy and edifying story that excises the complexities of lives lived in space and time. We must pay particular attention to the difference between what Justo González calls the "innocent readings" of history and "responsible remembrance."[4] Innocent readings are a selective forgetfulness, a heuristic device for our own agendas and power struggles. Responsible remembrance, on the other hand, sets us free from "the crippling imprisonment of what we can grasp and take for granted, the ultimate trivialising of our identity."[5] Responsible remembrance leads to responsible action. Doing history well, then, is irreducibly a moral affair.[6]

Engaging in this cultural anthropology of imagination will help us understand why the peculiar Christian call to nonviolence was unrecognizable by the culture around them; for it took the form of *civil disobedience* as the mark of a transnational community bound together with the bonds of baptism and the Eucharist. This was a community that honored Caesar by disobeying his commands and receiving upon their bodies the only response a state based on the power of the powerful could mete—in imitation of Christ.

WITH THE GODS ON OUR SIDE: RELIGION AND PATRIOTISM

The world into which Christianity first appeared was quite different from ours.[7] For one, unlike us who accept too easily the secularity of the state, in the religious demography of the Roman world such a concept did not exist. As with all other ancient peoples, for the Romans, too,

> political order was not a question, as it has become for us following the Eighteenth-century Enlightenment, of the functioning of a depersonalized machinery of government from which any final divine purpose or end is excluded.

---

[4]Justo L. González, *Mañana: Christian Theology from a Hispanic Perspective* (Nashville: Abingdon, 1990), p. 79.

[5]Rowan Williams, *Why Study the Past? The Quest for the Historical Church* (Grand Rapids: Eerdmans, 2005), p. 24.

[6]Ibid., pp. 24-25.

[7]For a fuller description and analysis of these themes see George Kalantzis, *Caesar and the Lamb: Early Christian Attitudes on War and Military Service* (Eugene, OR: Cascade, 2012).

Rather, political order consisted in the exercise of legitimate authority within a space that had been sacralized, and therefore under the control of the gods, who willed order and therefore peace (*pax*).[8]

Religion was intimately connected to the idea of sacred space, and the dominant religiopolitical themes of *sacrifice, power* and *social order* saturated the very air ancient peoples breathed. Worship of the gods and the sacrifices offered to them were essential for all aspects of life. Even from Rome's founding narratives, the close relationship between the Romans and the gods who had given the city her expanse in the centuries that followed her mythical founding was always at the core of *Romanitas*, Roman identity, and sacrifice was at the center of that identity.

Sacrifice was the primary means by which Romans communicated with the gods, discerned their will, and established order and balance between the people and the state and between the state and the gods—a balance that would also secure Rome's privileged position. This relationship of *do ut des* ("I give that you may give"), a perpetual cycle of reciprocal exchanges in the form of sacrifices and blessings, underscored the mutual obligations of gods and humans and not only characterized the contractual nature of Roman religion but extended to all forms of life, including social interactions.[9] The secrets of the future would be read in the entrails of the slaughtered animals. Contracts, decrees and laws were sealed with sacrifices. Marriages would be blessed and households would become prosperous. Disease and illness would be averted, and the daily meal would be rendered safe and a welcomed gift from the gods to whom a sacrificial libation was offered in return. Armies never marched without a favorable divine omen and a reading of the entrails of animals. Nor would the cohorts of the legions neglect to honor their divine guardians before battle or give them thanks afterward.

Romans did not separate religion from politics or localize the gods to their allotted spheres. The ubiquity of local shrines and temples, festivals and sacrifices, votive offerings and oracles created for the world of the empire a narrative discourse in which the sacred and the secular, the political and the religious were infinitely intertwined. However (and perhaps somewhat surprising

---

[8]Allen Brent, *Cyprian and Roman Carthage* (Cambridge: Cambridge University Press, 2010), p. 29.
[9]Kalantzis, *Caesar and the Lamb*, pp. 12-16, 18-21.

to us), Roman religion was not concerned with distinguishing true from false *beliefs*: it was simply the proper *behavior* that characterized the life of the Roman citizen. Whether domestic or public, religion in Rome "was more correctly understood as an existential category, discerning the proper actions that would ensure the success of the people and the state."[10]

The many and varied forms of both domestic and public sacrifices also functioned as key forms of social discourse. Ancient peoples used such social discourses to maintain not only their identity but also political and social power. Roman institutions were created and sustained by such political and religious "public transcripts" (that is, societally agreed upon and recognizable public statements concerning how those in dominant positions of authority wish to be perceived) that formed social understandings of power, obligation, expectations, honor and dishonor.[11] These public transcripts also set the boundaries that identified the community first to itself and then to those outside.[12]

Sacrifice is such a public transcript. As a public transcript, personal and corporate sacrifice was at the heart of *Romanitas* and defined the Roman world as *Roman*; it evoked a sentiment of loyalty, of belonging both to the Roman family and to the state. "To be Roman was to be religious. To be religious was to sacrifice in a variety of specified and ritually controlled ways."[13]

During the period of Christianity's early existence, the imperial cult was reinterpreted as an overarching symbol of everything connected with Roman religion, including the very notion of the state. The *pax Romana* ("Roman peace") could not be separated from the *pax deorum* ("peace of the gods"), and that peace was based on and sustained by sacrifice. Sacrifices were performed on behalf of the emperor, not necessarily offered *to* him. The imperial cult functioned as a political identity marker for an expansive empire and focused on the person of the emperor as the vicar of the gods on earth and as the people's representative to the gods, in the locus of the *paterfamilias*. In his very office as monarch and chief priest (*pontifex maximus*), the emperor was

---

[10]George Heyman, *The Power of Sacrifice: Roman and Christian Discourses in Conflict* (Washington, DC: The Catholic University of America Press, 2007), p. 12.

[11]Ibid., pp. xiii-xvi.

[12]See Mary Douglas, *Purity and Danger: An Analysis of Concepts of Pollution and Taboo* (London and New York: Routledge, 1966); also Catherine Bell, *Ritual Theory, Ritual Practice* (Oxford: Oxford University Press, 1992).

[13]Heyman, *Power of Sacrifice*, p. 43.

responsible for universal order under the auspices of the gods.[14] By the end of
the first century emperor Domitian (81–96 C.E.) assumed upon himself not
simply the cognomen of *divi filius* ("son of god"), which Augustus had embraced and used often in his ubiquitous imperial iconography, but that of a
living god, a *Dominus et deus* ("Lord and god").[15] Roman rhetoric presented
participation in the imperial cult within the framework of civic obligation and
the patriotic duty of Roman citizens. By the time of Diocletian (284–305 C.E.)
and the dawn of the fourth century, Rome had been transformed from the
Augustan ideal of a Principate to a Dominate—the absolute rule of a *Dominus*,
a god on earth.[16]

Worship of the omnicausal gods was world formative, not simply epistemic,
and the gods demanded sacrifice. The Christian rejection of the sacred cosmos
created by the Roman civic and religious system was not a mere substitution
of religious allegiances, nor were the prescriptions against idolatrous practices
limited to the *cultus*. It was a *tout court* rejection of this sacred world as the
Romans knew it, of the religion that created it and of the practices that gave it
expression. The Christian refusal to participate in the sacrificial system was
not simply a rejection of Roman religion: it was a fundamental challenge to
Roman identity and to that carefully crafted balance between the Roman state
and the gods.

The conflict between Rome and the church was thus inevitable.

A Radical Shift in History: The Resurrection of Jesus

The first mention of the Christian movement by a Roman writer is found in the
correspondence of Pliny the Younger (c. 61–113 C.E.). Pliny was appointed governor of the province of Bithynia (modern Turkey) at the beginning of the
second century and wrote a number of letters to the emperor Trajan seeking

---

[14]James H. Oliver, *Morals and Law in Ancient Greece* (Baltimore: John Hopkins Press, 1960), pp. 160-63.

[15]The Romans understood various gradations of divinity and made a somewhat consistent distinction
between *divus* ("divine") and *deus* ("god") that is lost in English translation. While the emperor was
recognized as *divus* (a/the "divine one") and his sons as *divi filii* ("sons of the divine"), their divine status
was conferred on them by the Senate by means of the proper offering of sacrifice and correct ritual—it
was not an ontological category. *Deus* ("god"), on the other hand, was a title reserved primarily for the
Olympians and their equals. Latin-speaking Christians used the title *Dei Filius* ("Son of God") for Jesus.
For more details see Mary Beard, John North and Simon Price, *Religions of Rome: Volume 1, A History*
(Cambridge: Cambridge University Press, 1998).

[16]David S. Potter, *The Roman Empire at Bay: AD 180-395* (London and New York: Routledge, 2004), p.
290.

advice on various matters, including how to engage this new group of whom he had never heard before: the Christians. Pliny identified Christianity as another of the fanatical groups of the Roman world, a *superstitio*, a cult—and a foreign one at that. For the Romans, *superstitio* was the opposite of *religio*; it was the improper or even excessive forms of behavior that could threaten the fine balance of divine favor to the state. Since the piety of the Romans was civic, communal and public, Roman society grew increasingly suspicious of religious practices that advocated the role of personal belief, private piety and secret rituals.[17]

For almost a century, small Christian communities arose primarily within a few urban centers around the Mediterranean basin and went unnoticed by most women and men in the Roman Empire. By the beginning of the second century, the earliest Christian writings, "highly theological and directed at Christian readers, present the life of Jesus and the beginning of the church as the turning point in history, whereas non-Christians see the Christian community as a tiny, peculiar, antisocial, irreligious sect, drawing its adherents from the lower strata of society."[18] As a nondominant subgroup within the empire, the nascent Christian movement began to formulate its own public transcript, for there was little common ground of understanding between Christians and non-Christians. The inevitable clash between Romans and Christians occurred as a result of Christianity's expansion and its ideological collision with the Roman religiopolitical transcript. The locus of this clash was none other than the very bodies of women and men who were called in front of Roman magistrates like Pliny to "give an account for the hope" that was in them (1 Peter 3:15 NASB).[19]

The self-sacrificial motif on behalf of one's convictions or for the benefit of others was well known among the Greeks and the Romans, as well as within the Jewish tradition.[20] For the Greeks and the Romans, valorizing the

---

[17]Suspected *private* piety should not be confused with *personal* piety, which was the expected norm.

[18]Robert Louis Wilken, *The Christians as the Romans Saw Them*, 2nd ed. (New York and London: Yale University Press, 2003), pp. xviii-xix. See also Robin Lane Fox, *Pagans and Christians* (San Francisco: HarperCollins, 1988).

[19]The accounts of these collisions between Christians and the state are often told in the form of stories under the designation of *martyrium* (report of the martyr's death), or *passio* (passion narrative), or *acta* (acts of the martyrs). *Martyrologies*, as these texts are known collectively, were very popular among the faithful, and a number of them survive.

[20]Unlike classical antecedents where the protagonist almost never had to face the willing sacrifice of one's life for religious reasons, the Christians looked especially to the martyrdom accounts of the Maccabees who defied Antiochus IV and Seleucid domination and were killed for their unyielding faithfulness to

deaths—that is, the very process of dying—of those who went to their deaths voluntarily infused the community with a potent rhetoric of divine call to sacrifice, something Plato recognized in the death of Socrates and which the heroic traditions exalted.[21] Because Christian thought, however, "arose in response to the facts of revelation, its idiom was set by the language and imagery of the Bible, and the life and worship of the Christian community gave Christian thinking a social dimension that was absent from ancient philosophy."[22] The Christians' *primary* inspiration was the power and hope of the resurrection of Jesus (1 Cor 15:13-14), whose life and example they were called to emulate. The descriptions of the suffering servant in Isaiah 53 and their obvious connections with Jesus were from very early on the interpretive matrix through which Christians understood their own experiences and times. To quote Robert L. Wilken,

> The church gave men and women a new love, Jesus Christ, a person who inspired their actions and held their affections. This was a love unlike others. . . . The Resurrection of Jesus is the central fact of Christian devotion and the ground of all Christians thinking. The Resurrection was not a solitary occurrence, a prodigious miracle, but an event within the framework of Jewish history, and it brought into being a new community, the church. Christianity enters history not only as a message but also as a communal life, a society or city, whose inner discipline and practices, rituals and creeds, and institutions and traditions were the setting for Christian thinking.[23]

Early Christian writers most often began with the demands of the gods of the Empire for obedience and sacrifice and blood and showed *how* and *why* Christians could not participate in such models of being and worship: that is, because Christians acted out of the abiding conviction of the power and hope present in the resurrection of Jesus.

God. Origen, for instance, exalted to the martyrdom of the Maccabees and acknowledged it as "a magnificent example" (*Exhortation to Martyrdom* 23). See W. H. C. Frend, *Martyrdom and Persecution in the Early Church: A Study of a Conflict from the Maccabees to Donatus* (New York: New York University Press, 1967), p. 54; also, W. Brian Shelton, *Martyrdom from Exegesis in Hippolytus: An Early Church Presbyter's Commentary on Daniel* (Milton Keynes: Paternoster, 2008), pp. 35-77.

[21]See for example Plato's *Phaedo* 57. Also, Brent D. Shaw, "Body/Power/Identity: Passions of the Martyrs," in *Journal of Early Christian Studies* 4, no. 3 (1996): 269-312.

[22]Robert Louis Wilken, *The Spirit of Early Christian Thought: Seeking the Face of God* (New York and London: Yale University Press, 2005), p. 3.

[23]Wilken, *Spirit of Early Christian Thought*, p. xv.

The incarnation provided early Christians with a new interpretive lens, a radical shift in history, and the dominical juxtaposition in Matthew, "You have heard that it was said . . . but I say to you . . ." (Mt 5:21-48) was understood as the fulfillment of the law (Mt 5:17-20). Tertullian used the formula "For though . . . but now the Lord . . . ," and the language of the "old law" being fulfilled by the "new law": "The old law vindicated itself by the vengeance of the sword, to take an eye for an eye and to repay injury for injury. But the new law was to focus on clemency and to turn bloodthirsty swords and lances to peaceful uses and to change the warlike acts against rivals and enemies into the peaceful pursuits of plowing and farming the land."[24] Origen, too, understood that Jesus is the kingdom of God in his own person, the *autobasileia*: "For he is the king of heaven, and as such he is *autosophia* [wisdom in person], and *autodikaiosyne* [justice in person], and *autoaletheia* [truth in person]. Is he not therefore, also *autobasileia* [the kingdom in person]?"[25]

The Christian idea of the *basileia tou theou*, the "kingdom of God," inaugurated in Luke 4:19 and given structure in the Sermon on the Mount (Mt 4:23–7:29, especially 6:9-13), could not but be seen as a threat to the "kingdom of Caesar," and the peace that Christ bequeathed the disciples (Jn 14:27) threatened the *pax deorum* that guaranteed Rome's eternal place. From the earliest expressions of self-identity, Christians rejected the dominative claims of Rome and instead confessed Jesus as *Dominus et Deus,* not Caesar—a public declaration with grave temporal as well as eternal implications (cf. Jn 20:28; Rom 10:9; 2 Pet 3:18, etc.).

I believe that most early Christian writers saw that there was a radical shift in the move from a bordered national identity with a religion to defend and a people and lineage to protect, to a universal call to discipleship and a new family of God through Jesus, a family that transgresses national identities and gender and societal constructs through the realigning effects of baptism (Gal 3:28; Eph 2:14), a family that brings all into a new kingdom (Rom 6:1-3; Gal 3:27) whose only defense is the empty tomb (1 Cor 15)—the proof that all violence has been subsumed and conquered on the cross.[26] The result is a

---

[24]Tertullian, *Against the Jews* 3.10.

[25]Origen, *In Ev. Matth.* 14.7, author's translation.

[26]The anonymous second-century *Epistle to Diognetus* had already presented to the Roman authorities the case that Christians were not seeking power and prestige, and that even though they "obey the established laws" and were orderly in their civic affairs, in truth they were "foreigners" and "nonresidents," for "their

resounding alienation from the structures of loyalty and ownership that orient this world because of the new Lord, Jesus.

MARTYRDOM AS THE NEW SACRIFICE:
PASSIVE COOPTATION OF POWER

Jesus had warned his followers that in response to his call they would be persecuted at the hands of the *status quo* (e.g., Mt 10:16-42; Jn 15:18-25). He had called his disciples to see themselves as blessed when reviled and persecuted on *his* account, and had assured them of the kingdom of heaven (Mt 5:10-12; Rev 21:7).

Persecutions directed specifically against the Christians as an identifiable group were too sporadic and local to be counted as normative before the sustained empire-wide persecutions of the mid-third century under Decius (249–251). Intolerant as they were of religious practices that undermined the relationship with the gods or defied the state, for the most part Romans were not in the business of making martyrs. They preferred that the accused recant and profess loyalty to the emperor and the gods.[27] Yet even from the earliest years Christians had felt the power and whims of the mob in multiple and various local instantiations (e.g., Acts 14; 16; 19), and had indeed suffered persecutions at the hands of Nero, Domitian, Trajan, Marcus Aurelius and Septimius Severus.

The stories of those who had suffered for their faith were preserved in various martyrdom accounts. These accounts were meant to reinterpret the way both Christians and non-Christians understood themselves and their situation, and to reshape the conventional categories of power. The Christian "athletes of piety," as Eusebius called the martyrs,[28] were not the expected heroes of Greco-Roman literature, nor were they limited to the classes of the

---

citizenship is in heaven": "They are cursed, yet they bless; they are insulted yet they bless; they are insulted, yet they offer respect. When they do good, they are punished as evildoers; when they are punished, they rejoice as though brought to life. By the Jews they are assaulted as foreigners and by the Greeks they are persecuted, yet those who hate them are unable to give a reason for their hostility." *Ep. Diognetus* 5.1-6.4, translation from Michael W. Holmes, *The Apostolic Fathers: Greek Texts and English Translations*, 3rd ed. (Grand Rapids: Baker Academic, 2007), pp. 701-5.

[27]Emperor Trajan was quite explicit in his instructions to Pliny: "In the case of anyone who denies that he is a Christian, and makes it clear by offering prayers to our gods, he is to be pardoned as a result of his repentance however suspect his past conduct may be." Pliny, *Letters* 10.97.

[28]Eusebius, *Ecclesiastical History* (henceforth, *H.E.*), bk. 5, introduction.

nobiles. The Christian martyrs were a mixed bag of characters, young and old, educated and uneducated, women and men, slaves, free persons, citizens and foreigners, almost none of whom shared in the classical ideal of the *hero.* They were women and men who challenged directly the authority of the state to dictate their conscience and responded "with a classic instance of a public 'no'—the open rejection of a ritualistic litmus test of types of sacrifice and publicly performed ceremonials that constituted an essential surrender of community and the self."[29]

As alternative public transcripts of sacrifice, appositional to the ones demanded by Rome, martyrdom accounts were the most powerful accounts of reversal of power.[30] The young are shown to be mature, both in faith and oratorical skill; women exert their autonomy and self-control; slaves are proclaimed to be the brothers and sisters of their masters, not only the equals of citizens who share their fate but often their teachers as well. The infirm, the old, those who in the eyes of the world ought not to have power to resist the force of Rome emerge victorious.

To the magnificent and terrifying display of state power, the Christians in these accounts responded with calm defiance, even joy. They did not recoil. These were theatrical performances, and the audience expected the customary responses from the accused: "Convicted of their own guilt by the overpowering rituals of court and 'awe of the law' with which they were faced,"[31] they were expected to blush, to sweat, to show signs of fear and shame, bowing, scraping and weeping to proclaim their repentance and remorse and to ask for forgiveness and life. The Roman writer Seneca had spoken of the expected

---

[29]Shaw, "Body/Power/Identity," p. 275. This is how Shaw describes the Maccabean opposition to Roman domination, which is also a very apt description of the Christian response, for it stems from the same understanding of the unique and exclusive relationship of the Christian with God.

[30]From the wealth of excellent scholarship on martyrdom, language and identity formation, see Shaw, "Body/Power/Identity," p. 274; also Sinclair Bell and Inge Lyse Hansen, eds., *Role Models in the Roman World: Identity and Assimilation* (Ann Arbor: University of Michigan Press, 2008); Daniel Boyarin, *Dying For God: Martyrdom and the Making of Christianity and Judaism* (Stanford: Stanford University Press, 1999); Elizabeth A. Castelli, *Martyrdom and Memory: Early Christian Culture Making* (New York: Columbia University Press, 2004); Michaela DeSoucey et al., "Memory and Sacrifice: An Embodied Theory of Martyrdom," *Cultural Sociology* 2, no. 1 (March 2008): 99-121; Rona M. Fields, *Martyrdom: The Psychology, Theology, and Politics of Self-Sacrifice* (Westport, CT: Praeger, 2004); Frend, *Martyrdom and Persecution in the Early Church*; Johan Leemans, ed., *More Than a Memory: The Discourse of Martyrdom and the Construction of Christian Identity in the History of Christianity* (Paris: Peeters, 2005); and Elaine Scarry, *The Body in Pain: The Making and Unmaking of the World* (Oxford: Oxford University Press, 1985).

[31]Shaw, "Body/Power/Identity," pp. 302-3.

"recoil effect" as one faced the real danger: the absolute limit of death. It was not so with the Christians.

In each of the martyrdom accounts, through their movements and gestures, accepting their impending torture and execution not as fate but as welcomed destiny, the martyrs signified the drastic shift of hierarchies of power that was occurring before the prurient eyes of the crowds. By refusing to conform to the expected prescriptions, Christians defeated all three propositions of the anticipated social transaction: first, they refused to obey an order; second, they denied the crowd the chance to witness the final display of state power over the subjects; and third, they denied the crown and the governing authorities what Brent Shaw calls "the production of truth," the uttering of the prescribed words of confession and "the performance of the required public ritualistic acts of assent."[32] The Stoic Seneca had expressed a deeply rooted Roman sentiment when he wrote to his friend Lucilius that one ceases to fear only when one ceases to hope.[33] The martyrdom accounts taught Christians that one ceases to fear when one recognizes that Jesus Christ is "our hope" (1 Tim 1:1). Bishop Irenaeus of Sirmium (d. 304) summed up this new paradigm at his trial when he professed that "Christians are wont to despise death because of the faith they have in God."[34]

It would be misleading to read the accounts of the martyrs primarily as refusals by Christians to offer sacrifice, as their pagan counterparts did.[35] Almost sacramental in character, each of these accounts is a rich sacrificial narrative that rejects the dominant religiopolitical paradigm and reinterprets assumed perceptions of power dynamics. The example of Christ, his response during trial and torture, even his physical posture of calm silence and assurance had given Christians a new vocabulary. It transformed profoundly deep-rooted ideologies about human beings, power, the world and history. The classical Greek concept of *arete* and its Roman equivalent *virtus*, both linguistic derivatives of "male/man," signified the ideal of individual greatness.

---

[32]Ibid., p. 278. See also *M. Frucuosus* 6.3 for death as confirming the life of the martyr and proving the truthfulness of Christian teaching.

[33]Seneca, *Ep.* 5.7.

[34]*M. Irenaeus, Bishop of Sirmium* 4.12, in H. Musurillo, *The Acts of the Christian Martyrs* (Oxford: Oxford University Press, 1972), p. 299.

[35]E.g., *M. Polycarp* 12; *Acts of the Scillitan Martyrs* (or *Mart. Scill.*) 3-4. Also, Tertullian, *Apology* 10 says that the chief charge against Christians was that they refused to sacrifice.

Based on the heroic ideal, Aristotle identified a virtuous person as someone who is prepared to sacrifice himself (women who entered this category were lauded as "manly women") for one's friends or family or homeland.[36] Many of the philosophers from the classical to the imperial era expressed similar views. To be humble was to be weak, poor, submissive, slavish and womanish; it was the physical position of shame, humiliation, degradation and, therefore, to be understood as morally bad. The New Testament revolutionized these values wholly by their total inversion. It presented Jesus who "endured the cross, disregarding its shame" (Heb 12:2) as the one Christians ought to emulate (1 Pet 2:19-20), and Paul's boasting in his lowly status (*tapeinos*) and sufferings in imitation of Christ gave new meaning to humility, transforming it into a virtue. In this new paradigm, endurance (Greek *hypomone*, Latin *patientia*) replaced the ancient ideal of glory, and humility (*tapeinophrosyne*), the voluntary abasement of one's self and body, "to be low, base, prone, and exposed, was now at the heart of the definition of being good."[37] In the "theater of the national pornography of the Roman state—its public executions,"[38] the new economy of the body displayed by the martyrs transformed humility into power, and *virtus* was manifested in the form of a slave woman, Blandina (martyred in Lyon in 177 C.E.).

Martyrdom was a baptism of blood that brought forgiveness of sins to the martyr,[39] and a eucharist in which one drank the cup of sufferings of Christ (Mt 20:22). Paul had also spoken of the redemptive role of suffering for the faith in his letter to the church in Philippi (Phil 3:10).[40] The martyrs were filled by the Holy Spirit, who gave them words to say to the authorities and to each other, visions of heaven and supernatural strength to endure sufferings (cf. Mt 10:19; Mk 13:11; Lk 12:11-12).[41] These were not the stories of naive and idealistic bishops and academic philosophers blind to the affairs of the world. These were people who had experienced the cruelty of war and persecution.

---

[36] Aristotle, *Eth. Nic.* 1169a.

[37] Shaw, "Body/Power/Identity," pp. 303-4.

[38] Ibid., pp. 304-5.

[39] E.g., Ignatius, *Romans* 5-6; also, Tertullian, *On Baptism* 16.

[40] Tertullian, *C. Marcion* 4.39.5, followed the same principle when he presented martyrdom as atonement for sin.

[41] See, for example, Perpetua's account of her visions in *Passio Sanctarum Perpetua et Felicitatis* 3-9, in Elizabeth A. Clark, ed., *Women in the Early Church*, vol. 13 of *Message of the Fathers of the Church* (Collegeville: Liturgical Press, 1983).

Justin's sobriquet is *Martyr*. Origen and Tertullian had witnessed the cruelty of the Septimian persecutions, the imprisonment, torture and execution of family members and fellow Christians. Irenaeus was a presbyter of the church in Lyon when members of his own congregation were condemned *ad bestias*. Cyprian was beheaded. They understood that wars were inevitable and that social order may necessitate violence on the part of the magistracy, but they also understood that that was not an option for the Christian.

Theirs was a realized eschatology in which the martyr participated already in the events of the eschaton. To the sacrifice of incense and grain demanded by the state as signs of the loyalty expected from those living under the protection of the gods who promised *Roma aeterna*, the Christian martyrs offered an alternative sacrifice that rejected these illusory claims and guaranteed true eternal life: they offered themselves. In imitation of Christ.[42]

"FEAR GOD. HONOR THE EMPEROR": SEDITION OR CIVIL DISOBEDIENCE?

The first account of a Christian martyr is the stoning of Stephen (Acts 6:1–8:2), and the earliest recorded prayer of the church for the state is found in the *First Letter of Clement* (60.4-61.3) sent by the church of Rome to the church in Corinth at the end of the first century (c. 90–95).[43] Scarcely a generation earlier, Paul had written to the churches in Rome to "be subject to the governing authorities; for there is no authority except from God, and those authorities that exist have been instituted by God" (Rom 13:1). Paul had also instructed the Romans to "pay to all what is due to them—taxes to whom taxes are due, revenue to whom revenue is due, respect to whom respect is due, honor to whom honor is due" (Rom 13:7; see also 1 Tim 2:1-2). Jesus had talked about rendering to Caesar what is Caesar's (Mt 22:21). To

---

[42]R. Jacob, "Le Martyre, épanouissement du sacerdoce des Chrétiens, dans la littérature patristique jusqu' en 258," *MScRel* 24 (1967): 57-83, 153-72, 177-209; Everett Ferguson, "Spiritual Sacrifice in Early Christianity and Its Environment," *ANRW*, 11.23.1 (Berlin: DeGruyter, 1980), pp. 1169-70, 1180, 1186. Also, *M. Dasius* 5.2; *M. Polycarp* 14; *M. Conon* 6.7; *M. Felix the Bishop*, p. 30. See also Ignatius's letter *To Polycarp*: "We must endure everything especially for God's sake, that he may endure us. . . . Await the one who is beyond the season, the one who is timeless, the one who is invisible, who became visible for us, the one who cannot be handled, the one who is beyond suffering, who suffered for us, enduring in every way on our account" (3.1-2).

[43]For a fuller description and analysis of the themes of civil disobedience and the peace-making character of the earliest Christian communities, see Kalantzis, *Caesar and the Lamb*, pp. 21-68.

these, Peter added: "For the Lord's sake accept the authority of every human institution, whether of the emperor as supreme, or of governors, as sent by him to punish those who do wrong and to praise those who do right. . . . Honor everyone. Love the family of believers. Fear God. Honor the emperor" (1 Pet 2:13-14, 17).

It was the same Peter, however, who, along with John, defined for the Christian community what honoring the governing authorities meant and why submitting oneself to the authorities did not mean acquiescing to the demands of the state. Following the example of Jesus before the Sanhedrin and Pilate, Peter and John affirmed that obedience to the command of God superseded the orders of the state: "We must obey God rather than any human authority" (Acts 5:29; also 4:19). With this seemingly simple declaration, the apostles exposed the true nature of the conflict and identified every other authority, secular or religious, as subordinate to God. The good news of God's imminent kingdom (Mk 1:15) was interpreted as "the rejection of one emperor, Caesar, by the proclamation of another, namely, Jesus" (cf. Acts 17:6).[44]

Unlike the Maccabees who rebelled against Hellenistic domination because of the Seleucid imposition of religious practices antithetical to Judaism (1 Macc 11:21) and as a sign of Jewish apocalyptic revivalism (1 Macc 6:16), the apostles neither rebelled against Rome nor sought a particular national identity separate from the eschatological kingdom of Christ (e.g., 2 Thess 2:1-2).[45] The witness of the New Testament and of the early Christians was not one of an autonomous Christian political order, and yet it was a wholly new political order. Christians insisted that they were taught to respect the authorities.[46] Christians had never rebelled, Tertullian declared; they were not seditious, nor did they take revenge, or even resist, for they were taught differently.[47] They honored the emperor by putting him in his proper place,

---

[44]Agnes Cunningham, S.S.C.M., *The Early Church and the State* (Philadelphia: Fortress, 1982), p. 2.

[45]There are numerous resources on Paul's eschatology and on the eschatology of the NT. Some of the best essays are found in Thomas E. Schmidt and Moisés Silva, eds., *To Tell the Mystery: Essays on New Testament Eschatology in Honor of Robert H. Gundry* (Sheffield: JSOT Press, 1994); see especially the essay by Gordon D. Fee, "Pneuma and Eschatology in 2 Thessalonians 2.1-2: A Proposal About 'Testing the Prophets' and the Purpose of 2 Thessalonians," pp. 196-215.

[46]*Diognetus* 5.9; *M. Polycarp* 10; Tertullian, *De Idol.* 15.8-11; Origen, *C. Celsum* 8.65.

[47]Tertullian, *Apology* 37.

under God, and commending him to divine favor.[48] "I will honor the emperor," wrote Theophilus of Antioch (c. 170), "not by worshipping him, but by offering prayers for him. . . . He is not God. He is a man whom God has appointed to give *just* judgment, not to be worshipped."[49] The distinction is crucial: the emperor has been given authority by God to govern according to *God's* justice, not Rome's.

Throughout the writings of this period the point is made frequently that it is God who appoints the king and who dispenses kingdoms,[50] and it is to this God that Christians owed their loyalty and in whose kingdom they held citizenship (Jn 18:36; Phil 3:20). As for now, Christians "live in their own countries, but only as nonresidents; they participate in everything as citizens, and endure everything as foreigners. . . . They live on earth, but their citizenship is in heaven."[51]

Christians *honored the emperor* and the governors as his appointed authorities not by acquiescing to the demands of the state, but by following the example of Christ in refusing their consent *and* submitting themselves to the consequence of rejecting the demands of the state—including scourging and death. That is what "rendering to Caesar what is Caesar's" would look like in the new economy: a simultaneous yes and no that points back to God as supreme. In doing so, they overturned yet again the normative paradigms of the classical traditions and showed how, for the Christians, power is gained through submission, not violence. This was a truly countercultural movement the Romans did not comprehend.

The Christian refusal to submit to the orders of the emperors, obey the law, honor the gods and participate in the public rituals of civic religion that preserved order was seen by the Romans as an act of civic and religious blasphemy. It was an act of sedition; or that is how the state saw it.[52] Christians, however, insisted that their refusal to acquiesce to the simulacra of justice and worship ought not be interpreted as subversion or disloyalty but as a call to

---

[48]Tertullian, *Apology* 30, 33-34; Origen, *C. Celsum* 8.74.

[49]Theophilus, *Ad Autolycum* 1.11, emphasis added.

[50]Tertullian, *Apology* 26; Hippolytus, *Daniel* 3.4; Origen, *C. Celsum* 8.68; *M. Polycarp* 9, 17; Eusebius, *H.E.* 5.1.55; *Acts of the Scillitan Martyrs* 6; *M. Conon* 3-4.

[51]*Letter to Diognetus* 5.5-8.

[52]See *M. Perpetua and Felicitas* 6.3; *M. Crispus* 1; *M. Apollonius* 7; *M. Fructuosus* 2.6; *M. Carpus* 4, 21; *M. Agapê* 3.4; *M. Justin* (B) 2.1. Even though the contest was expressed primarily as between God and idolatry and only secondarily as between church and state, there were profound political implications that persecution brought to the fore.

the state to repent and acknowledge its proper place under the authority of God (see Jn 19:11). It was *civil disobedience*.

A first principle of civil disobedience is the proposition that one cannot act contrary to conscience, even under compulsion.[53] An equally important feature of civil disobedience is its nonviolence—an incontestable principle early Christians inherited from the teachings of Christ and the New Testament (e.g., Mt 26:52).[54] These two, then, civil disobedience and nonviolence, go hand in hand throughout the stories that formed the character and identity of the earliest church.

"LOVE YOUR ENEMIES AND PRAY FOR THOSE WHO PERSECUTE YOU"

Martyrdom was not the fate of the powerless, those finally forced to submit to the grandeur of the state. Martyrdom was a witness *to* the state of its subordination to the God of heaven. Paul had already given expression to that concept: "'For your sake we are being killed all day long; we are accounted as sheep to be slaughtered.' No, in all these things we are more than conquerors through him who loved us" (Rom 8:36-37). This explicit cooptation of power through passive resistance is at the heart of the early Christian response to the power of the state. It was the very definition of nonviolent resistance.

To the dismay of the world around them, Christian nonviolent resistance was not a fatalistic acceptance of the world as they knew it, the *pepromenon*. On the contrary, the Christian response was rooted in Jesus' call for his disciples to engage in active peacemaking. In this peacemaking, this *eirenopoietic* relationship with the world, Christians were mandated to "cultivate piety, justice, love of humanity (*philanthropia*), faith, and hope, the kind that comes from the Father through the crucified one."[55] The earliest Christians understood too well that the scriptural call to nonviolence locates the positive call to love—especially toward the enemy—at the nonnegotiable center of the

---

[53]The martyr *Agapê*, for example, declared, "I refuse to destroy my conscience" (*M. Agapê* 3.3), and the martyr Phileas added that "Our conscience with respect to God is prior to all" (*M. Phileas*, col. 9).

[54]Everett Ferguson, "Early Christian Martyrdom and Civil Disobedience," in *Journal of Early Christian Studies* 1, no. 1 (1993): 81. Here Ferguson follows David Daube, *Civil Disobedience in Antiquity* (Edinburgh: Edinburgh University Press, 1972), pp. 1-4, 43.

[55]Justin, *Trypho* 110.3, my translation. For full text see *St. Justin Martyr: Dialogue with Trypho*, trans. Thomas B. Falls (Washington, DC: Catholic University of America Press, 2003), p. 165.

Christian message.[56] This reversal of power that originates voluntarily from the one in the perceived position of weakness and is directed toward the strong finds expression in the form of prayer for one's persecutor and aims to bring the enemy into the Christian communion (cf. Rom 12:21).

Love of enemy as an overwhelming apologetic of love of God and as a pious Christian obligation is a theme that permeates Christian writings of this period. From the *Didache* to Justin's *Dialogue with Trypho*, the *Second Letter of Clement*, the writings of Irenaeus, bishop of Lyon, Athenagoras's *Plea on Behalf of the Christians*, the *Letter to Diognetus*, the writings of Clement of Alexandria, as well as Tertullian, Origen, Cyprian, Arnobius and Lactantius, all speak of the irreducible relationship between love of enemy and the Christian call to nonviolence.[57] Tertullian insisted, as we have already seen, that love of enemy is a peculiar idiom found among Christians alone, and it separates them from all other people.[58]

So understood, the peacemaking character of the early Christians has to be interpreted as a concrete social event that gives the command to love the enemy a public and implicitly political dimension, "a fully rounded religio-philosophical and political position."[59] Christians are called to be peacemakers and, for their early writers, that *eirenopoietic* articulation of the kingdom on earth had its roots in their understanding of the imminence of the eschaton and the very character of Jesus.

A Practical Example: Could a Christian Participate in Military or Civil Service?

By the middle of the third century, the eschatological enthusiasm of the second seems to have dissipated, and the numerical growth of Christianity meant that a number of practical issues that were not imaginable before had

---

[56]On the positive call to love versus "negative counterpart and normal mode of realization," nonviolence, see John Helgeland, Robert J. Daly, J. Patout Burns et. al., *Christians and the Military* (Philadelphia: Fortress, 1985), p. 15.

[57]Cf. Mt 22:37-39; Mk 12:30-31; Lk 10:27. The theme of love of enemy is almost ubiquitous in early Christian literature. See, for example, 2 *Clement* 13; Justin, 1 *Apology* 11-16 (esp. 16.1-4), and *Trypho* 85, 96; Irenaeus, *Adversus Haereses* 2.32, 3.18, 4.13; Athenagoras, *Legatio* 1.4; Clement of Alexandria, *Paidagogos* 3.12; *Protrepticus* 10; *Stromata* 4.8; Tertullian, *Apology* 31, 37; *Adv. Iudaeos* 3.10; *De Corona* 11.2-3; *De Spectaculis* 16; *De Patientia* 6, 8.2; *Adv. Marcionem* 4.16; *Ad Scapulam* 1; Origen, *C. Celsum* 7.25, 7.58-61, 8.35; Cyprian, *Adv. Iudaeos* 3.48; *De Patientia* 16; Lactantius, *Divine Institutes* 5.10, 6.20.

[58]Tertullian, *Ad Scapulam* 1.3: *Amicos enim diligere omnium est, inimicos autem solorum Christianorum.*

[59]Helgeland, et. al., *Christians and the Military*, pp. 1, 14-15.

to be addressed. Tertullian and Origen were not alone in raising objections. The church-order document known as the *Apostolic Tradition* is almost a contemporary witness to the complexities facing the growing Christian movement. The document contains instructions for ordination, ministry, catechesis, baptism and so on, and versions of it were widely used for many centuries. Like Tertullian, the *Apostolic Tradition* recognizes the realities of life and the practical issues facing women and men who want to join the church. It recognizes that people come to Christ from all walks of life: women and men with established professions and lucrative careers, and those who are poor or need to find jobs; rich who became such by keeping brothels or selling slaves; slaves who have no control over their bodies, and free citizens who do; those who were raised as pagans, and those who grew up in Christian families. The church had to account for all these and many more. The church-order document addresses the trades and professions that are permissible for Christians and the ones that are forbidden. In section 16, it speaks to the catechumens and lists a number of professions: pimps and brothel keepers, prostitutes, magicians, makers of spells and pagan priests, astrologers and soothsayers should desist immediately or be rejected from baptism and the church. So should gladiators, who were most often slaves, or public officials of gladiatorial games, who were free citizens. The church recognized that among those who wanted to join and participate in the mysteries were also soldiers who had been converted while in service. Section 16.8-9 gives explicit instructions: "A soldier in command must be told not to kill people; if he is ordered so to do, he shall not carry it out. Nor should he take the oath [the *sacramentum*]. If he will not agree, he should be rejected. Anyone who has the power of the sword, or who is a civil magistrate wearing the purple, should desist, or he should be rejected."[60] As for those who professed to be Christians, whether catechumens or already baptized, and sought to join the military, the instructions were also very clear: "If a catechumen or a believer wishes to become a soldier they should be rejected, for they have despised God."[61] Parallel to the *Apostolic*

---

[60]*Apostolic Tradition* 16.8-9. This translation is from the Sahidic and is found in Alistair Stewart-Sykes, *Hippolytus: On the Apostolic Tradition* (Crestwood, NY: St. Vladimir's Seminary Press, 2001), p. 100.

[61]*Apostolic Tradition* 16.10, in Stewart-Sykes, *Hippolytus*, p. 100. Another variant is known as *Canons of Hippolytus*. In canons 13 and 14 of *Hippolytus* the instructions read: "[13] Whoever has received the authority to kill, or else a soldier, they are not to kill in any case, even if they receive the order to kill. They are not to pronounce a bad word. Those who have received an honor are not to wear wreaths on their

Tradition is the variant known as *Testamentum Domini*, which preserves this wording of canon 14: "Let a catechumen or a believer of the people, if he desires to be a soldier, either cease from his intention, or if not let him be rejected. For he has despised God by this his thought, and leaving the things of the Spirit, he has perfected himself in the flesh, and has treated the faith with contempt."[62]

Those who came to faith while in military service were to refuse the order to kill and were to leave the army, if they could—just like brothel keepers and pagan priests were to abandon their (often lucrative) professions and careers—or else suffer the consequences of their disobedience to carry out the orders they were given, just like gladiators who refused to kill or other slaves who refused the will of their masters. As for those who were already Christians but wanted to join the military out of a sense of civic obligation or as a profitable career, the ecclesiastical pronouncement was as clear as it was severe: such persons have "despised God by this thought" and have "treated the faith with contempt."

Then, there were those who argued that they could serve without truly "meaning the words of the oath" or being soiled by the office and its responsibilities. In his *Apology* 1.9, Justin had already argued that, contrary to the Roman dichotomy between interiority of belief and the external proper ritual practice, not to affirm what the oath says would be simply a moral oxymoron, a lie, to which Christians could not assent. Tertullian applied the same argument to Christians seeking positions of power and influence within the magistracy under the pretext that they would not be tainted or corrupted by its structures and demands.

> A dispute has lately arisen as to whether a servant of God can hold a position of honor or authority if he can keep himself free of any appearance of idolatry by means of some special grace or through his own wisdom, just as Joseph and Daniel, who served with honor and power, wearing the insignia and the purple

---

hands (i.e. reject the honor). Whosoever is raised to the authority of prefect or the magistracy and does not put on the righteousness of the gospel is to be excluded from the flock and the bishop is not to pray with him. [14] A Christian must not become a soldier, unless he is compelled by a chief bearing the sword (i.e., conscription). He is not to burden himself with the sin of blood. But if he has shed blood, he is not to partake of the mysteries, unless he is purified by a punishment, tears, and wailing. He is not to come forward deceitfully but in the fear of God." In Paul Frederick Bradshaw, Maxwell E. Johnson and L. Edward Phillips, *The Apostolic Tradition: A Commentary*, vol. 85 of *Hermeneia* (Minneapolis: Augsburg Fortress, 2002), p. 91.

[62]*Testamentum Domini* 2.2, in Bradshaw et. al., *The Apostolic Tradition*, p. 91.

of the governor of Egypt and Babylonia, yet without being tainted by idolatry. We may grant that someone could hold a position in a purely honorary way if you can believe that it is possible for him to avoid sacrificing or authorizing sacrifices, without paying for victims [viz. sacrificial animals], without managing the upkeep of temples, without taking care of temple taxes, without putting on shows [spec-tacula] at his own or at public expense or presiding over the staging of them, without issuing solemn pronouncements or edicts or even taking an oath. Pro-vided he can do this and also avoid the functions of his office, i.e. without passing judgment on a man's life [i.e. capital punishment] or honour—for you can put up with a decision on financial matters—without condemning or forejudging, without putting anybody in chains or prison or torturing, if it is believable that all this is possible, [then he may serve].[63]

And he concluded:

So what will you accomplish, if you use this attire [viz. of purple of the magis-tracy] but do not perform the function connected with it? Nobody can give an impression of cleanness in unclean clothes [i.e. the office is already polluted by long standing practice and tradition]. If you put on a tunic soiled of itself, it may perhaps not be soiled through you, but certainly you will not be able to be clean because of it.[64]

The writers of the early church decried the thinly veiled attempts by the state to hide the horrors of war in language of valor and justice, and lamented the pretense of arguments based on peace. Cyprian identified the problem well: "When individuals slay a man, it is a crime. When killing takes place on behalf of the state, it is called virtue."[65] Even in self-defense or in pursuit of a just cause, wrote Arnobius, echoing the long patristic tradition, "it is not right to repay evil for evil; it is better to suffer an injury than to inflict one and to shed one's own blood rather than pollute one's hands and one's conscience with the blood of another."[66] The Fathers rejected a double standard for private and public morality, even in this area, and a number of them made the

---

[63]Tertullian, De Idol. 17.2-3, ed. and trans. J. H. Waszink and J. C. M. van Winden, vol. 1 of Supplements to Vigiliae Christianae (Leiden: Brill, 1987).

[64]Tertullian, De Idol. 18.4.

[65]Cyprian, Ad Donatum 6. In the early fourth century Lactantius repeated the same sentiment and insisted that violence and war were one issue on which Christians differed decisively form pagans; Div. Inst. 1.18.8-10, 5.8.6, 6.6.22-24.

[66]Arnobius, Adv. Nationes 1.6.

explicit connection between bloodshed and moral pollution, enunciating an inherent conflict between acts of violence and the celebration of the Christian mysteries. Addressing himself specifically to Christians, Cyprian insisted that "after the reception of the Eucharist the hand is not to be stained with the sword and bloodshed."[67]

Christians countered the Roman *libido dominandi* with a new language about power based on the hope of resurrection and the sovereignty of God, and the church's ethical teachings were an expression of that hope. The prohibitions against killing, war and resisting evil did not simply derive from an assumption about violence as inherently evil, but rather from the early Christian understanding of the sovereignty of God. To the coercive power of the state, articulated in the demand for devotion to the gods of the empire and the emperor as their vicar on earth, the example of Christ provided Christians with a new interpretive matrix that allowed them to follow a completely new paradigm of power and sacrifice—and the undergirding instrumentalities of violence in all its pluriformity, including killing—based on civil disobedience and a passive cooptation of power that found its strength in nonviolent resistance, in imitation of Christ. In the end, Louis J. Swift puts it best: "If violence had any place in the Christian's life, it would appear that it must be a violence which is endured rather than inflicted, a violence which is suffered in imitation of the Founder as a way of transcending human passions and breaking the endless cycle of injury and retaliation."[68]

This was the Christian witness to the nations.

---

[67]Cyprian, *De Bono Patientiae* 14. See also Louis J. Swift, *The Early Fathers on War and Military Service* (Wilmington, DE: Michael Glazier Books, 1983), pp. 48-50.
[68]Swift, *Early Fathers*, p. 17.

6

NOT SO PRIVATE

A Political Theology of Church and Family

Jana Marguerite Bennett

When I told some close friends I'd be presenting on political theology, they all reacted similarly: "What? What are *you* doing presenting on political theology?" I write on marriage and singleness and adoption, and most recently on technology, topics that many would say have little or no interest for political theology. My friends had a knee-jerk reaction: *how* exactly do marriage and family fit with more familiar political theology topics such as just war and the economy?

They are not alone in that assessment; again and again marriage and family are discussed in opposition to what is seen as the political sphere. My friends' knee-jerk reaction comes, I suggest, from the ways Americans conceive of the family in relation to the nation-state, to their faith, and especially to the ways people want to put barriers between state, church and family.[1] Even in the case of homosexuality and marriage, which has become a large part of contemporary American political discourse, the discussions (as I shall show later) still revolve around thinking of marriage and family in contradistinction to nation-states.[2] I focus here on the idea of government as a public space *vis a*

---

[1]For example, corporate interests tend to counter government laws with an insinuation that the government is acting as a nanny state if and when it tries to impose rules about family leaves, similar to the ways that individuals protest against government encroachment on their "individual" rights. I note that the recent controversy about New York City's law banning the sale of large-size sodas involved discussions of encroachment against "individual" rights on the part of individual people, but that it tended to be corporations who were leading the charge against this infringement of the individual. See, for example, Joseph Ax, "Judge Blocks New York City Large Soda Ban; Bloomberg Vows Fight," Reuters, March 11, 2013, www .reuters.com/article/2013/03/11/us-sodaban-lawsuit-idUSBRE92A0YR20130311.

[2]I would note here that it need not only be these three entities; I am struck by how little we discuss family

vis church and family as private because these are the three that show up again and again in the way people discuss what is public and private, and how public and private are interrelated.

The words used to describe that relationship are *public* and *private*, words that frequently appear in both secular and Christian conversations about marriage and family. We name "family" and "church" as *private* matters, parts of life that are necessarily held distinctly from *public* matters, as in political life. At the same time, because Christians rightly understand family as a place where people learn discipleship and a place where formation and evangelization happen,[3] we care very much about how to think about families in relation to church and state. There is a relationship between these three entities, American Christians insist, and the work that we need to do is to determine exactly how to properly balance that relationship in order to ensure the best possible marriages and the best possible families.

Yet what I argue in this chapter is that the current conversation, which tries to delineate how family, state and church are public or private, derails Christian discipleship. This is because Jesus Christ upends the very notions of public and private; the risen Christ causes us to realize that not only do we have no common views of what is public and private, but that the very ideas are reconfigured to the point that the public/private distinction is shattered. First, then, I discuss some of the several ways Americans, especially Christians, make use of the words *public* and *private*, showing how this dichotomy is utterly unhelpful for Christians. Then I support my claim by discussing what Jesus' life, as attested by Scripture, shows Christians about family, state, church, public and private. Finally, I suggest that for Christians there can't be "public" and "private" in the ways we have tended to name, that we are called to be the church first, and I conclude with some practical implications of making this claim.

---

in relation to the modern corporation, for example, and how often the modern corporation tries to name itself as a private entity much like family and church, though traditionally it too has been named as part of a public sphere. Yet that must be a paper for another time.

[3]In my own Catholic tradition, for example, the church document *Familaris Consortio* states: "in the family the human person is not only brought into being and progressively introduced by means of education into the human community, but by means of the rebirth of baptism and education in the faith the child is also introduced into God's family, which is the Church." John Paul II, *Familaris Consortio: Apostolic Exhortation on the Family* (November 22, 1981), § 15, Libreria Editrice Vaticana, www.vatican.va/holy_father/john_paul_ii/apost_exhortations/documents/hf_jp-ii_exh_19811122_familiaris-consortio_en.html.

NAVIGATING THE PUBLIC AND PRIVATE REALMS

What is meant by the words *public* and *private* depends a great deal on historical context and the changing ways in which we use those words. Language about family and church being part of a private sphere and the government (and sometimes business) being part of a public sphere has a long, changing history. Philosopher Hannah Arendt shows that ancient Greek cultures tried to conceive of a separation between public and private spheres: "the human capacity for political organization is not only different from but stands in direct opposition to that natural association whose center is the home (*oikos*) and the family. The rise of the city-state meant that man received 'besides his private life a sort of second life, his *bios politikos*.'"[4] That is, men were raised in families that supported their subsequent participation in the political life of the city. Well-functioning families meant well-functioning states, but the two were also cordoned off from each other; they were two different ways of life.

In contemporary conversation, Christians sometimes describe the distinction between public and private in this Aristotelian way. Consider this quote from theologian Emil Brunner, who is often cited by Vision Forum and other evangelical groups interested in the well-being of families:

> Every state will learn by experience that it cannot allow the divine order of creation to be infringed with impunity. All political anarchy in the state begins with anarchy in marriage. The state in which adultery and divorce are the order of the day is also ripe for political decay. No house can be built with mouldering stones; no sound body can grow out of diseased cells. If the social basis, marriage, is rotten, the whole community is rotten.[5]

Brunner sees the importance of both careful distinctions and connections between the family and the state: the family, and with it, the church, provides the building blocks for a good state, thus the state has a stake in making sure that families are "sound."[6] In a discussion about gay marriage, Vision Forum

---

[4]Hannah Arendt, *The Human Condition* (Chicago: University of Chicago Press, 1998), p. 24.

[5]Quoted by William Einwechter, "The Debate Over Same-Sex Marriage," Vision Forum Ministries, June 21, 2006, www.visionforumministries.org/issues/family/the_debate_over_samesex_marria_1.aspx.

[6]Brunner has a much more carefully developed sense of ecclesiology in relation to family than his most-often-used quotes suggest. See Emil Brunner, *Dogmatics III: The Christian Doctrine of the Church, Faith and Consummation* (Philadelphia: Westminster Press, 1962), and also *Misunderstanding of the Church* (Cambridge: Lutterworth Press, 2002).

author William Einwechter uses Brunner to distinguish between responsibilities of Christian families, of churches and of the "civil sphere":

> But if Christians are really serious about "saving marriage," then let them begin
> by first making sure that they save their own marriages; let them begin by prac-
> ticing moral purity and marital faithfulness in the home. . . . The church must
> also rise up and begin to teach the biblical standards of marriage and divorce,
> and then enforce those standards by church discipline. In the civil sphere, the
> call to protect marriage should not be limited to the homosexual issue, but
> should also include the repeal of "no-fault divorce" and the reconstruction of
> divorce law to reflect the standards of biblical law.[7]

Einwechter makes a clear distinction between church discipline and participation in the "civil sphere"; the first key is that individual Christians are working on their own marriages first and foremost, which is supported by their churches. This effort then necessarily builds up the public sphere, which should support antidivorce and antiadultery laws that in turn advocate for the private sphere.

The more well-known organization Focus on the Family shows an even more carefully laid barrier between the private family and the public state. "Helping families thrive" is the organization's motto, and topics on their website address specific relationship issues: "how to prepare for marriage," "what it means to be intimate," "money and finances" and "adoption." From the point of view of the site's authors (and their presumption about what readers think), the ways to develop good families are so distinctive from the nation-state that in the site's "Christians in Politics" section, the authors are almost apologetic about asking people to participate in discussions about government. They write:

> Have you ever wondered why Focus on the Family encourages its friends to be
> involved in the culture around them as part of their faith? How being involved
> in biblical citizenship is part of living our lives as "salt and light" to the world
> around us?
>
> Or have you wondered if it's even appropriate or legal for Christian beliefs
> to help shape our government and policies?[8]

---

[7]Einwechter, "The Debate Over Same-Sex Marriage."
[8]Focus on the Family, "Christians in Politics," www.focusonthefamily.com/socialissues/christians-in-pol itics.aspx (accessed September 20, 2013).

The rhetoric is that the Christian family, supported by churches, is and should be almost entirely distinct from government participation.[9] Indeed, in recent years that distinction has been made even more explicit with the formation of the Family Research Council, Focus on the Family's "political issues" arm. Once again, we appear to have Aristotle's view that we live two separate lives—one the life of the home (private), and the other the life of the city (public).

Yet there is more going on in our rhetoric about what is public and what is private than simply the idea that public and private are separate but support each other. Note, for example, another Vision Forum Ministries author's description of the relationship between the presumed private sphere of religion and the presumed public sphere of the state:

> Federal and state governments, in matters of religion, are forbidden to coerce or prohibit individual choice and action. Within the states, the people are free to decide by constitutional majority the nature and extent of the state's expression of religious belief. This leaves individuals free to make their own choices with respect to religion, but it also secures the right of the people of the states to live under a government that reflects their religious inclination.[10]

While here we do see the idea that the nation-state is responsible for upholding and undergirding the private sphere, in this case specifically religion, we also see the specific reason why there is a connection between public and private: it is the *individual*. On this particular view, the individual's choice of religion is protected by the US Constitution; most scholars would agree to that view. Vision Forum Ministries goes one step further, suggesting that when there are enough individuals in a locality who profess a certain religion, the state should reflect that religious identity because that reflects the col-

---

[9]In another section, Focus on the Family suggests: "It's easy to think that 'politics' and 'social issues' are disconnected from your everyday life, or are something that matter only when elections roll around every couple years. . . . Do you know what you'd do if your child's school started teaching material contrary to your beliefs? Would you know how to respond if your child accidentally accessed 'adult material' on a computer while at the public library? These are family issues. But they are also social policy issues." Focus on the Family, "Defending Your Values," www.focusonthefamily.com/socialissues/defending-your-val ues.aspx (accessed March 15, 2013).

[10]Alan Keyes, "The Rule of Law Must Be Upheld: What the Constitution Really Says About Establishment of Religion," *Puritan Rising*, February 12, 2012, http://puritanrising.com/2012/02/the-rule-of-law -must-be-upheld-what-the-constitution-really-says-about-establishment-of-religion.

lective will and right of those individuals—which the US government, via the Supreme Court, has tended not to uphold.

What is significant is not so much the articulation (or lack thereof) of the US Constitution but rather the way this quotation displays the role of the individual in maintaining both the public and the private spheres. It is the individual who votes, the individual who is responsible for creating the public sphere alongside other individuals. It is also the individual who chooses his or her participation in the private sphere: chooses his religion, chooses how to maintain her family. Aristotle did not conceive of the individual person in this kind of way; entities like family and state supported the individual, not the other way around, and the individual certainly did not maintain that kind of control (if any) on the public sphere. While we tell a story that suggests good families maintain good governments and vice versa, the underlying story is that good *individuals* maintain good families and good governments.

Focus on the Family also utilizes this emphasis on the individual, and especially the individual's responsibility to maintain both public and private spheres. "Be aware. As parents and taxpayers you have the right—and responsibility—to know what your child is being taught in public school classrooms."[11] The message to be aware and take on individual responsibility is repeated often, in relation to myriad issues from Internet pornography to school choice to homosexuality.[12] Know what is going on; get involved. While the social-activism messages at Focus on the Family's website are often (though not entirely) limited to the realm of public schools and institutions related to raising children, the underlying message is that individuals are the ones with the choices (and the responsibility) for engaging in the public sphere in order to ensure that the state, at all levels, is supporting the kinds of families we want to raise. The acknowledgment of the role of the individual in upholding both public and private spheres puts pressure on individual parents to raise their children to make sound individual choices. In the section on Internet pornography, for example, we see: "Even if you make your own home secure, at some point your children will walk out your door and have to make

---

[11]Focus on the Family Issue Analysts, "What You Can Do," www.focusonthefamily.com/socialissues/defending-your-values/homosexual-curriculum/what-you-can-do.aspx (accessed March 31, 2013).

[12]For instance, in the section on religious liberties: "Be aware of school policies before inappropriate material gets into classrooms, or your child's hands," www.focusonthefamily.com/socialissues/defending-your-values/religious-liberties/what-you-can-do.aspx (accessed April 3, 2013).

their own decisions. . . . Teach them about healthy sexuality and help prepare them with a plan for what to do if they are exposed to pornography or an online predator." Indeed, for all its focus on the family, the rhetoric focuses much more on the individual parent, who in turn is utterly responsible for his or her own family.

This turn to the individual as the upholder of both public and private spheres showcases how much we Americans conceive of the world in terms of individuals even more than of entities like "public" and "private." Hannah Arendt writes: "The emergence of the social realm, which is neither private nor public, strictly speaking, is a relatively new phenomenon whose origin coincided with the emergence of the modern age and which found its political form in the nation-state."[13] On Arendt's view, the social sphere arises from the emergence of mass culture and consumer capitalism, both of which focus on the production of private, individual desires. The modern nation-state, which has its underpinnings in an Enlightenment age that privileged the individual's ability to make free, rational choices, found a major champion in the work of thinkers such as John Stuart Mill.[14] Mill suggested that the only reason people and states should interfere with individuals was if they were doing something both out of ignorance and that they would almost certainly regret. The nation-state functions to uphold individualism so that, in effect, everything becomes turned inward toward the individual and his or her rights and rationality.

Given the way we tend to discuss both public and private in relation to the individual, it should come as no surprise that our discussions of hotly debated issues like gay marriage focus on individual rights. Any discussion of church, state and family is couched in terms of how to maintain the individual's precarious sense of self in relation to all these entities. Thus, the advocacy group beyondmarriage.org offers the following bullet points for what it hopes to achieve: "Separation of church and state in all matters, including regulation and recognition of relationships, households and families. Freedom from state regulation of our sexual lives and gender choices, identities and expression."[15] Liberal-minded commentator Laurie Shrage argues:

---

[13]Arendt, *The Human Condition*, p. 28.
[14]See John Stuart Mill, *On Liberty* (n.p.: Dover Thrift Publications, 2002).
[15]"Executive Summary," Beyondmarriage.org.

The state should not promote marriage among adults as a way to establish parent responsibility or to avoid poverty. The state can pursue these aims less intrusively—by formalizing agreements of child support and custody between both unmarried and married parents, that is, independently of marriage. . . . When these arrangements exist in tension with widely shared public values— like those that subordinate wives and daughters and limit their opportunities— privatizing and deregulating marriage will curtail the government's ability to promote gender equality within families structured by marriage.[16]

Churches and other religious groups are, in her view, the inegalitarian groups she advocates against.

At the same time, conservative commentator Ed Morrissey argues for the privatization of marriage in relation to the individual:

Imagine if government had no interest in the definition of marriage. Individuals could commit to each other, head to the local priest or rabbi or shaman—or no one at all—and enter into contractual agreements, call their blissful union whatever they felt it should be called and go about the business of their lives. . . . I believe your private relationships are none of my business. And without any government role in the institution, it wouldn't be the business of the 9th U.S. Circuit Court of Appeals, either.[17]

Such questions are not limited to gay marriage. The hotly debated, recent Health and Human Services mandate entailed similar arguments by people who might call themselves conservatives, who say "Stay out of my bedroom" as they protest a mandate requiring artificial contraception and potentially abortifacient drugs to be covered by nearly all insurance plans. "If you want the church to stay out of your bedroom, then don't ask the church to pay for the consequences of what happens there."[18]

American discourse sharply dichotomizes public and private, liberal and conservative, suggesting that they are far apart and should be kept distinct from each other. Yet at the heart of most language about politics and family is a key similarity: the importance of the individual and his or her choices. For

---

[16]Laurie Shrage, "The End of 'Marriage,'" *The New York Times*, November 4, 2012, http://opinionator.blogs .nytimes.com/2012/11/04/the-end-of-marriage.

[17]Ed Morrissey, "Why Is the State Involved in Marriage at All?" Hot Air, August 7, 2012, http://hotair.com/ archives/2010/08/07/why-is-the-state-involved-in-marriage-at-all.

[18]Kellie Red, "Our Phony Contraception Debate," *Building Cathedrals*, March 6, 2012, www.patheos.com/ blogs/buildingcathedrals/2012/03/our-phony-contraception-debate.

those like Morrissey, individual choice is exercised in choosing one's religion, which then can dictate whether and how marriage functions. For those like Shrage, that individual choice is best exercised by choosing family forms first, and only then choosing religion (if, indeed, one chooses a religion at all). Where they disagree is on the question of where individual rights are infringed: are they chiefly infringed by the government, or are they chiefly infringed by the church?

As Christians, we should worry about this turn to the individual for at least two main reasons. One is the point many theologians and other scholars have named: an Enlightenment focus on individual choices and autonomy turns us away from proclaiming Christ. I am struck again and again by how often Christian arguments (and not just the ones I have mentioned here) about the place of family in relation to the state utilize the idea of the individual's right to choose, rather than grounding their arguments in Christ himself. That is, though the Family Research Council names the family as the "the foundation of civilization, the seedbed of virtue, and the wellspring of society,"[19] in each of the descriptions I have given of family, state and church, it is the individual and his or her choices that become the bedrock of civilization. On the individual's shoulders rest decisions about how to form families, participate in governments and maintain the two spheres.

This view, in turn, leads me to wonder whether we thereby reject God's grace. I have long believed that in our culture we are guilty of making the family into an idol; our rhetoric, both secular and Christian, about families suggests that we think if we can just get the perfect family, we will have a more perfect society.[20] Our views of what counts as a perfect family differ, of course, and we have arguments about that. But while I still think it is true that we make families into idols, I think at root we make families into idols because we have already made individuals into idols. The pressure on individuals to make precisely the right choices that strike precisely the right balance between upholding individual liberty on one hand, and fostering good society by the choices we make on the other, puts each individual in an untenable pressure cooker. It suggests that everything that is wrong about the world

---

[19]Family Research Council, "FAQs," http://frc.org/faqs (accessed March 15, 2013).
[20]See especially chapter 1 of my book *Water Is Thicker than Blood: An Augustinian Theology of Marriage and Singleness* (New York: Oxford University Press, 2008).

stems from the fact that we do not take responsibility for our actions and for knowing about our world enough. This denies the fact that we already know Christ saves and Christ redeems this world in spite of itself. By participating in and focusing on our culture's intense love of the individual and intense inward turning, we simply make our world more the world, more of the same. We imitate the world, rather than being witnesses for Christ, because we are drawn inward by the ways the arguments about private, public, family and state are made. We are not able to see, then, that God's grace is meant to draw us away from ourselves and away from the tired conversations about the place of the individual that never go away in American political discourse.

CONSIDERING SCRIPTURE

In this next section, therefore, I discuss Scripture and what it might have to say about family and state, public and private, and the nature of the individual. Most theologians discussing marriage begin with the Genesis account of God creating male and female and commanding them to be fruitful and multiply and have dominion over the earth. While this is fruitful, and while the Genesis text remains the underpinning of what I say in this chapter, in view of my concern about the place of Christ in the conversation as I have outlined it so far, I wish instead to think about family and state in relation to the Gospels, Acts and Paul's letters, so my aim here will be a rather broad, sweeping vision presented in the New Testament. What I argue in this section is that the fact of God coming into this world reconfigures a public/private dichotomy and leaves aside a privileging of individual autonomy in favor of bringing in a new creation of public/private, family/state and individual.

So I begin with the birth of Christ, which is significant for the fact that Jesus, Son of God, fully human and fully divine, is born into a *family*. It is especially significant that he has both a human mother and a human father, however much that human father is not his biological father. I say this not to negate the fact that the Father begets the Son or that Mary became with child through the Holy Spirit but to bring up a couple of points about Joseph's relationship with Jesus that are often overlooked but that are also intensely important for rightly seeing public and private, family and state, in Jesus' life.

For example, it is important that in Luke's Gospel we read that around the time of Jesus' birth a census was taken by Caesar Augustus on the basis of

Joseph's family of origin. Joseph was related to David and had to return to Bethlehem for the census to be taken. So that is one way in which Joseph is important—it shows Jesus' connection to King David, the premier king of Israel. But the significance is even greater than this. In a homily on the birth of Christ, second- to third-century Christian Origen imagines someone asking him: "Evangelist, how does this narrative help me? How does it help me to know that the first census of the entire world was made under Caesar Augustus; and that among all these people the name of *Joseph, with Mary who was espoused to him and pregnant*, was included; and that, before the census was finished, Jesus was born?"[21] Origen answers the question:

> To one who looks more carefully, a mystery seems to be conveyed. It is significant that Christ should have been recorded in the census of the whole world. He was registered with the world for the census, and offers the world communion with himself. After this census, he could enroll those from the whole world in the book of the living (Rev. 20.15 and Phil. 4.3) with himself.[22]

Such a view coincides, too, with the importance of Adam being named as part of Jesus' genealogy in Luke's Gospel (Lk 3:38), which identifies Jesus as related to the whole world.

Via his family, especially Joseph his father, Jesus is presented politically to an empire. Being named in the census also names this Son of God as fully human, as really a part of our world. Family and politics are tied together in order to make the incarnation of God present to us. But it is then precisely *because* the Word is made flesh, and becomes part of our world as symbolized in this census, that the Word saves the world. This holy family is imbued with political meaning from the outset. At Jesus' birth, there is little or no distinction made between Jesus' familial beginnings and his political beginnings.

When the wise men visit King Herod and tip him off that there is a baby king somewhere about to usurp the throne, Herod responds with an extraordinary amount of violence directed against all children two and under—but as we know Jesus escapes. Why does he escape? Because he is part of a human family and has a human father, Joseph, who hides Jesus and speeds him to Egypt, and thus participates in God's mystery of the incarnation. Joseph, just

---

[21]Origen, Sermon 11.
[22]Ibid., Sermon 11.6.

as much as Mary, knows that the all-powerful and ever-living God has improbably come to earth as a tiny, helpless human infant in need of all the protections a human family can give. Yet it is also precisely because that infant is the all-powerful and ever-living God that Joseph, the poor carpenter, is empowered to make that journey to Egypt. Mary and Joseph thereby protect Jesus not for themselves, not out of horror of losing a child, though surely that is there too—they protect Jesus for all of humanity. Thus family becomes vastly opened. Mary and Joseph, in taking Christ the Son of God as their son, suddenly find that their family is opened, radically. It is made fully public, for Jesus becomes radically all of humanity's.

Jesus underscores this vast openness and public nature of his family in his ministry. Consider the scene toward the beginning of Jesus' ministry when his mother and brothers come to greet him. In Matthew, for example, we hear:

> While he was still speaking to the crowds, his mother and his brothers were standing outside, wanting to speak to him. Someone told him, "Look, your mother and your brothers are standing outside, wanting to speak to you." But to the one who had told him this, Jesus replied, "Who is my mother, and who are my brothers?" And pointing to his disciples, he said, "Here are my mother and my brothers! For whoever does the will of my Father in heaven is my brother and sister and mother." (Mt 12:46-50)[23]

There is here both a radical acceptance of and a radical rejection of the standard family as determined by culture. While Jesus clearly acknowledges the need for and presence of mothers, brothers, sisters, fathers and so on, he also places a claim on those families in a much larger way. In other words, Jesus accepts the fact of the family and of course embraces marriage and family as instituted by God. Yet at the same time, marriage and family both become absorbed into the new creation, which turns away from an inward focus directed almost solely between the couple and their children, toward outward discipleship to Christ. Family, rightly oriented toward God, cannot be a private entity.

As a further example, note what happens on the cross and the mixture of family and state powers that appear there. In John's Gospel, one of Jesus' last deeds is addressing his beloved disciple and his mother: "When Jesus saw his

---

[23]All Scripture quotations in this chapter are from the NRSV.

mother and the disciple whom he loved standing beside her, he said to his mother, 'Woman, here is your son.' Then he said to the disciple, 'Here is your mother.' And from that hour the disciple took her into his own home" (Jn 19:26-27). All this happens while Jesus' crucifixion is surrounded by and imbued with political implications. Notions of what constitutes family once again become changed radically. But similarly, Jesus' death on the cross is noted by many as not being the standard kind of political activism people were expecting. This is no Jesus raising up an army and thus no so-called public sphere in the way that we think about it. In a sense, the cross is a uniquely private event: "Into your hands I commend my spirit," Jesus cries (Lk 23:46). It is him alone calling to God. Yet the cross, too, is ultimately and radically made public for all humans, and indeed all of creation. Violence brings in a new kingdom—but it is reverse violence. The one who will be king is killed; it makes all the difference in the world that he is also resurrected. The one who is a son of his mother loses a mother in the act of saving the world. Thus even on the cross, family and politics become enmeshed, and they become both public and private. Just as Jesus' birth entailed that the incarnation of God swallowed the whole of the world, family and politics with it, so in the cross and resurrection the whole of creation is absorbed in that redemption.

What is perhaps most significant of all, though, is that following the resurrection, discussion of family and state doesn't appear in relation to Jesus. The fact of the cross and the resurrection changes everything. Family and state can no longer take on the significances they did preresurrection. Jesus appears to his followers and breaks bread with some unrelated disciples, but the motifs of family and political state do not appear again until after Pentecost, when the church as Christ's body is made known to the world. Now we Christians are meant to see that in the resurrection, family and politics simply don't matter in the ways that we thought they did. The resurrection leaves us both hopeful and perplexed because the world looks entirely different. Part of that difference is exactly found in the institution of the church.

Reinhard Huetter has shown that we tend to understand the church as one entity among many, equivalent to the ways we name business, government and families as entities.[24] As I mentioned above, our language about the

---

[24]Reinhard Huetter, *Suffering Divine Things: Theology as Church Practice* (Grand Rapids: Eerdmans, 2000), especially part 4.

church as a private entity matches this kind of language. Yet because of the incarnation, cross and resurrection, the church simply cannot be seen in this way, as one entity among many. Rather it transcends those entities, even as it takes on those entities in a radical way.

The apostles greatly wrestle with the apparent paradox of being part of an institution that is both in the world and radically distinct from it. How can Christians live in Christ faithfully in a world where family and state matter, but yet follow Jesus, who has transformed both family and state? Thus it is no mistake that we see the disciples wrestling with what it means to be married and have families, or what it means to participate in politics. In Acts, for example, we see the disciples complicating standard household rules by living all together as a church household, sharing everything in common (Acts 2:42-47).

In 1 Corinthians 7, Paul clearly privileges a single life to marriage—obviously wrestling with what, exactly, it would mean to live as a person in a post-resurrection world and whether family ought to have the same kind of status and importance as it did in a preresurrection world.[25] In his letter to the Ephesians Paul writes: "So then you are no longer strangers and aliens, but you are citizens with the saints and also members of the household of God" (Eph 2:19).[26] This is meant to remind Christians that, again, the church is no entity among other entities and that family and state take on a different kind of significance in light of Christ. Christ becomes the site for being both citizen and household, together. Here there is no room for the kind of dichotomies that we saw earlier in the discussion about public and private.

Scripture constantly attests that when our focus is on Jesus, family and state, public and private get overturned. Contemporary liberal conceptions of public as being about citizenship get transcended by this view of the church with members as citizens. As well, contemporary liberal conceptions of private space as being about households get transcended here—for members are members of the household of God.

CONCLUSIONS AND IMPLICATIONS

What are the implications of all that I have said here? I think what becomes

---

[25]In ancient Palestine, family mattered because it was the means by which a person belonged to society as a whole and the way in which a person received an identity.

[26]Reinhard Huetter develops this point in *Suffering Divine Things*, p. 163.

clear, first and foremost, is that any attempt to divide family, state and church into spheres called "public" and "private" is more a concession to a modern Enlightenment-based culture than it is a response to Christ. There can be no sense that a proper division between public and private somehow "saves" our society, or more particularly, that it saves the individual. As Christians in the church, our understanding of family necessarily morphs because we have a broader vision of what it means to belong to a family—just as our understanding of the state and politics changes in the ways my colleagues mention in this book.

This does not mean that there is no distinction between state and family and their functions; what it does mean, however, is that Christians should not merely acquiesce to the perceived cultural boundaries of public and private. Instead, what counts as public and private is transgressed and transformed. Indeed, I suggest that rather than of thinking in terms of "public" and "private," Christians ought to think in terms of the virtues of charity and justice and the ways in which the individual, family and state relate to each other in living out these virtues. I do not have time to develop this idea further, but I think justice and charity stand as much more significant than the public/private distinction for the Christian tradition. Charity calls us to love each other as God loves us; justice calls us also to seek right relationships with each other while being able to speak to the world's range of organizations, government among them.

Living with justice and charity instead of public and private means that family cannot be turned in on itself. Indeed, Christians are called radically to embrace other members of the body of Christ as their family. I am reminded of a church in Chicago where, if the pastor discovers that a teenager has become pregnant and been thrown out by her family, he asks his congregation if anyone will take her in and care for her as their own daughter. This is not because they think that out-of-wedlock pregnancy is a good thing or that premarital sex is good—but rather that, regardless, this girl is part of their Christian family. If she is Christ's, then she must be theirs too. And that means a call to radical discipleship.

I am reminded, too, of the example of Jonathan Wilson-Hartgrove and his wife, Leah. They run the Rutba House, a community in inner-city Durham, North Carolina, where they, a white couple, live in the poorest, most racially diverse part of Durham, an area known as Walltown. And from the beginning of their marriage they have opened their house to anyone who needed a bed because that person was Christ, coming to them. Their household is not just themselves and their children; it is a whole host of people who live with them and cook with them and raise their children with them.

That is my suggestion for the so-called private sphere: families become more public, more engaged, more radically involved in treating each other as the body of Christ. In the public sphere, the implication is somewhat different. I am not calling on people to decline to vote, though that may be an outcome. I hope that people will decide that for the sake of Christ they cannot go to war anymore, and I hope that they will decide to find ways to curtail participation in a global capitalist economy. That means more engagement with families and their local neighborhoods and economies.

The most important implication, I think, is that Christians need to learn to live being betwixt and between. Just as Jesus breaking into this world is so radical that the world doesn't quite know what to do with him but is also utterly changed by him, so we Christians who follow him must realize that there is no easy way to be Christians in the world. Following Jesus means that we never neatly fit into a box. I was amused by how, following the 2013 election of Pope Francis, people were immediately trying to label him as "liberal" or "conservative," but he keeps defying those categories. No political party, no human family, will every fully be all that we want it to be—and indeed we should be suspicious when we think it is.

That, then, is why I think I have something to say about political theology as someone who writes on marriage and family. Marriage, family and politics are swallowed up in Jesus' great embrace, as we wait in joyful hope for his coming again to bring us home.

7

ARE CORPORATIONS PEOPLE?

The Corporate Form and the Body of Christ

William T. Cavanaugh

In January of 2010, the United States Supreme Court handed down its landmark five-four decision in *Citizens United v. Federal Election Commission*, which overturned limits on political expenditures by corporations and unions. The Court was asked to rule on the narrow question of whether or not the advocacy group Citizens United could advertise for and air a film critical of Hillary Clinton close to the Democratic primary, but the Court decided to broaden the case out to rule on the constitutionality of campaign finance laws. In doing so, they struck down significant parts of the McCain-Feingold Act of 2002. Although corporations and unions are still barred from making direct contributions to political candidates, in order to avoid quid pro quo corruption or the appearance thereof, they can now spend freely on electioneering communications that attack or advocate for candidates within sixty days of a general election or thirty days of a primary, without the inconvenience of having to set up a separate PAC (political action committee) to do their speaking for them.[1]

The decision was immediately hailed and decried as a major turning point in US law, not simply because of the decision reached but because of the way the majority argued. Corporations and unions were clearly regarded as being the subjects of speech; they could speak like human beings, and therefore their free speech rights should not be "chilled." Although the Supreme Court had

---

[1] *Citizens United v. Federal Election Commission*, 558 U.S. 310 (2010). The McCain-Feingold Act is more formally known as the Bipartisan Campaign Reform Act of 2002 (BCRA).

long given some First Amendment protections to corporations, the majority in *Citizens United* argued against the law's ability to make any sort of distinctions among speakers in First Amendment cases. Reaction against the decision by the 80 percent of Americans who oppose it[2] has tended to echo the conviction of Justice John Paul Stevens's furious dissenting opinion: the speakers in this case "are not natural persons, much less members of our political community."[3] "Corporations are not people" is the refrain of politicians, books, websites and blogs dedicated to overturning *Citizens United*.[4] Only individual human beings are people, and therefore only individual human beings should be the subjects of a democracy.

In this article, I am going to take issue with that type of criticism from a theological point of view. The fact is that corporate personhood is central to Christianity; the people of God and the body of Christ are corporate persons, recognition of which should prevent Christians from thinking that only individuals are actors in the world. At the same time, however, I think that *Citizens United* is a disastrous and distorting decision, not because it recognizes corporate persons as such but because of the kind of corporate person it privileges, the business corporation. To critique *Citizens United* we must go deeper than trying to privilege the individual actor in the marketplace of ideas; we must critique the integration of politics and markets that lies underneath the distortion of any ideas of citizen participation.

I will begin with a brief look at bodies politic in the ancient world, compared and contrasted with biblical views of corporate personhood. Then I will discuss the simultaneous rise in modernity of states and corporations, and why they fall short of a truly participatory politics. I will examine the *Citizens United* decision in more detail and argue that although the idea of a corporate person is coherent and important, the privileging of the business corporation

---

[2]According to an ABC-*Washington Post* poll conducted February 4-8, 2010; see Dan Eggen, "Poll: Large Majority Opposes Supreme Court's Decision on Campaign Financing," *Washington Post*, February 17, 2010, www.washingtonpost.com/wp-dyn/content/article/2010/02/17/AR2010021701151.html?sid =ST2010021702073.

[3]*Citizens United*, Opinion of Stevens, p. 32.

[4]For example, Ari Berman, "Elizabeth Warren to Romney: 'Corporations Are Not People,'" *The Nation*, September 5, 2012, www.thenation.com/blog/169773/elizabeth-warren-romney-corporations-are-not-people; Jeffrey D. Clements, *Corporations Are Not People: Why They Have More Rights Than You Do and What You Can Do About It* (San Francisco: Berrett-Koehler Publishers, 2012); corporationsarenotpeople .com; Thom Hartmann, *Unequal Protection: How Corporations Became "People" and How You Can Fight Back* (San Francisco: Berrett-Koehler Publishers, 2010).

is a distortion of the kind of communal body that the church is called to promote and enact.

BODIES POLITIC IN THE ANCIENT WORLD
AND THE CHRISTIAN TRADITION

The idea of a corporate person can be found in the ancient Greek analogy of a body politic. Plato begins the *Republic* by treating society on analogy with the human body, which can be either feverish or healthy. Aristotle develops the idea further: "The state has a natural priority over the household and over any individual among us. For the whole must be prior to the part. Separate hand or foot from the whole body, and they will no longer be hand or foot except in name."[5] The *polis* is therefore not a human creation but reflects the order of nature; it is "both natural and prior to the individual."[6] The individual receives life by participation in the larger whole; the whole is not constructed of preexisting parts. The individual, then, receives fulfillment by participation in the *polis*, but that participation for Aristotle was not on an equal basis. The body analogy allowed for a hierarchical relationship; just as the head governed the body, so certain people were naturally fit for rule. Citizenship was limited to propertied men; women, children, slaves, resident foreigners and many laborers were excluded. Aristotle was not a democrat in the modern sense because he did not think that the *demos* (people) had either the leisure to commit to informed decision making or the means to hire someone else to represent them.[7] Democracy in the ancient world excluded the working class; it was taken for granted that to be a citizen one could not be dependent on others for employment. In other words, contrary to what we have been taught to think today, one could not have democracy in a class-divided society.[8]

Corporate personhood is inflected differently in the biblical tradition, beginning with the creation of all human beings in the image of God. It is not the case that only individuals are made in the image and likeness of God. The image of God in Genesis 1:27 seems to apply to the whole human race: "in the image of God he created him [*adam*, singular]; male and female he created

---

[5]Aristotle, *Politics*, trans. T. A. Sinclair and Trevor J. Saunders (London: Penguin, 1981), p. 60 [1253a18].
[6]Ibid.
[7]Ibid., pp. 254-55 [1292b21-34], 368-72 [1318b6-1319b27].
[8]C. B. MacPherson, *The Life and Times of Liberal Democracy* (Oxford: Oxford University Press, 1977), pp. 12-13.

them [plural]" (ESV), which is why many versions of the Bible translate *adam* with a corporate noun like "humankind." Indeed, the concept of corporate personhood is a dominant theme throughout the Bible. Israel is regarded as God's son (e.g., Ex 4:22-23; Hos 11:1). The suffering servant in Isaiah (52:13–53:12) is Israel as corporate person and/or the Messiah who takes the collective sins of all onto his own body. This sense of corporate personhood is crucial to Paul's soteriology. According to Paul, Christ is able to undo Adam's sin because Christ, like Adam, incorporates the whole human race.

> Therefore, just as sin came into the world through one man, and death came through sin, and so death spread to all because all have sinned—sin was indeed in the world before the law, but sin is not reckoned when there is no law. Yet death exercised dominion from Adam to Moses, even over those whose sins were not like the transgression of Adam, who is a type of the one who was to come.
>
> But the free gift is not like the trespass. For if the many died through the one man's trespass, much more surely have the grace of God and the free gift in the grace of the one man, Jesus Christ, abounded for the many. (Rom 5:12-15 NRSV)

Here the concept of *type* illustrates the essential unity of the human race.

The reality of corporate personhood is fundamental to the thought of the patristic writers. As Henri de Lubac explains, "The unity of the Mystical Body of Christ, a supernatural unity, supposes a previous natural unity, the unity of the human race. So the Fathers of the church, in their treatment of grace and salvation, kept constantly before them this Body of Christ, and in dealing with the creation were not content only to mention the formation of individuals, the first man and the first woman, but delighted to contemplate God creating humanity as a whole."[9] De Lubac writes that when pagans like Celsus and Porphyry jeered at the Christian idea that the whole human race could be united in the same faith, Christians could reply that it was simply the reuniting of all people who are made in the image of the one God.[10] This "monogenism" was at the core of the reality of the body of Christ; Christ comes to restore the original unity of humanity by gathering all into his body. His incarnation was not just a *corporatio*, a corporation, but a *concorporatio*, as St. Hilary says. "Christ the Redeemer does not offer salvation merely to each one; he effects it,

---

[9]Henri de Lubac, *Catholicism: Christ and the Common Destiny of Man*, trans. Lancelot Sheppard and Elizabeth Englund (San Francisco: Ignatius Press, 1988), p. 25.

[10]Ibid., pp. 30-31.

he is himself the salvation of the whole, and for each one salvation consists in a personal ratification of his original 'belonging' to Christ, so that he be not cast out, cut off from the Whole."[11] There is thus a horizontal as well as a vertical dimension to salvation; we are reconciled with each other as we are reconciled to God. Augustine famously describes this as the formation of a different kind of city—what Aristotle would call a *polis*—the city of God, which is formed by the unity of people around the altar, in the becoming of the body of Christ.[12]

Gerhard Lohfink has shown how biblical soteriology in both the Old and New Testaments is founded on this idea that unity is not only an effect of salvation but *is* salvation, the restoring of the primordial harmony of a creation torn apart by sin. This is why *gathering* is a fundamental theme in both the Old and New Testaments.[13] When the early church borrowed the Greek word *ekklesia* for itself, it took on some of the resonances of the Greek body politic, in which the *ekklesia* was the gathering of all those who had the rights of citizens in the city-state, as opposed to the smaller group of elected officials that made up the council (*boule*).[14] The church thus claimed to be more than a club organized around private interests; it was a fully public gathering concerned with the whole of life. At the same time, it was not the earthly *polis* but an anticipation of the eschatological gathering of the people of God. According to Lohfink, the origin of *ekklesia* was ultimately not the Greek city-state but the "day of the assembly" at Mount Sinai when the Israelites received the Decalogue (Deut 5:22).[15]

Paul's strong identification of the *ekklesia* as the very body of Christ is no doubt indebted to Greek concepts of corporate personhood in the body politic, but at the same time it is a radical departure from Greek ideas of citizenship and class. The wholeness of the human race in biblical thought, rooted in the essential equality of all and coparticipation of all in the image of God, is recapitulated and redeemed in the one man, Jesus Christ. Christ's crucified

---

[11]Ibid., p. 39.

[12]Augustine, *City of God*, trans. Henry Bettenson (Harmondsworth: Penguin, 1972), X.6.

[13]Gerhard Lohfink, *Does God Need the Church? Toward a Theology of the People of God* (Collegeville, MN: Michael Glazier, 1999), pp. 51-60, 218-36.

[14]Robert L. Wilken, *The Christians as the Romans Saw Them* (New Haven: Yale University Press, 1984), pp. 32-34.

[15]Lohfink, *Does God Need the Church?*, p. 219.

and resurrected body thus becomes the whole of humanity, restored to the primordial unity in which it was created. The distinctions with which Greek concepts of citizenship operated simply disappear: "There is no longer Jew or Greek, there is no longer slave or free, there is no longer male and female; for all of you are one in Christ Jesus" (Gal 3:28).[16] As the image of the body makes clear, there remains differentiation among the members; some are eyes, some are hands, some are feet and so on. But this means that equality is not a mere formal equality, in which all are treated as the same before the law. In fact, differentiation produces a kind of attraction among the members—for as Paul tells the Corinthians, the eye realizes that, because it is not the hand, it needs the hand, and the head realizes that it needs the feet (1 Cor 12:19-21). What holds the body together is not mutual interests or rights or fear of external enemies but *agape*, love (1 Cor 13:1-13). This love is the fruit of the Spirit (Gal 5:22), in whom all were baptized into the one body of Christ (1 Cor 12:4-13). Not only are the weakest members not excluded from citizenship or membership in the body, but there is a preferential option for the weakest in the body: "the members of the body that seem to be weaker are indispensable, and those members of the body that we think less honorable we clothe with greater honor" (1 Cor 12:22-23). Paul takes the body analogy even further by implying that a kind of nervous system connects all the members, for "if one member suffers, all suffer together with it; if one member is honored, all rejoice together with it" (1 Cor 12:26).

The corporate nature of the church is further intensified beyond the Greek model by the Eucharist, which serves to bind the members together into the body of Christ by an act of bodily consumption. In a move that must have seemed exceedingly odd and even perverse to the Greeks, the body of Christ was identified with both the corporate person of the church and the food on which the members of the church fed. "The cup of blessing that we bless, is it not a sharing in the blood of Christ? The bread that we break, is it not a sharing in the body of Christ? Because there is one bread, we who are many are one body, for we all partake of the one bread" (1 Cor 10:16-17). By eating the Lord's body, we become assimilated to the Lord's body, consumed by what we consume. We do not thereby eat ourselves, because there is no self, properly

---

[16]All subsequent Scripture quotations in this chapter are from the NRSV.

understood, before we enter into communion with God and with one another. As the work of John Zizioulas has made clear, the patristic anthropology is not one in which preexisting individuals subsequently enter into communion with each other. It is instead the case that we become who we really are only by entering into that communion. Being is not a mere biological fact but an ecclesial reality. In pagan Greek thought, person, or *prosopon*, referred to the mask that actors would wear on the stage. The substance (*hypostasis*) of the human being was a given reality unrelated to the person. The human actor could don a mask and fight with the gods and his fate on stage, but ultimately there is no true freedom for him; his person is nothing but a mask, with no ontological bearing on his substance. Once the biblical writers had traced human freedom back to God's free act of creating from nothing, however, then the ontology of the human being could be unified with her person. The person is called out of nothing and into freedom by participation in God.[17] This act is realized in the re-creation of the person in Christ, the summit of which is the becoming-Christ of the Eucharist. We do not first have our being and then subsequently enter into communion with Christ and others; being is communion. This is why Zizioulas makes the provocative claim that the Eucharist *"is the reality which makes it possible for us to exist at all."*[18]

What the body of Christ inaugurates, therefore, is a new type of sociality, one that is bodily but simultaneously eschatological. Its being is received from another, God, and so it is aware of the other in its midst, the stranger and poor one who is the personification of Christ (Mt 25:31-46). There was nothing new about the followers of Jesus forming associations of like-minded people based on common interests. By the time of Jesus, associations were common in the pagan world. They were social clubs based on a particular trade—fruit merchants, for example—or funerary societies to ensure each member a decent burial, or societies based on the cult of a particular deity. They shared meals together and achieved a sense of belonging, even brotherly love.[19] What made the church different, however, was not only its choice of an explicitly public and political term like *ekklesia*—as opposed to terms like *koinon* and

---

[17]John Zizioulas, *Being as Communion: Studies in Personhood and the Church* (Crestwood, NY: St. Vladimir's Seminary Press, 1993), pp. 27-41.

[18]John Zizioulas, quoted in Paul McPartlan, *The Eucharist Makes the Church: Henri de Lubac and John Zizioulas in Dialogue* (Edinburgh: T & T Clark, 1993), p. 270. Italics in original.

[19]Wilken, *Christians as the Romans Saw Them*, pp. 35-40.

collegium that designated associations—but its transgression of ordinary social boundaries to include women, men, children, slaves, Jews, Greeks, rich and poor all within the same gathering. There was originally meant to be only one church, presided over by the bishop, in each city, instead of many parishes into which people could self-separate. The eucharistic assembly therefore gathered people from across all kinds of natural and social divisions. The church came to be seen as a third race, a *tertium quid*, that was not only neither Jew nor Greek but also superseded all kinds of divisions of class, gender, age and so on. The Acts of the Apostles makes clear that economic relationships were not exempt from this breaking down of barriers. The early Christians are said to have had no private ownership, but rather shared all things in common, taking special care of any in need (Acts 2:44-45; 4:32). Such was the ideal, anyway. The account is no doubt somewhat romanticized. As Paul's scolding of the Corinthians in 1 Corinthians 11:17-34 makes clear, the ideal in practice was not always so. But the type of corporate person that the body of Christ called into being was clearly a challenge to existing social, economic and political stratification.

In the medieval period, the body of Christ continued to be a powerful image of the corporate nature of human relations. The body of Christ produced a relation of *agape* among the members that differed from the Greek and Roman body politic, and suffused the body with a mystical sense quite alien to the classical world. The body of Christ also radically divided the political loyalties of Christians. Among the Greeks there could be no doubting one's membership in the body politic; although one could question this law or that tyranny, one's membership in the *polis* was a necessary condition for one's development as a human person. The Christian, on the other hand, could have doubts about political participation because she belonged to another type of body, a body that was already a colony of heaven.[20] According to Sheldon Wolin, when participation had been stifled in the later Roman Empire by centralized power, Christianity revivified political life by projecting a new type of body politic whose full citizenship was in heaven.[21]

Christian ideals and Christian realities were not the same things, however,

---

[20]Sheldon Wolin, *Politics and Vision: Continuity and Innovation in Western Political Thought*, expanded ed. (Princeton: Princeton University Press, 2004), p. 92.
[21]Ibid., pp. 86-87.

and the corporate nature of the Christian community was recruited into use for a more hierarchical and uniform vision of society. John of Salisbury's *Policraticus* in the twelfth century, for example, draws on Plutarch, not Paul, to establish the image of the political community on the analogy of a human body, with the king as the head, priests as the soul, soldiers as the hands, the treasury as the stomach and peasants as the feet.[22] Marie de France similarly draws on Livy and Aesop in her "Fable of a Man, His Belly, and His Limbs," which justifies taxation, collected by the belly, because the belly provides strength for the limbs.[23] As Henri de Lubac famously documented, beginning in the eleventh century the term *corpus verum*, true body of Christ, increasingly referred to the Eucharistic elements on the altar, not to the church. The *corpus mysticum* came to refer to the church, but the sacramental and eschatological elements of the image were muted as the church became increasingly bureaucratized. The term *corpus mysticum* was increasingly used in a legal context to refer to the church's structure, which was seen less as an effect of the Eucharist and more on analogy with human bodies. It became possible then to refer not to the mystical body of Christ but to the mystical body of the church.[24] As Ernst Kantorowicz writes, "Undeniably the former liturgical concept of *corpus mysticum* faded away only to be transformed into a relatively colorless sociological, organological, or juristic notion."[25]

Of even greater importance was the migration of the concept of mystical body to the nascent state in the late medieval and early modern periods. Building on de Lubac's work, Kantorowicz's famed study *The King's Two Bodies* showed how the state borrowed theological body language to take on the trappings of divinity. By the fifteenth century, theologians like Jean Gerson and jurists like Jean de Terre Rouge were referring to the "mystical body of France."[26] What Wolin found so politically promising about Christianity is also what he found so dangerous. Classical thought had conceived of political

---

[22]John of Salisbury, "Metalogicon and Policraticus," in Cary J. Neederman and Kate Langdon Forhan, eds., *Medieval Political Theory—A Reader: The Quest for the Body Politic, 1100–1400* (London: Routledge, 1993), pp. 37-53.

[23]Marie de France, "The Fable of a Man, His Belly, and His Limbs," in Neederman and Forhan, *Medieval Political Theory*, p. 25.

[24]Ernst H. Kantorowicz, *The King's Two Bodies: A Study in Medieval Political Theology* (Princeton, NJ: Princeton University Press, 1957), pp. 200-206.

[25]Ibid., p. 202.

[26]Ibid., pp. 218-20.

solidarity in a body politic, but never as a mystical body. "Christianity helped father the idea of a community as a non-rational, non-utilitarian body bound by a meta-rational faith, infused by a mysterious spirit taken into the members."[27] This mysticism would gradually be transferred to the nation-state, spawning nationalism and all of its ills.

CORPORATE BODIES IN A MARKET SOCIETY

In a previous work I have looked at the story of the nation-state as a kind of mystical body.[28] What I want to do now is look at the business corporation as another kind of body, one that arose in conjunction with the state and one whose power has now come to rival and in many cases has merged with the state. What we see in the modern era is a new type of corporate person, the business corporation, which has taken on powers of speech. The rise of a market economy along with the modern state is often depicted in terms of the rise of the individual over against more communal forms of living that are associated with the medieval period. The organic metaphor of the body was largely replaced by social contract theory, in which preexisting individuals band together to form a state and society based on mutual interests and mutual fears. Hobbes's *Leviathan* bridges these two traditions by depicting the state as an artificial body constructed of many individuals. In later political theory the body analogy, for the most part, disappears. At the same time that the body analogy was dropping out of political theory, however, and the new science of economics was fixated on the encounters of individuals in markets, each pursuing his or her own interests, the primary use of collective body language outside of the church became that of the business corporation. The idea of individuals coming together in a legally recognized body with rights and liabilities that transcend any of those individuals dates back to the Roman *collegia*. What was new about modern corporations like the Dutch and British East India Companies, chartered in the seventeenth century, was their incorporation for the pursuit of profit on behalf of private shareholders.

The rise of the corporation was predicated on the creation of the capitalist and of the wage laborer, a creation that was in turn predicated on the libera-

---

[27]Wolin, *Politics and Vision*, p. 119.
[28]See my book *Migrations of the Holy: God, State, and the Political Meaning of the Church* (Grand Rapids: Eerdmans, 2011).

tion of the individual from the confines of the traditional social group. Medieval feudal arrangements, towns, guilds, clans and other bearers of local custom were swept away by the rise of the sovereign state with one centralized political center and legal structure. The rise of market economies depended on the state and the establishment of standardized systems of law, currency and taxation. All individuals were now, in theory, equal before the law, and all were "liberated" to sell their labor or purchase the labor of others—to deal with each other on the basis of contract, in other words, rather than as members of a social body. This process of freeing wage labor included dispossessing masses of individuals from control over their means of production, through the enclosure of common lands and other coercive means.[29]

We are accustomed to telling the story of the simultaneous rise of the modern state and the rise of market economies and the rise of the corporation and the rise of democracy as if they were all one story. The *Citizens United* case, however, demands that we consider the possibility that they are not all one story. The rise of corporate power is not the same as the rise of democracy, and in fact can threaten democracy. As Charles Lindblom argued in his landmark book *Politics and Markets*, there is no essential relationship between democracy and markets. The reason that polyarchies—systems in which no monolithic elite controls the political process—are always associated with market systems has to do with the constitutional liberalism in which both polyarchies and market systems were born. Liberalism, however, is not necessarily democracy. Liberalism was not democratic in origin but an attempt to protect and enlarge the liberties first of nobles and then of a merchant middle class. The job of liberal states was and is to protect property and provide the necessary conditions for market competition. Popular rule, or democracy, was sometimes seen as a means toward the attainment of liberty, but liberty and equality were often at odds, and when they were at odds, liberty has usually trumped equality,[30] as in the case of *Citizens United*. In *Citizens United*, both the majority and the dissenting opinion agreed that the First Amendment is designed to protect liberty, the freedom to speak, but it is not meant to

---

[29]Anthony Giddens, *The Nation-State and Violence* (Berkeley: University of California Press, 1987), pp. 148-60. Also Michael Perelman, *The Invention of Capitalism: Classical Political Economy and the Secret History of Primitive Accumulation* (Durham: Duke University Press, 2000).

[30]Charles E. Lindblom, *Politics and Markets: The World's Political-Economic Systems* (New York: Basic Books, 1977), pp. 161-69.

equalize the power of those who speak. In his dissenting opinion, Justice Stevens emphasizes that equalizing the relative influence of speakers on elections is not the basis on which the McCain-Feingold Act had sought to restrain corporate electioneering.[31]

C. B. MacPherson writes, "Liberalism had always meant freeing the individual from the outdated restraints of old established institutions. By the time liberalism emerged as liberal democracy this became a claim to free all individuals equally, and to free them to use and develop their human capacities fully."[32] Despite the claim to equality, however, liberal democratic theorists accepted class division. The equality envisioned was a formal equality before the law. "The first formulators of liberal democracy came to its advocacy through a chain of reasoning which started from the assumptions of a capitalist market society and the laws of classical political economy. These gave them a model of man (as maximizer of utilities) and a model of society (as a collection of individuals with conflicting interests)."[33] Early theorists of liberal democracy did not give up on the goal of full democracy through equality but did their best to reconcile a competitive market economy with equality. John Stuart Mill, for example, saw liberal democracy as a moral project for the improvement of humanity that would progressively overcome class divisions. Mill saw that the current system was grossly unfair, in that rewards were inversely proportional to the amount of labor a person did, but Mill thought this inequality was only accidentally related to the market system. He thought that participation in the competitive market would allow the working class to develop its own human potential, but in the meantime, the elite should be given a disproportionate share of votes, since in their present debased condition the lower classes could not be trusted to vote in the interest of the common good.[34]

Mill had the virtue of recognizing that class division and inequality were a problem for democracy, and he attempted to institute a political solution, however elitist, to market inequities. As MacPherson shows, however, theorists of democracy in the latter half of the twentieth century, beginning with Joseph

---

[31]*Citizens United*, Opinion of Stevens, p. 51.
[32]MacPherson, *Life and Times of Liberal Democracy*, p. 21.
[33]Ibid., p. 24.
[34]Ibid., pp. 44-64.

Schumpeter, have tended to conflate the political and economic processes so that liberal democracy is envisioned on the model of a market. Any concern about class division and the improvement of humankind has tended to give way to a more ostensibly empirical model of all people as individual rational maximizers who choose political candidates as they choose salad dressing at the supermarket. Democracy is a marketplace in which elections register people's desires as they are, just as purchases do in the economic marketplace.[35] There is no overriding *telos* or common good; each person chooses his or her own good based on his or her own preferences, and individual preferences will inevitably conflict. The market is the mechanism in both the economic and political realms that determines whose preferences prevail, with one important difference. In the economic market, minority preferences may still be met by some suppliers; in the political market—in a two-party system especially—it is winner take all. The preferences of the majority always trump those of the minority.

The model of democracy as a marketplace is certainly not the only theoretical model of democracy available,[36] but the Supreme Court seems to take it for granted. Both the majority and the dissenting minority in *Citizens United* repeatedly use the model of marketplace to describe the political arena. The majority argues that restricting corporate speech will impede the "uninhibited marketplace of ideas,"[37] by restricting the ability of corporations to "compete" in the "'open marketplace' of ideas protected by the First Amendment."[38] One of the precedents that *Citizens United* overturned—*Austin v. Michigan Chamber of Commerce*—had sought to prevent "an unfair advantage in the political marketplace" by using "resources amassed in the economic marketplace,"[39] but the majority knocked down this attempted barrier between the two marketplaces by arguing that the Court had already rejected as

---

[35]Ibid., pp. 78-80.

[36]The widely influential account of John Rawls is less competitive and more cooperative, though it still depends on envisioning the individual as a rational maximizer of his own interests who, under conditions of moderate scarcity, will choose principles of justice behind the "veil of ignorance"; John Rawls, *A Theory of Justice*, rev. ed. (Cambridge, MA: Harvard University Press, 1999). Jeffrey Stout's theory of democracy as a moral tradition based on a background of agreement rather than competition is an interesting alternative, though I find it hard to square with the actual empirical condition of democracy in the United States; Jeffrey Stout, *Democracy and Tradition* (Princeton, NJ: Princeton University Press, 2004).

[37]*Citizens United*, Opinion of the Court, 19, citing a previous case, *Virginia v. Hicks* (2003).

[38]Ibid., p. 38; the internal quotation is from a previous case, *New York State Board of Elections v. Lopez Torres* (2008).

[39]Ibid., p. 34. Here the majority is quoting the *Austin* decision.

unconstitutional the goal of "equalizing the relative ability of individuals and groups to influence the outcome of elections."[40] Speech is held to be "the means to hold officials accountable to the people," and so "the First Amendment stands against attempts to disfavor certain subjects or viewpoints or to distinguish among different speakers, which may be a means to control content."[41] The logic of the economic marketplace—that more choices are better and no one can prejudge which choices are good—is applied also to the political marketplace: "There is no such thing as too much speech,"[42] as Justice Scalia has written. Justice Stevens in dissent also recognizes the legitimacy of the "market for legislation,"[43] but wants to create "breathing room around the electoral 'marketplace of ideas'" in order to allow competition in that market to be more fair.[44]

The marketplace in Adam Smith's vision assumes supply responds to demand because many sellers respond to many buyers. What happens when many individuals band together to form a corporation? The majority in *Citizens United* assumes that corporate persons have the same speech rights as individuals; democracy is the process by which all speakers, including groups of individuals, have their say, and then the citizens or consumers choose which speech is true; the electoral system responds to consumer demand, one person, one vote. The problem is that the political market, in fact, is an oligopoly. The buyer confronts not multiple sellers but two in a two-party system such as that of the United States. The sellers need not respond to the buyers'/voters' demands as they would in a fully competitive system; demand is dictated by the sellers. It is true that the system gives one vote to each individual natural person. But the candidates and issues that are voted on, and the information provided to the individual voter, are largely determined not simply by demand but by *effective* demand. In an economic market, the only demand that counts is demand backed by purchasing power. In an economic market, the person with a million dollars has a million times more "votes" than the person with one dollar. And so it is in the political market. The Su-

---

[40]Ibid. Here the majority is quoting *Buckley v. Valeo* (1976).

[41]Ibid., Syllabus, p. 3.

[42]This quote from Justice Scalia is from his dissenting opinion in the *Austin* decision; Stevens quotes Scalia in his dissenting opinion in *Citizens United*, Opinion of Stevens, p. 83.

[43]Ibid., p. 82.

[44]Ibid., p. 83.

preme Court recognizes that money is the equivalent of speech. Those with a
lot of money are much more effective at creating demand than those without.
Where there is substantial inequality of wealth, there is no true democracy,
unless democracy is defined in a minimal way as a lack of tyrannical dicta-
torship. What we have are competing elites with low citizen participation.[45]
The majority in *Citizens United* astonishingly uses heavy corporate spending
on elections as evidence that the people are in charge: "The fact that a corporation, or any other speaker, is willing to spend money to try to persuade
voters presupposes that the people have the ultimate influence over elected
officials."[46] The Court therefore dismisses the idea that people will cease to
participate, even though nearly half of the electorate already sits out national
elections. Wolin's view of American democracy is probably closer to the mark:
"The citizen is shrunk to the voter: periodically courted, warned, and confused
but otherwise kept at a distance from actual decision-making and allowed to
emerge only ephemerally in a cameo appearance according to a script com-
posed by the opinion takers/makers."[47]

Early theorists of liberal democracy feared that giving the lower classes
the right to vote would overturn the class system and result in chaos. It never
happened. As Wolin points out, Americans are apolitical but not alienated,
patriotic and resigned or relieved to turn over their civic obligations to the
experts. Why? I think it has to do with the kinds of social bodies that have
largely replaced the church in the modern era. The first is the nation-state.
The mysticism of nationalism has tended to occlude any discussion of class
divisions. We are convinced that we are *e pluribus unum*, one united from
many. Policy debate shies away from any discussion of class; those who raise
the issue of class are accused of making class warfare, which strikes me as the
equivalent of accusing the fire department of arson because they keep
showing up at house fires. We rally around the flag and support our troops
so that we can ignore the brute fact that those who kill and die on our behalf
come overwhelmingly from the lower classes. The second type of social body,
whose interests have largely merged with those of nation-state elites, is the
business corporation. Here too corporations have succeeded in convincing

---

[45]MacPherson, *Life and Times of Liberal Democracy*, pp. 87-92.
[46]*Citizens United*, Opinion of the Court, p. 44.
[47]Wolin, *Politics and Vision*, p. 565.

us that their interests are not private but fully public. The welfare of the whole society depends on the success of business—"It's the economy, stupid," as President Clinton's personal reminder ran—and so public officials are remarkably solicitous of business demands for favors, which include everything from direct subsidies to fighting wars for economic interests. Lindblom quotes a DuPont executive as saying "the strength of the position of business and the weakness of the position of government is that government needs a strong economy just as much as business does, and the people need it and demand it even more."[48] Lindblom comments, "The duality of leadership is reminiscent of the medieval dualism between church and state, and the relations between business and government are no less intricate than in the medieval duality."[49]

Michael Novak has notoriously applied the suffering servant passages in Isaiah to "the modern business corporation, a much despised incarnation of God's presence in the world."[50] Naomi Klein, on the other hand, has documented a corporate chic in which branding creates a kind of salvific mysticism around corporate identities.[51] Either way, corporations embody powerful social processes and, in some cases, effect a kind of mystical union among managers and consumers, a charmed circle from which workers are largely excluded. Novak is right to emphasize the inherently corporate nature of the corporation; market economics is primarily about social bodies, not lone individuals. Business corporations can and do serve social purposes in the pursuit of private profit, and Novak argues that business corporations are not just economic but moral, social and political actors.[52] The problem is that when political discernment has been subsumed into a competitive market model based on preferences rather than any substantive *telos* or conception of the common good, there is no standard on which to judge which social purposes are to be pursued. Markets are designed for the maximization of preferences; in the absence of any equalizing considerations, those preferences with the most power win out. And power in a corporate-dominated society is based

---

[48]Quoted in Lindblom, *Politics and Markets*, p. 175.

[49]Lindblom, *Politics and Markets*, p. 175.

[50]Michael Novak, "A Theology of the Corporation," in *The Corporation: A Theological Inquiry,* ed. Michael Novak and John W. Cooper (Washington, DC: American Enterprise Institute, 1981), p. 203.

[51]Naomi Klein, *No Logo: Taking Aim at the Brand Bullies* (New York: Picador, 1999).

[52]Novak, "A Theology of the Corporation," pp. 220-24.

on class division, the fundamental divide between the owners of capital and those who have nothing to sell but their own labor. The business corporation embodies class antagonism, not a true social solidarity, not simply because the corporation is divided between capital and labor but because the managers of the corporation understand their task as the maximization of shareholder value, which often comes at the expense of labor: one significant way to increase profits is to cut labor costs, that is, to decrease wages paid to workers. In the political sphere, corporations commonly use the profits generated by labor to support the interests of shareholders, often opposing the interests of labor. What we have then is our current situation: patriotic assurances that the nation and the corporation enact truly social processes that bind us all together as one, combined with a reality of ever-greater class division and political participation that is driven by and serves those with access to large amounts of money.

Justice Stevens makes a number of powerful arguments demonstrating the corrupting influence of corporate speech, but his main move is to claim that free speech rights are meant to protect individuals, not corporations. He stops well short of questioning the legal personhood of corporations, but he writes of the framers of the US Constitution, "Unlike our colleagues, they had little trouble distinguishing corporations from human beings, and when they constitutionalized the right to free speech in the First Amendment, it was the free speech of individual Americans that they had in mind."[53]

The problem with Justice Stevens's dissent, as I see it, is that it does not fundamentally call into question the marketization of the political process. He hopes that envisioning society as a collection of individuals will make for a fairer competition, but fairer competition is not the same as full participation, much less the pursuit of any real common good. To see society as a collection of individuals both occludes the reality of class division and prevents any true attempts to overcome those divisions through a deeper kind of solidarity. If we do not see each other as members or potential members of the same body, we cannot begin to see the political process as a healing process for the weakest of our members.

From a Christian point of view, we have a strong stake in corporate

---

[53]*Citizens United*, Opinion of Stevens, p. 37.

personhood. The church as the body of Christ is called to see the joys and sufferings of all God's children as intimately bound together. The scandal of the rich feasting while the poor go hungry cannot be reconciled with the enactment of the body of Christ, as Paul makes clear in 1 Corinthians 11. The option for the poor is the church's response to class division. The church must furthermore be able to speak as a body, not a mere collection of individuals. In the recent debate over contraception and the HHS health care mandate, the government privileged the rights of individuals over the rights of corporate bodies like the church. For this reason, some within the church welcomed *Citizens United* as a vindication of the rights of corporate persons like the church to speak. I think this is a mistake. The majority in *Citizens United* disavows any sort of distinctions among types of corporate bodies, or indeed among speakers of any kind; according to the Court, "the First Amendment generally prohibits the suppression of political speech based on the speaker's identity."[54] The Court thus claims to be blind to the exercise of power while eliminating the ability to make political decisions on the basis of anything but raw power. But Christians need not feign such blindness; there are important distinctions between class-divided business corporations whose goal is the pursuit of profit, and churches, unions, farmer cooperatives, nonprofit corporations, charitable organizations, credit unions and other bodies who can make greater claims to promote solidarity and common good.

The church's goal in society is to speak as a corporate person on behalf of the poor, to promote organizations of true social solidarity and also to encourage businesses to pursue legitimate profit within the wider *telos* of an economy of love. As Pope Benedict XVI writes in his encyclical *Caritas et Veritate*, love must be "the principle not only of micro-relationships (with friends, with family members or within small groups) but also of macro-relationships (social, economic, and political ones)."[55] What it means to enact

---

[54] *Citizens United*, Opinion of the Court, p. 34.

[55] Pope Benedict XVI, *Caritas in Veritate*, §2, www.vatican.va/holy_father/benedict_xvi/encyclicals/documents/hf_ben-xvi_enc_20090629_caritas-in-veritate_en.html. Pope Benedict writes, "When both the logic of the market and the logic of the State come to an agreement that each will continue to exercise a monopoly over its respective area of influence, in the long term much is lost: solidarity in relations between citizens, participation and adherence, actions of gratuitousness, all of which stand in contrast with *giving in order to acquire* (the logic of exchange) and *giving through duty* (the logic of public obligation, imposed by State law). In order to defeat underdevelopment, action is required not only on improving

the body of Christ in this context is not to despair of the state of corporate-state power but to build businesses and communities of true participation and solidarity.

exchange-based transactions and implanting public welfare structures, but above all on gradually *increasing openness, in a world context, to forms of economic activity marked by quotas of gratuitousness and communion.* The exclusively binary model of market-plus-State is corrosive of society, while economic forms based on solidarity, which find their natural home in civil society without being restricted to it, build up society"; ibid., §39, emphasis in original.

8

Violence

Peter J. Leithart

From beginning to end, the Bible is utterly opposed to violence.[1] Scripture never commands or endorses violence, never permits violence, never allows for a minimal level of violence, never treats violence as a good or as a necessary evil. Biblical ethics and politics are nonviolent ethics and politics.

The God revealed in the Bible is utterly opposed to violence. He never commands or endorses violence, never allows a minimal level of violence, never treats violence as a necessary evil. The God of Israel never commits violence himself, and violence (Hebrew חמס) does not describe what God does, or commands, or is, or loves.[2] On the contrary: God hates (שׂנא) hands that shed innocent blood, hearts full of wicked schemes, feet that run to do evil, false witnesses and those who spread strife among brothers (Prov 6:16-19). He hates the one who robes himself with violence (Mal 2:16). "The one who loves violence His soul hates" (Ps 11:5 NASB). As far as I have found, lovers of violence are the only thing God hates down to his "soul."

These claims will come as a surprise to many, not all of them named Dawkins, Dennett, Hitchens or Harris.[3] Many Christians will be surprised,

---

[1]Attempts to define violence are numerous and inconclusive. See Christopher Yates, "Introduction," in *Philosophy and the Return of Violence: Studies from this Widening Gyre*, ed. Nathan Eckstrand and Christopher Yates (London: Continuum, 2011).

[2]Terence E. Fretheim, "God and Violence in the Old Testament," *Word & World* 24, no. 1 (2004): 20n8, notes what he claims are a few exceptional passages (Job 19:7; Jer 20:8; Lam 2:6).

[3]For responses to the claim that religion or Christianity are inherently violent, see, in brief, Miroslav Volf, "Christianity and Violence," in *War in the Bible and Terrorism in the Twenty-First Century*, ed. Richard Hess and Elmer Martens (Winona Lake, IN: Eisenbrauns, 2008), pp. 1-17. More expansively, William T. Cavanaugh, *The Myth of Religious Violence: Secular Ideology and the Roots of Modern Conflict* (Oxford: Oxford University Press, 2009). On Cavanaugh's thesis, see Ephraim Radner, *A Brutal Unity: The Spiritual Politics of the Christian Church* (Waco, TX: Baylor University Press, 2012), pp. 19-61.

and the surprise is understandable. After all, the God of Israel regularly gives orders such as: "You shall destroy their altars, break their images, and cut down their groves" (Ex 34:13).[4] And the objects of destruction are not always inanimate. He tells Moses to smite the Midianites (Num 25:17), and sends his people into the land to carry out *herem* warfare: "You shall smite [the Canaanites], and utterly destroy them. . . . You must destroy the peoples Yahweh your God gives over to you. Do not look on them with pity" (Deut 7:2, 16). Dutifully fulfilling everything Moses commands, Joshua "totally destroyed all that breathed, just as Yahweh, the God of Israel, had commanded" (Josh 10:40).[5] Yahweh rewards Phinehas for impaling a fornicating couple in the camp of Israel (Num 25), and tears the kingdom from Saul for failing to carry out the ban against the Amalekites (1 Sam 15).

The God who gives these instructions appears to be as savage as his people. He strikes (Gen 8:21; Ex 3:20; 12:12-13, 29) and smites. He wages war (Ex 14:14; Deut 1:30), judges (Ezek 7:27), repays (Deut 7:10), punishes (1 Sam 15:2; Jer 9:24; 44:13; Hos 12:2), afflicts (1 Sam 16:14; the NASB has "terrorize") and avenges (Judg 11:36). He tramples the mighty, crushes young men and treads Jerusalem like grapes in a wine press (Lam 1:15). He dashes to pieces (Ex 15:6) and "swallows" (Ps 21:9) or "eats" (Num 16:35) his enemies in his fiery wrath. He spreads fear (Deut 2:25), confusion and panic (Is 22:5). He destroys (Gen 6:7; 7:4, 23; 18:28; Ex 17:14; Deut 7:10), he kills (1 Sam 2:6).[6] Yahweh not only commands *herem* war. He is the chief *herem* Warrior. He threatens "utterly to put out the remembrance of Amalek from under heaven. . . . Yahweh will have war with Amalek from generation to generation" (Ex 17:14, 16), and he zealously exterminates Jewish "Canaanites" who have taken over the temple: "My eye will have no pity nor shall I spare; and though they cry in my ears with a loud voice, yet I shall not listen to them" (Ezek 8:16-18).

We cannot escape the discomfort of these texts with the Marcionite strategy of honing close to the New Testament, for the God of destructive

---

[4]Translations throughout are the author's, modified from the KJV and NASB.

[5]Philip Jenkins compiles many of these texts in *Laying Down the Sword: Why We Can't Ignore the Bible's Violent Verses* (San Francisco: Harper, 2012), pp. 36-39.

[6]Cheryl Kirk-Duggan estimates that God is the subject of "violent" verbs more than a thousand times in the Bible, while human beings are subjects of violent verbs only about six hundred times; "Violence," in *Eerdmans Dictionary of the Bible* (Grand Rapids: Eerdmans, 2000), p. 1328. But she confuses the point by using the word "violence" to describe these actions.

wrath is the God and Father of Jesus. According to Paul, God used to "wink" (Acts 17:30) at ignorant idolatry and show "forbearance" with sin (Rom 3:25). God's treatment of sin in the Old Testament was mild, almost jocular. Only *now* is the wrath of God revealed from heaven against all the ungodliness and unrighteousness of men (Rom 1:18). As the Lamb, Jesus himself bursts out in wrath to make the sky fall and mountains collapse, sending the survivors scurrying for cover (Rev 6:12-17). The saints watch the spectacle not with horror but with relieved praise. When the harlot city becomes infested with plagues, pestilence and famine, and is burned with fire, a great multitude in heaven greets the event with "Hallelujah! Salvation and glory and power belong to our God because his judgments are true and righteous, for he has judged the great harlot. . . . Hallelujah! Her smoke rises forever and ever" (Rev 19:1-3).

In sum: The God who hates lovers of violence orders his people to destroy altars and shrines. The God who hates those who cover themselves with violence prohibits Israel from showing pity to Canaanites. One and the same God hates violence with his whole soul and burns the harlot city so that her smoke rises forever, while saints in heaven rejoice. We are left with an existential tension, if not a conceptual contradiction, for which we can imagine several explanations: perhaps the Bible is internally incoherent; perhaps, more charitably, it houses incommensurate theologies; or perhaps it offers an understanding of "violence" different from our current usage.

Imagine a rather extreme practical syllogism: God condemns violence; any use of force that causes physical harm or pain to another human is an act of violence; therefore, God condemns all uses of force that cause physical harm or pain. If one is convinced of this, he might renounce all force, or he may decide that, for practical reasons (keeping children in order, protecting his wife from a mugger), he must occasionally hold the nose of his conscience and commit unavoidable acts of violence.

This paper aims to combine a vigorous defense of the major premise combined with a vigorous challenge to the minor premise. God hates violence, but the question is, What does the *Bible* call violence? Superficially, my point is semantic or rhetorical. But rhetoric and semantics are ethically and politically, and therefore pastorally, relevant. I hope to be able to clear some ground and provide a fresh basis for rethinking our theology of violence. I admit that "fresh basis" is a piece of marketing. What I offer here is little more than a summary of the collective wisdom of the Christian political tradition in a biblical idiom.

GOD'S WAR AGAINST VIOLENCE

It is often observed that the Bible opens with a creation account radically different from those of other ancient cultures. Instead of a combat myth, we have a poetic speech, a rhythmic song. The God who is love speaks a word in the power of the Spirit, and so brings worlds into being. Violence intrudes into a world made without violence. The first fall, that of Adam, is an act of disobedience and idolatry; the second fall, of Cain, is an act of violence. With the third fall, the intermarriage of the sons of God with the daughters of men, violence is globalized. Before the flood, the whole earth is filled with violence, which "corrupts" or "destroys" the whole earth (Gen 6:11-13). By one man, sin entered the world, and death through sin, and so death spread to all men in that all sinned. "Violence" describes both sin and its destructive effects.

It intrudes everywhere, for Israel's story too is plagued by violence. Jacob curses Simeon and Levi for their violence (Gen 49:5) after they slaughter the circumcised men of Shechem to avenge their sister Dinah (Gen 34). Jacob renounces their violent conspiracies and their murderous assembly. Abimelech slaughters the seventy sons of Gideon on a single rock, a massive human sacrifice (Judg 9, esp. v. 56). David is consistently surrounded by enemies trying to take away or diminish his life (Ps 7:16; 11:1-5; 25:19; 140:1).[7] Nebuchadnezzar's destruction of Jerusalem is violent, and Zion prays that violence will fall on Babylon in turn, as ruler turns against ruler in the destruction of its idols (Jer 51:35-47). Edom commits violence against his brother Jacob by killing fugitives, taking prisoners, plundering and gloating over the results (Obad 10-14). Yahweh sends Gentile nations to discipline his people, but when they use excessive force he chastises and judges them in turn.

Violence is not, however, limited to physical assault or harm. Courtroom testimony can be violent. "You shall not put your hand with the wicked to be a witness of violence" (Ex 23:1; cf. Ps 35:11). A (suspected) witness of violence is required to appear before the priests and judges, and if his testimony is found to be false, he suffers the same harm he intended to do to his brother

---

[7]No book of the Bible speaks of violence more often than Psalms. In sheer statistical terms, Psalms contains twice as many uses of *hamas* (14x) as the nearest competitor, Proverbs (7x).

(Deut 19:16-19). In these passages, speech is violent in part because the false witness intends physical harm to his victim. Even outside court, words may be violent (Prov 10:6, 11; 13:2). Job complains that his "comforters" crush him with false charges and insults, and in response he cries, "Violence" (Job 19:7). David prays that slanderers who murder his reputation will be hunted down the way they have hunted him (Ps 140:11), and he asks Yahweh to deliver his soul from the "breathers of violence" (Ps 27:12). Scripture often represents history as courtroom drama, played out before the Judge of all the earth, and within this setting slander, libel, media smears and the like constitute violence just as much as false testimony in a court case.

Dante distinguished sins of violence from sins of fraud, but in Scripture fraud comes under the heading of violence. Micah condemns the violent wealthy who deceive with unequal weights and measures (Mic 6:11-12). Tyre's traders become luxurious through their violent commerce (Ezek 28:16). Rulers too can perpetrate violence. In Psalm 58, David charges that the civic "gods" do not "judge uprightly": "in heart you work injustice, on earth you weigh out the violence of your hands" (Ps 58:1-2). Bribes entice judges to overlook abusive practices of the wealthy. Rulers are also violent when they fail to suppress economic abuses. Jeremiah warns the kings of Judah to deliver victims of robbery from their oppressors, and not to "mistreat or do violence to the stranger, the orphan, or the widow" (Jer 22:3). These three categories of vulnerable people are given special protections and privileges in the law. They are allowed to glean and scrump in Israel's fields, and Yahweh commands Israel to treat strangers as brothers, since Israel had been abused as strangers in Egypt. Though Jeremiah does not specify what violence strangers, orphans and widows suffered, it is likely that it involved economic oppression by a denial of privileges and rights, the all-too-common practice of taking advantage of those who are too weak to fight back. Ezekiel warns the princes to put away violence and to stop their exactions (Ezek 45:9).[8] He condemns Jerusalem as a city of violence in a land filled with judicial murders, "judgment of bloods" (Ezek 7:23). By contrast, the ideal king of Psalm 72 acts on behalf

---

[8]The noun for "expropriation" is *gerushah*, from the verb *garash*, meaning to "drive out, thrust out." When Yahweh expels Adam and Eve from Eden (Gen 3:24) and Cain from the land (4:14), this verb is used. The princes of Judah in Ezekiel's day appear to be driving the people from their land, perhaps through exorbitant taxation.

of the humble and needy, taking the role of kinsman-redeemer (Ps 72:12) to deliver them from the oppression of the violent (Ps 72:14).

Violence can be traced to anger and "self-will" (Gen 49:5-6). It arises from hatred (Ps 25:19), arrogance, complacency. People act violently to protect their own comfort (Ps 73:1-6). The violent are serpents and adders, with poison in their mouths (Ps 140:1-3; see also "venom" in Hab 2:15). Like the great serpent, they seduce others to violence (Prov 1:8-19) and, because violence works, it is tempting to envy and emulate the ways of the violent (Prov 3:31). They form diabolical communities (see "join hands" in Ex 23:1; "assembly" in Gen 49:6). Joined in a parody Eucharist, they eat the bread of wickedness and become boisterous, intoxicated, even addicted to the wine of violence (Prov 4:17). Solomon warns his son to stay away from that table of demons (Prov 4:14).

Violence can become the key signature of social and political life. David sees a city where violence and litigious strife parade on the walls. In the bowels of the city are iniquity and mischief; destruction, oppression and deceit are on every street corner (Ps 55:9-11). Violence hides in dark places. Enemies revile and threaten the afflicted (Ps 74:18-20). Isaiah gives a vivid picture of a city of violence:

> Your iniquities have made a separation between you and your God,
> And your sins have hidden His face from you so that He does not hear.
> For your hands are defiled with blood
> And your fingers with iniquity;
> Your lips have spoken falsehood,
> Your tongue mutters wickedness.
> No one sues righteously and no one pleads honestly.
> They trust in confusion and speak lies;
> They conceive mischief and bring forth iniquity.
> They hatch adders' eggs and weave the spider's web;
> He who eats of their eggs dies,
> And from that which is crushed a snake breaks forth.
> Their webs will not become clothing,
> Nor will they cover themselves with their works;
> Their works are works of iniquity,
> And an act of violence is in their hands.
> Their feet run to evil,
> And they hasten to shed innocent blood;

Their thoughts are thoughts of iniquity,

Devastation and destruction are in their highways.

They do not know the way of peace,

And there is no justice in their tracks;

They have made their paths crooked,

Whoever treads on them does not know peace. (Is 59:2-8 NASB; see also Is 1:4)

Habakkuk is undone by the violence, wickedness and injustice that dominate Judah. Justice is perverted, discord and strife are common, the people contend with one another in court and everywhere else. Torah is impotent to arrest violence or to establish order (Hab 1:2-4). With the destructive Chaldeans on the march, the only prospect is yet more violence (Hab 1:9; cf. Jer 36:29).

In the beginning, God creates a world in which man is to be fruitful and multiply until he fills the earth (Gen 1:28). Human beings instead fill Yahweh's earth with violence, and Yahweh does not tolerate the ruin of his world. When the earth becomes filled with violent destructiveness in the days before the flood, Yahweh unleashes his power to destroy it, destruction for destruction (Gen 6:11-13, 17).[9] He clears away the ruins of the world and starts fresh with Noah, a new Adam called to be fruitful, multiply and fill (Gen 9:1). Yahweh's later interventions follow the same pattern. Surrounded by enemies, David prays that Yahweh be his Rock, Shield, Horn, Tower, Refuge and Savior from the violent. Yahweh comes with arrows and blasting a storm from his nostrils (2 Sam 22:15-16).[10] The Lord turns the violence of the violent on their own heads, when the predatory enemy falls into the trap that he prepared for David (Ps 7; 25:3; 27:11-12; 140:1-11). Yahweh prosecutes his *herem* warfare against the idolaters of Jerusalem to remove the abomination of violence.

For the biblical writers, God's wrath is not violence but a sign of God's refusal to overlook and be indifferent to evil. As Abraham Heschel put it, "All

---

[9]The structure of Genesis 6:11-13 reinforces the reciprocal character of the punishment:

  A. And **corrupted** the earth before the face of God

      B. and filled the earth **violence**

           C. and looked God the earth and behold it was corrupt,

           for corrupted all **flesh** his way on earth

                D. And said God to Noah

           C'. End of all **flesh** comes before me

      B'. For fills the earth **violence** from before their face

  A'. Behold I will **corrupt** them with the earth

[10]Though *hamas* is never used to describe it, Pharaoh's attack on Israel was an act of violence. It arose from hatred and fear, and aimed at the destruction of the people of Israel.

prophecy is one great exclamation: God is not indifferent to evil!" His indignation at human malice and ruthlessness seems excessive to us only because we are all complicit, passively if not actively. "The exploitation of the poor is to us a misdemeanor," Heschel observes, but "to God, it is a disaster. Our reaction is [mild] disapproval [at best!]; God's reaction is something no language can convey." Is it violence, Heschel asks, when "God's anger is aroused when the rights of the poor are violated, when widows and orphans are oppressed?"[11] God is a warrior, and one of his chief enemies is violence. His hypersensitivity to evil is the reflex of his unblemished goodness, his absolute innocence.

Yahweh's war against violence is the paradigm for human judgment. Rulers are to be deacons of God's avenging wrath. A witness who testifies falsely to convict a brother suffers the same punishment he intends to do to his brother (Deut 19:16-19). It is an application of the *lex talionis*, which Moses reinforces with a form of the *herem* formula: "your eye shall show no pity" (Deut 19:21). By punishing the violent witness, "you shall purge (burn away) the evil from among you" and warn others not to "do such an evil thing among you" (Deut 19:19-20). Punishment is *not* counterviolence that keeps violence within bounds but an act of purgation. Punishment is a social good. It establishes justice, purges the land and instructs the people in the ways of the Lord. Israel's conquest of Canaan is likewise a purgation, destroying destructive idols so that God can plant his vine (Ps 80).[12] Force can be used not to oppress but to deliver the oppressed. Surprisingly to us, the martyr Stephen commended Moses for using deadly force to defend a Hebrew slave (Acts 7:23-25).

One of the central promises of Scripture is that God will win his war. Violence will not be victorious. God will pacify his world, repair the ruins, replant the garden, rebuild his peaceable city. He will destroy destroyers and their destruction. When wolves and lambs, lions and calves graze together, "they will not hurt or destroy in all My holy mountain." A fresh, new Adam, an eternal child, will lead them (Is 11:1-10 NASB). Death itself, the ultimate destroyer (Is 25:8) and final enemy (1 Cor 15:26), will be abolished. Death is violence itself, but Christ removes death's sting to swallow it up in victory.

It is important to notice what the Bible does *not* count as violence. Yahweh

---

[11]Abraham Heschel, *The Prophets* (San Francisco: HarperCollins, 2001), pp. 364-65.

[12]Idolatry is regularly described as self-destructive (Ex 32:7-9; Deut 4:16, 26, 31; 9:12; Judg 2:19). Yahweh wars against idols to save his people from suicide.

puts words of fire in Jeremiah's mouth, but the rhetorical intensity of prophetic speech is not violent. On the contrary, the prophet breathes Yahweh's
fire against violence. Sharp rebuke, and even insults, are not necessarily acts
of verbal violence. True testimony is not violent, even if it leads to punishment
of a person convicted by the testimony.[13] Though power is often abused, not
every exercise or insignia of authority is violent.[14] Neither physical discipline
nor punishment is violence.

All this might seem to evade the question by the subterfuge of redefinition.
By their own lights, Nazis and Soviets regarded all their surveillance, arrests
and torture, their imprisonments and executions as necessary uses of force
designed to purify society. One man's intervention on behalf of the oppressed
is another man's violence. Besides, as Philip Jenkins has recently demonstrated,
the very texts that I have characterized as nonviolent have regularly been used
to justify atrocities. Once you decide your enemy is an "Amalekite," genocide
follows pretty naturally.[15]

A full response to these objections would require a much longer work than
this chapter. As a shorthand answer, I would say that violence is unjust and
sinful use of force. But that only presents further questions that need to be
answered in detail, especially, What counts as a sinful use of force? In an-
swering this question, we should make use of the rich casuistry of the Christian
tradition, including, as its most well-known expression, just war theory. This
tradition is not without its lacunae and mistakes, and Christian practice has
hardly lived up to the standards proposed by the theologians. But the tradition
is full of deep reflections on Scripture, history and practice, and it provides a
touchstone as we struggle to answer contemporary questions.

Yet an overemphasis on detailed questions concerning the use of force can
distract attention from the more fundamental Christian response to violence.

VIOLENCE VALORIZED

Writing in 1908, George Sorel argued that violence is the source of creativity
since it manifests the vibrant life force of human beings. Exhibiting a Nie-

---

[13]This needs to be qualified. Open truth telling can ruin a reputation that should be preserved and protected.
It is possible to use the truth to destroy. Truth can in some circumstances be an instrument of violence.
[14]It seems that the Bible makes room for Bourdieu's category of "symbolic violence," provided it is not
understood to be inherent in all social relations.
[15]See Jenkins, *Laying Down the Sword*.

tzschean *juissance de la guerre,* he celebrated the American habit of viewing life
"as a struggle and not as a pleasure."[16] Mixing Marx with Henri Bergson in a
volatile compound, Sorel hoped that the enervated bourgeoisie and intelli-
gentsia would be energized by the violence of the proletariat. The great danger
is that the proletariat will be "hypnotized" into complacency. If they hold fast
to revolutionary ideas, their violence "carried on as a pure and simple manifestation of the sentiment of class struggle, appears thus as a very fine and
heroic thing; it is at the service of the immemorial interests of civilization."
Violence "may save the world from barbarism."[17] A half century later, Sartre
offered similar encouragement to the decolonized "wretched of the earth."
"Violence," Sartre said, "like Achilles' lance, can heal the wounds it has inflicted." Violence is creative, like the chaos of primeval myths: "irrepressible
violence . . . is man recreating himself." Sartre insists that it is through the "mad
fury" of violent action that "the wretched become men."[18]

Does anyone read Sartre anymore, much less Sorel? But everyone is reading
Zizek, who ends his treatise *Violence* with reflections on Walter Benjamin's
discussion of "divine violence." Benjamin distinguishes between mythic violence—violence as the "exception" that establishes state sovereignty—and
divine violence. Mythic violence is a means to an end; divine violence is a
"sign without meaning" that manifests the sheer injustice of the world and
shows that things are "ethically 'out of joint.'" Divine violence does not attempt to create anything. It comes "out of nowhere," from outside "the structured social field" and strikes blindly in an effort to enact "immediate justice/
vengeance." Zizek sees divine violence in the mobs in Rio that "descended
from the favelas into the rich part of the city and started looting and burning
supermarkets." Divine violence belongs to the order of Event, not the order
of Being; it is an unpredictable shock that breaks apart all our categories.
Divine violence is thus "radically subjective." It is "the subject's *work of love.*" It
is the capacity for violence and cruelty, in fact, that gives love its power. "Love
without cruelty is powerless," Zizek says, "cruelty without love is blind." What
gives love its "angelic" character is "its link with violence," which enables it (in

---

[16]George Sorel, *Reflections on Violence,* ed. Jeremy Jennings (Cambridge: Cambridge University Press, 2004), p. 232.

[17]Ibid., p. 85.

[18]Quoted in Hannah Arendt, *On Violence* (Orlando, FL: Harcourt, 1970), pp. 12, 20.

the words of Che Guevara) to transcend "the natural limitations of man." This is love in what Zizek calls the full "Paulinian" sense: *"the domain of pure violence, the domain outside law (legal power), the domain of violence which is neither law-founding nor law-sustaining, is the domain of love."*[19]

Behind this valorization of violence is Zizek's Hegelian conviction that violence is woven into the fabric of things. It is not simply that one must, unfortunately, sometimes use violence to suppress more destructive forms of violence. Rather, violence infiltrates the most apparently peaceable social interactions, for Hegel in the struggle for recognition between master and servant and for Zizek in the use of language. Zizek mocks liberal faith in the international-relations version of the talking cure. "What if," he queries, "humans exceed animals in their capacity for violence precisely because they *speak*?" Symbolization is already an act of violence that "mortifies" the thing by "reducing it to a single feature." Language dismembers and destroys the unity of a substance, treating its parts as autonomous and inserting it, forcibly, into a field of meaning of our making. By using the word "gold," we "violently extract a metal from its natural texture, investing into it our dreams of wealth, power, spiritual purity . . . which have nothing whatsoever to do with the immediate reality of gold."[20] We cannot open our mouths without doing violence to reality. No wonder Zizek is such a fan of Bartleby the scrivener, who would prefer not to.

Wild as he seems, Zizek exposes and exaggerates a valorization of violence that is inherent in the political thought of the past century or more. In her little classic *On Violence*, Hannah Arendt comments on the strange "consensus among political theorists from Left to Right to the effect that violence is nothing more than the most flagrant manifestation of power," and cites Max Weber's definition of the state as "the rule of men over men based on the

---

[19]Slavoj Zizek, *Violence: Six Sideways Reflections* (New York: Picador, 2008), pp. 196-205, emphasis in original. On Zizek and Benjamin, see Simon Critchley, "Violent Thoughts About Slavoj Zizek," in Eckstrand and Yates, *Philosophy and the Return of Violence*, ch. 4. Zizek does acknowledge that the same act might be violent or nonviolent depending on the context. See Sabine Reul and Thomas Deichmann, "The One Measure of True Love Is: You Can Insult the Other," *Spiked*, November 15, 2001, www.spiked-online .com/Articles/00000002D2C4.htm. Benjamin's essay is included in Bruce Lawrence and Aisha Karim, eds., *On Violence: A Reader* (Durham: Duke University Press, 2007), pp. 268-85. See also Eric Jacobson, *Metaphysics of the Profane: The Political Theology of Walter Benjamin and Gershom Scholem* (New York: Columbia University Press, 2003), pp. 193-232.

[20]Zizek, *Violence*, p. 61.

means of legitimate, that is allegedly legitimate, violence."[21] For Weber, the state cannot be defined by its activities, since "there is no task of which it could be said that it is always, far less exclusively, the preserve of those associations which are defined as political." It is not activities but means that define the state, and the means is physical violence. If violence withers away, then the state has disappeared along with it. Violence is not, Weber says, the "normal or sole means used by the state," but it is the "means *specific* to the state." The state is the institution that can say, "You must do as we say because we are allowed to kill you." Prior to the modern age, Weber notes, "the most diverse kinds of association—beginning with the clan—have regarded physical violence as a quite normal institution." What distinguishes the modern state in particular is its "claim to the monopoly of legitimate physical violence within a certain territory." Other entities can employ physical force only by the state's permission: "The state is held to be the sole source of the 'right' to use violence [*physischen Zwanges*]."[22]

To Arendt, this consensus reflects a basic confusion about power. If power is no more than the capacity to issue commands that are obeyed, it is reasonable to conclude that "there is no greater power than that which grows out of the barrel of a gun." On this basis, however, it is impossible to distinguish the policeman's gun from the robber's.[23] Arendt counters that power is the human ability "to act in concert." A person is said to be "in power" when empowered by a group to act on behalf of the group. When the group disappears or withdraws its empowerment, the individual's power evaporates. Violence by contrast has an "instrumental character" and uses "implements," designed and used, like all tools, "for the purpose of multiplying natural strength."[24] For violence to be effective, it must have the backing of power: "Where commands are no longer obeyed, the means of violence are of no use. . . . Everything depends on the power behind the violence"—*not* the violence behind the power. When soldiers refuse to fire on the mob, the commander is no longer "in power," even though he still has the tools of violence.[25] Threats of violence may be the most

---

[21]Arendt, *On Violence*, p. 35.
[22]Max Weber, "The Profession and Vocation of Politics," in *Political Writings*, ed. Peter Lassman and Ronald Speirs (Cambridge: Cambridge University Press, 1994), pp. 310-11.
[23]Arendt, *On Violence*, pp. 35, 37.
[24]Ibid., pp. 44, 46.
[25]Ibid., p. 49.

effective means of achieving obedience, but people rely on naked violence mostly when they have lost power. Terror is the extreme, violence used to gain obedience in the *absence* of power. Arendt concludes that violence and power "are opposites; where the one rules absolutely, the other is absent. Violence appears where power is in jeopardy, but left to its own course it ends in power's disappearance."[26] Violence is not the iron fist inside the velvet glove. It is the metal glove manipulated by the power that wears it.

Despite their fundamental differences, Weber and Arendt agree that what counts as violence is physical force that causes pain, harm, physical damage or ultimately death. As a result, for both, political entities are organizations that resort, at least in the face of extreme threats, to violence. Neither, as a result, is able to recognize the genuinely political character of the church. So long as the church does not kill anyone or break anything, it is, for political theory, no more than a metaphorical polity. By contrast, Augustine argued rightly that the church is the one true commonwealth.

Scripture is a manifesto neither for pacifism nor for law-and-order conservatism. Though the Bible does not condemn punishment or war as inherently a form of what it calls "violence," it also does not give hope that violence can be arrested and eliminated by rigorous and just use of force. As Habakkuk complained, in the face of violence Torah is numbed, ineffective (Hab 1:4). If Torah cannot restrain violence, neither can the US Constitution, the criminal code of Illinois or the Geneva Accords. As institutions of the *saeculum*, governments use force to curb worse violences, but all too often they become agents of violence themselves. Even at their best they do not have the kind of tools needed to carry on Yahweh's war on violence. Law enforcement is a good, and Christians may legitimately do this good work. But it does not swallow violence in victory.

Only Jesus does that. Jesus alone is the death-eater. God purges violence in the flood, clears out the violence of Pharaoh, destroys the Babylonian destroyers. It is Jesus who launches his decisive campaign against violence. He takes the role of Yahweh's Servant, the Arm of Yahweh, his power in action, his power unveiled to destroy the destroyers. The Servant does not look like the Lord's Arm. Disfigured, marred, mangled, he is not a man of war but a man of

---

[26]Ibid., p. 56.

sorrows. He is not acquainted with victory but with grief. He does not pierce dragons, as Zion hopes, but is himself pierced. He does not crush enemies but is himself crushed. He should be the scourge of Babylon. Instead, he is scourged. Zion wants the active arm of God. What she gets is a passion.

Zion herself contributes to the Servant's suffering. She regards the Servant as an outcast, a covenant breaker, "stricken, smitten by God, and rejected" (Is 53:4). In their fury against God, the people of Israel pierce, beat, crush, insult, scourge. They break the Servant with all the violence they can until he is cut off from the land of the living. To their surprise, they finally recognize that this is how Yahweh achieves his plan to save Israel and the nations. The violence they inflict on the Servant leads to their peace and healing. Jesus the Servant absorbs their every unjust attack, keeps silent as a lamb led to slaughter, refuses to return violence to violence or insult to insult, and so bears the violence of Israel to the grave. Yet he prolongs his days, and in this he is exalted as the "successful" Servant of Yahweh. This truly is the Arm of the Lord in person, Yahweh's power that surpasses the power of violence and of death. The Servant consumes death in being consumed by it.

In the resurrection of Jesus the Servant, he lays the foundation for a new city, a polity that follows the same way of the cross that Jesus himself followed. The church is not violent in either the biblical sense or in our usual sense of the word. She does not employ the normal forms of political force, but negative "nonviolence" is not her essence. Jesus' city is something far stranger. It is the community of the Suffering Servant that, in union with the Servant, bears insults, rejection, hatred, beatings, attacks and assaults, entrusting itself to the one who judges justly. Filled with the fire of the Spirit, the church is to preach God's fiery, furious words against the violent. The church is to stand apart from the clashes of the nations of the *saeculum*, refusing to choose among varieties of violence. The church is to be a shield between the violent and their victims. The church is to hold out hope of an absolute peace, and to be the sacrament of the holy mountain where "they neither hurt nor destroy." The church is a community of martyrs, suffering the violence of the world, swallowing death in dying with Christ. Among the polities of the *saeculum*, Jesus erects his strange city, filled with his own Spirit to carry on his zealous conquest of violence—a suffering city, called to love enemies and lay down its life for the life of the world.

A Sobering Conclusion

We cannot help but end on a sobering, not to say chilling, note, because the church has tragically failed to be what she is called to be. Let me give two brief illustrations.[27]

All told, the United States spends close to $1 trillion a year on defense and security. Military spending infiltrates every corner of American life. Hundreds of millions end up in university research programs.[28] Billions of dollars naturally flow from the Department of Defense to private companies for weapons, airplanes and other military equipment.[29] Nonmilitary industries are bolstered by the DOD's millions and billions. IBM, Time-Warner, Ford, General Motors, Microsoft, NBC, General Electric, Hilton, Columbia TriStar Films, Sony, Sara Lee, Proctor & Gamble, ESPN, Disney, Bank of America and Apple are all defense contractors.[30] In an analysis of the economic impact of proposed DOD spending reductions for 2013, Stephen Fuller estimated that the cuts would reduce GDP by $86 billion, a quarter of the projected GDP increase for 2013.[31] In our permanent war economy, we do not rely on the military simply to protect our commerce and industry from attack. We rely on consistent and growing military spending to keep our commerce and industry thriving in the first place.

One does not have to be a pacifist to be alarmed at how much of our university research, our intellectual energy, our economic inventiveness and productivity, and our enormous material resources are devoted to keeping us on a war footing. If this is not the modern equivalent of "multiplying horses and chariots," I cannot imagine what is (see Deut 17:16). We cover ourselves with

---

[27]This example comes from Viktor Mayer-Schonberger, *Delete: The Virtue of Forgetting in the Digital Age* (Princeton: Princeton University Press, 2009), p. 56.

[28]Henry A. Giroux, *The University in Chains: Confronting the Military-Industrial-Academic Complex* (Boulder, CO: Paradigm Publishers, 2007), pp. 53-54.

[29]Andrew Feinstein, *The Shadow World: Inside the Global Arms Trade* (New York: Farrar, Straus & Giroux, 2011), pp. 366-67.

[30]Nick Turse, *The Complex: How the Military Invades Our Everyday Lives* (New York: Macmillan, 2009), pp. 2-4. According to Turse, Proctor & Gamble received more than $350 million in defense contracts in 2006, and General Electric received $2.3 billion in the same year.

[31]Stephen S. Fuller, "The U.S. Economic Impact of Approved and Projected DOD Spending Reductions on Equipment in 2013," George Mason University, October 24, 2011, armedservices.house.gov/index .cfm/files/serve?File_id=33a3bd4e-fcaa-4eef-bea6-12bd39265f9a. On the development of the permanent war economy, see Thomas K. Duncan and Christopher J. Coyne, "The Origins of the Permanent War Economy: A Consequence of Government, not Capitalism," Social Science Research Network, March 19, 2013, papers.ssrn.com/sol3/papers.cfm?abstract_id=2235729.

talk of global responsibility and the burdens of empire. We tell ourselves that we want to stay home and be left alone. Our expenditures may say something else: We are a people that delights in war. If the God of the Bible is the Judge of all the earth, this is not a delight we should allow ourselves to indulge (see Ps 68:30).

And what does the church say to this? Thousands of American Christians support the US military virtually without question, as a sacred duty. It is not surprising that Chris Hedges, author of *American Fascists: The Christian Right and the War on America*, found that preachers on the Christian right attack every institution in America except "the military and law enforcement."[32]

Jingoism is one of the side effects of the church's more intractable and long-term complicity in violence, the plague of what the Prayer Book too nicely calls our "unhappy divisions." In a searching exploration of the connections between ecclesial divisions and political conflicts in Rwanda and elsewhere, Ephraim Radner suggests (partly in response to Cavanaugh):

> If Christians are responsible for violence, if conceptions of their motives are given in Christian terms, if these conceptions have been shaped and gathered together in their hostile force through particular decisions made on behalf of Christianity's ecclesial vocation, so understood, and if, finally, these decisions and their forms can be shown as bearing the power of violence, it is appropriate ... to speak of a specifically *Christian* responsibility for violence.[33]

Even if one agrees with Cavanaugh, as I do, that it is impossible to disentangle religion from other factors, Radner's challenge hits home. Why *can't* Christians extract ourselves from political conflicts? Is the church's polity too anemic to stand apart from political divisions to discern and condemn violence done by "our people"? Is the church too wispy, or too wimpy, to stand on her own?

And if we are, do we not have to confront an even more alarming question: Have we set ourselves against the God who hates violence?

---

[32]Chris Hedges, "America's Holy Warriors," Truthdig, Dec 31, 2006, www.truthdig.com/report/item/20061231_chris_hedges_americas_holy_warriors.

[33]Radner, *Brutal Unity*, p. 38. Radner argues that the Christian history of division has to be worked into our understanding of Christian unity, and sketches out a "sacrificial" and cruciform understanding of church unity. Despite the chilling power of his argument, I cannot agree. Jesus prays that we may be one not in a dialectic with division but as the Father and Son are one. Can't we hope that the Father answers his Son's prayer?

9

JUST WAR AS CHRISTIAN POLITICS

Daniel M. Bell Jr.

At first glance, the idea that just war might embody a distinctive Christian political witness is a rather odd claim. It is an odd claim for several reasons. First, most Christians do not have any idea of what a just war entails. Even after more than a decade of war at the start of the twenty-first century, most Christians in North America have little or no grasp of what just war involves beyond perhaps a vague recollection of one or two of the criteria mentioned in the media. Hence, given its insignificance in the Christian life and imagination, even in the midst of war, it makes little sense to suggest that just war is part and parcel of a distinctive Christian politics.

Second, just war clearly is not a distinctively Christian practice. To the contrary, just war is part of the secular political lexicon. Indeed, the history of the just war tradition clearly shows that Christians, like St. Augustine, first adopted the notion from classical pagan sources. Thus, insofar as Christians invoke just war they are sharing in a tradition, not offering a distinctive political witness.

Third, the way those contemporary Christians who are aware of the just war tradition tend to use it does not suggest that Christian advocacy of just war really amounts to a politics at all. Typically, when on the eve of war Christians dust off the "just war theory," they present a list of criteria as a kind of checklist to ascertain if a particular war would be a just one: "Let's see. Is the war declared by a legitimate authority? Check. Is there just cause? Check. Is it a matter of last resort? Check."

Indeed, the commonplace reference to "just war *theory*" is indicative of just how far this usage is from any kind of distinctive politics. Just war is treated as an abstract theory that is applied to a problem. In this way it more resembles a math problem than a politics. Its relevance to life is occasional, momentary, episodic—certainly not indicative of a way of life that might constitute a distinctive Christian politics.

Furthermore, if church pronouncements and publications are any indication, this checklist can be taken off the shelf and applied easily and quickly, perhaps in the space of a few hundred words or a couple column inches of an editorial or press release. Moreover, it can be applied pretty much by anyone, without any particular training, education or formation and certainly without being immersed in the life of any particular political community.

JUST WAR AND POLITICS

Of course, we all know how pronouncements by religious leaders on such matters tend to be received. If a leader's opinion corresponds with my personal opinion of the war in question, then his or her assertion is lauded. If it does not, then I am all too happy to dismiss it.

This last observation, regarding how the declarations of religious authorities are received, suggests that while the idea that just war might constitute a distinctive Christian politics or political witness appears on the face of it to be absurd, the idea that just war is bound up in politics is not.

Whether we recognize it or not, just war is part of a political vision, and whether we are aware of it or not, even the rather superficial way Christians invoke just war today is deeply embedded in a politics—the politics of contemporary North American political liberalism. As the typical response to pronouncements by religious authorities suggests, the church's political voice is subsumed by the politics of party, ideology and interest group.

So it comes to pass that the superficial checklist approach to just war serves contemporary North American politics well, assuring among other things that there will be no substantial challenge either to the nation-state's political sovereignty or to its wars from Christians as such.[1] For example, as a consequence of this subsumption, debating the "just war theory" is reduced to a kind of theopolitical theater or entertainment, at most providing Christians

---

[1]By "challenge" I do not mean simply "opposition." Rather, challenge could encompass correction as well.

an opportunity to feel like they are being responsible, doing something—either by supporting the troops or resisting what is deemed an unjust war.

But such resistance is not really oppositional. At best, one may opt out of the nation's wars if one is opposed to all war, which provides some consolation for pacifists but offers none to those who are the principal focus of this chapter: would-be just warriors. But even such pacifist resistance is more illusory than real insofar as there has not been a draft in a generation and the chances of a new draft are for the foreseeable future infinitesimally small. Besides, even pacifists support the nation's wars by means of their taxes, which effectively renders their witness merely platonic—a matter of the abstract and disembodied ideals and heartfelt aspirations of individuals that do nothing substantial to interfere with the material progress of the nation's wars. Indeed, such platonic opposition may ironically nurture the nation's wars as those who wage wars are inspired by such flaccid opposition to boast "we are fighting for your freedom to disagree."

Although it may be largely unrecognized, the idea that Christians ought to conceive of just war as part of a larger political vision is not new. A generation ago, as just war was beginning to reemerge on the public stage after a hiatus of several centuries, Paul Ramsey attempted to remind the church that its just war doctrine was part of a Christian theory of statecraft.[2] Just war, he said, was a "politico-military doctrine," by which he meant that just war did not stand alone but was intrinsically embedded in a larger vision and practice of human governance, or what he called "political agency," but which we can call simply "politics."

Ramsey made this claim to counter those whom he thought distorted just war by extracting it from its proper place in a comprehensive political vision, thereby reducing it either to a solitary military doctrine or a solitary moralistic doctrine. Those who misused just war by reducing it to a military doctrine alone were apt to invoke it on behalf of the use or threat of the use of force without regard for the political context and consequences of such action. Whereas those who reduced just war to a moralistic doctrine divorced it from both politics and military doctrine by using it as a casuistic checklist with which to delegitimize all wars one by one.

---

[2]Paul Ramsey, *The Just War* (New York: Charles Scribner's Son, 1968), p. xiii.

What follows is an effort to encourage the church to be more intentional in taking Ramsey's advice to heart, that is, to be more deliberate in considering how its advocacy and practice of just war is part and parcel of an expansive political vision.

At the same time, however, it goes beyond Ramsey, suggesting that he did not go far enough in articulating the distinctively Christian character of this political vision. In other words, while Ramsey helpfully reminds us that just war is properly at home in a broader vision of politics and so encourages us to consider the character of that political vision, he misses the mark to the extent that he identifies the appropriate Christian politics of just war as a matter of *statecraft*. He misses the mark because at its best, the Christian practice of just war is *not* a matter of politics as statecraft but of politics as church-craft. Using Ramsey's terminology, we might say that just war as Christian discipleship begins not with the state as the primary "political agency" but the church.

What follows, then, is an attempt to articulate just war as a distinctly Christian political witness, which means that it is an effort to recenter the Christian practice of just war in the church rather than in the state. While this does *not* mean that the church should raise an army, it does mean that just war as a distinctly Christian politics begins with and is anchored in the convictions and disciplines of the Christian community. Furthermore, as we will see, starting from the church rather than the state has significant implications for exactly what the discipline of just war entails, both in terms of the kind of people it calls for and the demands it makes upon such people.

TWO STRANDS OF THE JUST WAR TRADITION

To make sense of this claim, we begin by considering just war not as a theory but as a living tradition. Notwithstanding popular discourse, there is no such thing as the just war theory or doctrine. There is no single, set-in-stone, fixed account of what constitutes a just war. Instead, just war is a tradition. As such it resembles an argument extended across time and along the way it has developed in novel directions and taken a variety of shapes and forms. Thus, what constituted just war according to the ancient Romans was different from what just war meant to Augustine and different again from what it looked like a millennium later according to the great Catholic thinker Francisco de Vitoria. And it continues to develop today.

Recognizing that just war is a tradition, and calling to mind Ramsey's claim that just war is properly part of a larger political vision, we can distinguish within the just war tradition two strands, corresponding to different politics or to the political community they principally serve: the modern nation-state and the church. The one strand I call Just War as Public Policy Checklist (PPC) and the other Just War as Christian Discipleship (CD).

Just War PPC is rooted in nation-states and international law, and as such it is principally concerned with defining the moral responsibilities of states and politicians who guide them. Indeed, at its most extreme form the just war criteria are thought to be solely the concern of politicians; citizens and laity have no legitimate voice in judgments concerning just war. As a tool of state-craft, just war takes the form of a checklist of criteria meant to guide decision makers and public policy.

What is noteworthy about Just War PPC is that anyone can use the checklist. It requires little or no preparation or training to engage in just war. On the eve of war, all one has to do is memorize the list of criteria and then muster the willpower to abide by them. Furthermore, character does not matter. You can be a scoundrel, someone who has never cared before about your neighbor, and yet if you can check off criteria, you can claim to be a just warrior.

Just War CD, in contrast, finds its center in the life and convictions of the Christian community and is rooted in the church's commitment to follow Christ by loving and seeking justice for its neighbors—even enemy-neighbors—in war. As such, just war is not primarily a checklist of rules but an expression of the character of the Christian community. It is the extension of the character and virtues that mark the day-to-day life of the Christian community in peacetime into the time and space of war as well. Just as the church loves and seeks justice for its neighbors in times of peace, just as it acts with prudence and courage as it goes about its daily life and work of mercy, so it does in war.

What this means is that just war requires not just information and will-power but long-term preparation. Memorizing a checklist of criteria is not sufficient. Just warriors cannot be pulled like rabbits from a hat on the eve of war. This is the case because character and virtue are not formed in an instant but require time. It takes time to learn and inhabit the dispositions, instincts, judgments and vision associated with just war as a form of Christian discipleship. Just War CD recognizes that you are not likely to sustain justice, prudence, honor and courage (physical and moral) in the moral pressure cooker that is war (for both soldiers and civilians) if you have not learned to embody and sustain such virtues before war. Willpower alone is not reliable. If we do not learn to serve our neighbors with justice and mercy, if we do not care about our neighbors before war, if we have not learned to treat strangers with dignity and respect when we encounter them in our homes, neighborhoods, churches, jobs and so on, we are not likely to do so in war.

In sum, Just War CD recognizes the truth behind General Sir John Winthrop Hackett's observation, "What the bad man cannot be is a good sailor, or soldier, or airman."[3] An unjust people cannot wage a just war, no matter how many checklists they produce and try to complete on the eve of war.

THE DIFFERENCE JUST WAR AS CHURCH-CRAFT MAKES

Already in the course of distinguishing the two politics of just war, we can identify one difference between them. Just War CD requires formation; it requires a community of a particular character. Beyond the need for preparation, what is the distinctive shape of just war as one dimension of a distinctly Christian political witness? What difference does envisioning just war as a distinctly Christian practice make? For an answer to these questions we turn to the criteria, comparing and contrasting how they are understood according to the two strands of just war.

The just war criteria have been divided between those that govern going to war and those that govern the conduct of warfare. We begin with the criteria governing justice in going to war.

Legitimate authority. This criterion can be broken down into the question of who wages war and who determines whether a particular war is just. With regard to who may wage war, Christianity holds that God alone has authority over life and death, and the just war tradition asserts, on the basis of Scripture such as Romans 13:1-7, that God has shared that authority with the government. Likewise, Just War PPC holds that the right to wage war is lodged in the hands of states and heads of state.

This similarity regarding who may wage war, however, masks a significant

---

[3]John Winthrop Hackett, "The Military in the Service of the State," USAF Harmon Memorial Lecture #13 (1970), www.usafa.edu/df/dfh/harmonmemorial.cfm.

difference between the two politics. Just War PPC is at home in modern political liberalism, which is distinguished by the thinnest of common goods, namely, the liberty to pursue one's self-interest—with the result that government wages war primarily to defend its interests against others, and too often political office itself becomes a kind of prize with which to assert one's interests or a tool with which to pander for power. Just War CD, as an ecclesial politics, is distinguished by a thick conception of the common good as well as a corresponding account of political office as fundamentally a matter of responsibility for the common good. As we will see momentarily, these divergent understandings of the function of legitimate authority result in different understandings of just cause.

Before turning to that, we must consider who determines whether a particular war is just or unjust. Here, again, Just War PPC defers to heads of state. Just War CD is more complex and involves three levels of judgment. First, the head of state, with wise advisors, is expected to make such a determination. The assumption that the head of state will be surrounded by wise advisors indicates that the authority to determine justice in going to war is as much about formation as it is about information. The presence of virtuous advisors suggests that the determination to wage war is a matter not only of information but sound moral judgment for the sake of the common good. Just as warfare is taken out of the hands of private individuals in order to prevent vindictive feuds, so authority is lodged in the hands of the prince because it is assumed that a prince will be constrained from vengeance by wise advisors and by a commitment to the common good.

Second, individual soldiers are expected to give the prince the benefit of the doubt with regard to the justice of a war—but only the benefit of the doubt. In other words, soldiers are to defer to the judgment of the ruler unless they are certain a war is unjust, in which case they should refuse to fight. Although this may appear to be a rather flimsy qualification, it is nevertheless significant for the way in which it clearly distinguishes the identity and so allegiance of Christians to a politics that transcends the nation-state.

Third, as it developed within Christianity, determinations of the justice of a war were subject to the oversight of the church, particularly through the interventions of bishops in the affairs of princes and the practice of confession, where princes and soldiers were guided in the examination of conscience.

A political corollary of this ecclesial oversight is the recognition of selective conscientious objection (SCO). Just war Christians are not opposed to all wars (as per conscientious objection) but to unjust wars. Therefore, part of the political witness of Just War CD is advocacy for SCO and support of those who refuse to fight on just war grounds.

Just cause. Here a significant difference between Just War PPC and Just War CD emerges. International law has effectively reduced just cause to national self-defense. In contrast, the Christian tradition considers just cause from an other-regarding perspective. Just cause is about the defense of an innocent third party in the face of unjust aggression. In other words, for Christians just cause is not first and foremost a matter of self-defense. Indeed, as the just war tradition was developed by Christianity, the advocates of just war were clear that self-defense did not constitute legitimate grounds for a lethal response to injustice. After all, Christians, following Christ who accepted the cross instead of simply slaying sinners, and who told us to turn the other cheek and take up the cross, would rather be killed than kill an enemy-neighbor. This logic, however, does not leave societies defenseless. Rather, it means that government officials and Christians serving in a society's armed forces are to understand themselves not to be engaged in self-defense but in the defense of their neighbors who make up the society they are defending. Traditionally, this has meant repelling an attack underway, recovering that which has been unjustly taken and punishing in the sense of restoring a just order.

Furthermore, insofar as Christians are concerned with the common good and not self—or even national—interest, Just War CD has no particular qualms about humanitarian interventions and other military actions where national defense or interest are not at stake.

Right intention. Here, too, there is a significant difference between Just War PPC and Just War CD. The public policy checklist approach has reduced right intention to an unreflective peace and a perfunctory disavowal of revenge. This is to say, Just War PPC considers the criterion satisfied if the stated goal of a war is peace and revenge is foresworn.

As a matter of discipleship, the criterion of right intention is more substantial. First, it is a matter not simply of peace but of a just peace. As Augustine noted long ago, everyone desires peace; wars are always fought for a peace that better suits the aggressor. It is not sufficient, then, merely to be for peace. One must intend a peace that is not merely self-serving but truly just, that is, building up the common good. Second, right intent entails that even in warfare we love our enemy. In a just war we are not exempt from loving our enemy-neighbor (Mt 5:44). Indeed, in waging war the right intent is not to destroy the enemy but to bring them the benefits of a just peace. Even in war, our hope is that the enemy will turn and embrace the order of peace and justice. As Augustine said, "Therefore it ought to be necessity and not your will that destroys the enemy who is fighting you."[4] Thus the proper response to a war's conclusion is not celebration (although we are, of course, glad that the bloodshed has ceased), but grieving and repentance. In other words, the just war tradition at its best is about the formation of sad, reluctant killers. Again, as Augustine said, "Wars and conquests may rejoice unprincipled men, but are a sad necessity in the eyes of men of principle."[5]

Third, right intent entails what can be called "complete justice." This gets to the issue of character. Recall that just war as discipleship reflects the character of the people of God who love and pursue justice in the entirety of their life. Unlike Just War PPC, which assumes that anyone—saint or scoundrel—can wage a just war, Just War CD understands that a war can only be just if it is anchored in the life of a community that is deeply and constantly committed to love and justice for the neighbor. Right intent highlights character as it considers the consistency and completeness of the desire for justice. Right intention rules out the selective enforcement of or appeal to the tradition— the kind of use of the tradition that is concerned only about select injustices and select neighbors, while ignoring others. It entails the self-examination that is willing to confess and make amends for complicity with injustice in the past (cf. Mt 7:35). And it includes a commitment to carry through on the desire for justice after the shooting stops—that, for example, neither abandons the defeated enemy nor replaces one tyrant with another.

The connection of just war to a distinctively Christian polity is perhaps nowhere clearer than here. Loving enemies, confessing wrongdoing and making amends may all require a supernatural politics made possible by the means of grace available in the church.

---

[4]Augustine, *Augustine: Political Writings*, ed. E. M. Atkins and R. J. Dodaro (New York: Cambridge University Press, 2001), p. 217.
[5]Augustine, *The City of God*, trans. Marcus Dods (New York: Random House, 1950), 4.15.

Last resort. This criterion ensures that the resort to arms occurs not as a first resort but only after other feasible means of addressing injustice (like mediation, negotiation, arbitration, international tribunals, etc., but not compromise or appeasement) have failed.

There are subtle but important differences here between Just War CD and Just War PPC. The first concerns the applicability of the criterion. Increasingly, those who approach just war as a checklist are asserting that this criterion is no longer relevant, that a nation with a just cause may strike with military force whenever it is deemed strategically advantageous. Just War CD holds fast to the criterion.

The second difference concerns the commitment to diplomacy. The checklist approach says little about how diplomacy should be pursued, including whether the criterion is incompatible with deceit, humiliation and demonization of the enemy, refusing to consider grievances or setting unreasonable deadlines. Just War CD insists that last resort entails a commitment to diplomacy in good faith, thus forestalling such practices.

The third difference concerns a commitment to developing alternatives to war. The checklist approach says nothing about the requirement that a just war people devote time and energy to developing means other than war for addressing injustice. Just War CD recognizes that last resort entails developing ways and means that might indeed make the resort to war less necessary, ways and means like those identified as "just peacemaking."[6] Sanctions may or may not be part of the effort to forestall war; after all, some forms of sanctions may themselves violate justice in their infliction of harm that is indiscriminate and disproportionate.

Reasonable chance of success. This criterion states that the goals of a just war should be attainable. This means that even if one has met the other criteria, one nevertheless is not justified in waging war if there is little chance of succeeding. Just wars are limited wars. Their aim is to address or rectify a particular injustice, not to rid the world of evil, wipe out an ideology or attain absolute security. Such grand and widesweeping goals are not likely to be achieved and more closely resemble a crusade vision. Also part of the limited nature of a just war is the refusal to insist on unconditional surrender from the

---

[6]Glen Stassen, ed., *Just Peacemaking: Transforming Initiatives for Justice and Peace*, 2nd ed. (Cleveland: Pilgrim Press, 1998).

enemy. Rather, it includes a clear declaration of the conditions under which the unjust enemy can bring the hostilities to an end.

Questions concerning the cost of waging war, traditionally identified as "proportionality," may also be included here. Proportionality means that if the harm likely caused by a war (in terms of lives and resources, regional or global destabilization, curtailment of liberties, etc.) exceeds the harm suffered by absorbing or resisting the injustice in another form, then one may be obliged to forgo the resort to arms.

Where the two visions of just war diverge with regard to this criterion concerns the moral imperative to surrender. Just War CD recognizes that if one cannot begin or continue to wage war with a reasonable chance of success while abiding by the just war discipline, then one must not engage in or continue to wage war. Instead, the injustice in question must be resisted in other ways. This is the moral imperative of surrender. Some proponents of Just War PPC resist this imperative and instead argue that when faced with a supreme emergency, that is, when faced with annihilation, one can discard the criteria and do whatever it takes to prevent defeat.

Discrimination. We now turn to consider the just conduct of warfare, spelled out in two criteria. The first criterion states that civilians may not be intentionally and directly targeted and killed. For example, one may not legitimately target cities in order to undercut enemy morale, nor may one target civilians in order to reduce the number of combatant casualties. This criterion, however, does not mean that a just war prohibits all civilian deaths. Rather, it states that civilian deaths must only be the unintended, secondary effect of an attack on a legitimate military target.

Just War PPC interprets this criterion permissively. As long as one does not intentionally target civilians, and the military benefit is deemed to outweigh the cost, civilian deaths are permitted. Just War CD rejects such a permissive rendering of the criterion in favor of recognizing a responsibility to protect. Thus, it is not sufficient that civilians are not intentionally targeted. Because we are called to love our neighbors, we actively seek to avoid their deaths. Thus, we have a responsibility to avoid even unintentional deaths that are foreseen as likely.

Proportionality. This criterion concerns the force directed against military targets, asserting that the force used must be necessary, and it must only be used to advance the just purpose of the war. This is to say, in a just war, force should not be used for revenge or to pursue purposes that are not connected to the just cause of the war, such as access to natural resources or territorial enlargement. Here again Just War PPC tends to be permissive, reducing the criterion to a cost/benefit analysis, holding simply that the benefits of the use of force must outweigh the costs. As a result, it sanctions a policy of maximum allowable force.

In contrast, Just War CD insists that force be directed toward the legitimate just goals of a war and that the force used must be *minimized*. Thus, it restricts the just use of force to the minimum necessary.

JUST WAR AND WORSHIP

Comparing just war as a policy guide for nation-states and just war as a form of Christian politics leaves the impression that Just War CD is more demanding in terms both of the restraint and the responsibility it embodies.

Such a conclusion, however, only scratches the surface of the fundamental difference between the two politics. Initially I asserted that just war as a form of Christian discipleship was but an outgrowth or extension of the character and virtues of the Christian life in peacetime to the realm of war. This means that insofar as the character of the Christian life is a matter of worship, of glorifying God, of loving God and reflecting that love toward our neighbors, so too just war as a Christian discipline is a matter of worship. Herein lies the fundamental difference between these two politics. One is anchored in worship of the blessed Trinity, the other not.

There are two dimensions to this claim. First, to the extent that Just War CD demands extraordinary (some might even say supernatural) restraint and responsibility, it is clearly related to the love of God experienced and expressed in worship. It is this love that moves us to risk our lives and those of our loved ones for the sake of our neighbors, for the common good, even when our interests are not at stake. It is this love that drives us to strive to minimize the harm of war and avoid even unintended foreseeable noncombatant casualties. And it is this love shown toward our enemy-neighbors that prompts us to wage only limited wars against them, fighting only when we can succeed within the parameters of the just war discipline, using the minimum force necessary, hoping not to kill, and not abandoning them after the shooting stops.

The second way just war as Christian politics is related to worship concerns how the practice of worship may form and shape Christians into a people of the character and virtues necessary to wage war in accord with the restrained and responsible discipline of Just War CD. This is to say, just war as a distinctive Christian politics is connected to worship as a means of grace through which we are sanctified, made better than we otherwise would be, as we are infused with the theological virtues of faith, hope and love.[7]

At first glance, the connection between worship and just war is obvious in that worship, especially preaching, might inspire, motivate and instruct a just war people. But the connection goes deeper than this, beyond information and inspiration to formation. In what follows, I will briefly consider a few ways worship may form a people capable of embodying the discipline associated with the just war criteria.

The criterion of legitimate authority calls for the church to maintain an identity independent of the nation-state such that the church can exercise its proper oversight regarding judgments of when to wage war. The practice of baptism clearly establishes this identity. Yet worship that carefully adheres to the modern split of religion and politics, relegating worship to the immaterial spiritual realm, undermines the church's ability to exercise its proper political oversight. Likewise, the church's independent identity may be undercut by the inclusion of national flags and pledges of allegiance in worship insofar as such may reinforce the subordination of the church to the state. A similar thing may happen as well when the civic calendar overrules the liturgical calendar in worship, with Memorial Day trumping Trinity Sunday or the Fourth of July becoming a religious festival. It is also worth noting that the divided worship of the church—the denominational fractures of the body of Christ—also undermines the church's voice on the justice of war.

The criterion of just cause calls for a people who forgo self-interest and are willing to risk much in service to their neighbor. Whether it is a matter of kneeling, reciting the Lord's Prayer or being baptized, worship forms us as a people who die to the self turned inward and so are set free to turn outward in love toward our neighbors. The Eucharist forms us as a people of love and courage who, being incorporated into Christ's sacrifice, go into the world to give

---

[7]Of course, worship is not the only means of grace. As important are the disciplines of discipleship, such as the works of mercy.

ourselves (and our loved ones and resources) for others. Likewise the practice of offering forms us to give generously to others as we learn to see that all that we have is a gift given to us to be offered in service to God and our neighbors.

Furthermore, the practice of confession and the recognition of the season of Lent are crucial to being a people capable of discerning just cause, which includes being able to hear the just complaints of those whom we have wronged and so to recognize when we are guilty of offense and need to make amends.

By way of contrast, worship that is framed in terms of affirmation, therapy and meeting my felt needs only reinforces the self-interest that neglects our neighbors. Likewise, the absence of regular celebration of the Eucharist leaves us susceptible either to the wrong sacrifices (unjust wars) or to failing to sacrifice or risk for others when we should (humanitarian interventions).

With regard to right intention, worship is one of the principal means of grace whereby we are formed in the virtue of charity. From start to finish worship is about the reception of the love of God and its return by being directed toward our neighbors in the hope of extending communion, community and building up the common good. Thus from baptism, to the prayers of the people, to the Eucharist, our lives are directed toward others in the shared love that is the common good. For example, as we regularly and publically pray for our near and distant neighbors, including our enemies, and as we learn to be reconciled to our enemies in the Christian community, our hearts are being nurtured with the intent necessary to wage a just war.

Conversely, where our worship is riven by division of class, nation and race, or where we only pray for ourselves and our own, we are not likely to be a people capable of sustaining the right intention of love that underwrites Just War CD. Likewise, where we have discarded or diminished the practice of confession and penance we will be less likely to be capable of practicing the arts of forgiveness, healing, judgment and reconciliation that are crucial to justice after the shooting stops.

The criterion of last resort calls for discernment and the exercise of judgment that is neither too hasty nor too slow in entering into war. As such it calls for prudence, something we learn in worship as we become skilled in listening to the Word as well as to the promptings of the Spirit in the various liturgical forms it takes. This criterion also calls for patience and endurance, virtues that the church is schooled in as its liturgical life is directed by the seasons of Advent, with its patient expectation, and Lent, with its steadfast endurance. This criterion also calls for a people of hope, a people who hope that injustice can be addressed by means other than war. Such hope, however, is not anchored in human optimism but divine trust. We hope that God can soften hard hearts, and we learn such hope and see such hope answered in worship as sinners are raised up out of the waters of baptism and as the saints share their testimonies of redemptive change.

The criterion of reasonable chance of success, like the last, calls for discernment and judgment that is formed in worship. Insofar as it is also a matter of waging limited wars for limited ends, it calls for a temperance that resists vengeance and overreach. Worship may form us in such temperance through ascetical disciplines, like prayer and fasting, that moderate our desires between too much and too little.

One of the principal challenges presented by this criterion is the moral imperative of surrender. This is nothing less than a call to take up the cross, a call to the courage to risk suffering and loss for the sake of what is right. It is also a matter of faith in God, of trust that God will prevail though we may be defeated, that justice ultimately does not depend on the strength of our arm or the speed of our horses. Insofar as worship is about participation in the crucified Christ—whether that is through baptism into his death and life, being joined to his sacrifice at the altar, or funerals where we are reminded that whether we live or die we are the Lord's—it is a means of grace that can instill the faith and courage to abide by the just war discipline, even in the face of defeat.

The last two criteria—discrimination and proportionality—can be treated briefly and together insofar as the character they call for replicates the other criteria. They call for a prudent people, capable of exercising discriminating judgments about targeting, and a temperate people who can be measured in their use of force. They call for charity and courage, which inform the desire to minimize harm as well as the willingness to bear great risks in order to do so. And in the ways already mentioned, worship can indeed form such a people, infusing us with charity toward our neighbors, even our enemy-neighbors, such that even in waging war we do not wish them harm but rather to share in the benefits of a just peace.

CONCLUSION

Just war as a distinctly Christian form of politics asks a great deal of those who would abide by its discipline. It asks of Christians that they recognize that their identity is found first and foremost not in the nation-state but in Christ and his body, the church. This is no small task or petty challenge, given the pretensions of modern states. Just war also asks that Christians who would wage war do so not in defense of self and self-interest but out of love for their neighbors, including their enemy-neighbors. Accordingly, just war calls for a people who can bear great risks, shoulder heavy responsibilities and forgo the consolations of a more permissive politics of war.

Such risks and responsibilities are too much for any individual and too often contrary to the interests of modern nation-states. Indeed, they are too much for merely human communities and human politics. They require a different politics founded on a power greater than any nation-state can muster. That is why Just War CD is a matter finally not of statecraft but of church-craft. For it is in the church, through the means of grace, that God makes us better than we otherwise would be, forming us in the virtues of faith, hope and love. In the church, God makes a Spirit-formed people capable of bearing the cross, of taking the great risks and of shouldering the tremendous responsibilities that come with loving our neighbors, even our enemy-neighbors.

10

Repentance as Political Witness

Jennifer M. McBride

In spring 2006, several hundred people gather at the University of Southern Maine in Portland for a town meeting on the Iraq War. The program is simple. Any individual has the opportunity to speak for three minutes. Halfway through the night, an evangelical Episcopal priest approaches the microphone. He is new to the area, has no strong ties to a political party and no experience speaking in this kind of public arena. Wearing his collar and conscious of his role as a representative of the church, he opens by confessing that Christians have been in collusion with military might to the detriment of witnessing to Christ. He says to the crowd,

> As you can see, I am not a politician. I am not a military expert, nor an expert in international affairs. However, as a Christian pastor, I felt compelled to come tonight to bear witness to the witness of Christian Scriptures relative to these issues. Christian ideas and pieces of the Bible have been used so much in all this—particularly during the build-up to the war in Iraq, in an attempt to justify it—that I simply feel I must speak to give testimony to what the witness of the Christian Scriptures is if we read it as a whole and let it speak to us with integrity and . . . do not approach it trying to justify an end upon which we have already decided.
>
> And when I read the Bible with these issues in mind, I see one big thing that comes off the pages boldly. It is this: God will not be mocked. . . . God perhaps tolerates empires for a season, with all their swagger, all their might, all their . . . self-justification. . . . But that should not be mistaken for God's favor. And that should not be mistaken for God being on our side or fighting for us.
>
> Because, the witness of Christian Scriptures is that eventually . . . God

judges . . . hubris and violence, neglect of the poor and vulnerable, and exploitation of the good creation. . . . The witness of Scripture is clear that the God who incarnated himself into this world in Jesus knew suffering, was a friend of the poor and broken, confronted empire in his own day, loved justice, and cared for the good creation God made. God will not be mocked but will eventually bring righteous judgment.

Tim Clayton steps away from the microphone feeling like a fish out of water, so nervous that his mouth is parched, aware that what he said is not perfect. Yet, to his surprise, there is a certain dynamism, a tangible energy stirring in the room as he walks back to his seat. The Green Party candidate for governor speaks a few minutes later and says, "I think we ought to give one of Maine's Senate positions to Pastor Tim!" and the audience responds with a rousing cheer. In the lobby a diverse crowd surrounds Clayton to talk: local reporters, a devout Catholic who has devoted his life to social justice, a woman who says she has lost her faith because so many Christians support corrupt political acts, and many other people who simply say, "Thank you for what you said."[1]

Why does Clayton's political witness, expressed in particularly Christian language about God's love in Christ and God's judgment on human sin, receive *cheers* from a diverse and mostly secular audience? Why do reporters find his words newsworthy? What is it about Clayton's public witness that draws into conversation a mixture of secular citizens, devout Christians and those who describe themselves as having lost their faith? Is the audience's reception of Clayton's message a result of a shared political platform, or does his witness break through the dualisms partisan politics create and offer something unique and new? More generally, given that thoughtful Christians come to conflicting conclusions, how can Christians take a stand on specific social and political matters without binding the church to partisan politics, without allowing politics to define what is Christian? My concern in raising these questions is not *whether* the church should be involved in public life but *how* the church should be engaged.[2]

Christians so thoroughly disagree about issues like war, the death penalty,

---

[1]Tim Clayton, interview with author, April 24, 2006; email, April 21, 2006. This section is adapted from the opening anecdote of my book, *The Church for the World: A Theology of Public Witness* (New York: Oxford University Press, 2011), pp. 3-4.
[2]McBride, *Church for the World*, p. 4.

abortion, ecological care, immigration and race relations that we wind up on opposing sides of the political spectrum. The increasing polarization of our society and of our churches is cause for great concern, especially because it arises, I believe, from a triumphalism that contaminates all sides. By triumphalism I mean an arrogant or self-righteous confidence in the validity of a set of beliefs that closes down productive conversation. Instead of triumphalism, we need a *non*-triumphal witness, and for two reasons: the flourishing of the common good in our pluralistic society demands a humble witness; and even more, faithfulness to the character of the crucified Christ demands a humble witness. Triumphalism brings not peace, reconciliation and healing but divisiveness, judgmentalism and self-righteousness. It brings polarizing politics in which every side claims to be the standard bearer of morality and the rightful judge of all. And yet, given that there are certainly times when Christians must take a clear stand on issues that are divisive, we need a public witness that is bold. How then do Christians offer a witness that is simultaneously bold and humble? Said differently: How can the church remain faithful to that basic Christian proclamation that Jesus is Lord and also participate humbly in our pluralistic society? How may the church offer a *non-triumphal* witness to the *lordship* of Christ? I contend that Clayton's public witness is characterized by a disposition of confession and repentance, and that *this* is the way Christians offer a witness at once bold and humble. A public presence rooted in confession and repentance ignites the response described above and positions the church as a vehicle of concrete redemption and reconciliation.

Clayton's speech at the citizen's meeting is a vivid example of political witness because it is overtly public. This one explicitly public moment arises, though, out of the daily work and witness of the Eleuthero Community, a small, ecumenical evangelical, worshiping congregation (established by the Claytons) whose commitments and practices are born out of a disposition of confession and repentance. In 2005, Tim and Cheryl Clayton and two other families moved from Washington, D.C., to the predominantly unchurched region of Portland, Maine, with a desire to learn about ecological care from the surrounding secular culture. They joined in community with two other couples already living in Portland who were drawn to a vision of Christian faith that affirms this world as divine gift and thus understands ecological care as central to discipleship. Eleuthero's founding mission was, in the words of

Tim, that "Christian faith becomes a robust, recognized resource and inspiration for the care and dignifying of the natural world and of vulnerable populations." Central to Eleuthero's affirmation of the world, though, is self-critique and confession of sin. "We find ourselves living in a sharp irony," the mission reads. "As a culture arguably we have more—stuff, power, success—than any people who have ever lived. Yet it is not at all clear that the way we are on is sustainable. It is not . . . clear that the way we are on is life-giving to the world's poor and vulnerable. Indeed, it is not . . . clear that stuff, power, success feed our own souls, should we take the time to stop and look inside." Members of Eleuthero live into this vision by acknowledging their complicity in the excess of American culture, by establishing partnerships and learning from various environmental organizations, by forming relationships with marginalized populations (in particular a group of Sudanese refugees), and by seeking, as a community, practices of simplicity and sustainability. They are a church, in other words, with an identity and mission rooted in the confession of specific structural sin and organized around a common work of repentance. They are a community whose political witness is defined by confession and repentance.[3]

A DISPOSITION OF CONFESSION AND REPENTANCE

Although this short space does not allow for a robust description of the Eleuthero Community, I want to offer a few snapshots that further exemplify the way a disposition of confession and repentance finds expression in the work and witness of this community. By *disposition* I mean a *mode of being* in the world, encompassing presence, action and speech. By *confession of sin* I do not primarily mean a formal statement of confession, like an apology issued by a denomination, but a pattern of speaking arising from humble acknowledgment of complicity in specific injustice and of the church's inherent entanglement with society's structural sin. By *repentance* I mean the church's concrete social and political engagement that arises from it taking responsibility for such sin. Through creative and courageous repentant activity in public life, the church participates in God's healing transformation of this world.[4]

---

[3]Content from www.eleuthero.us, accessed 2006–2008; cited in McBride, *Church for the World*, pp. 153-54.
[4]McBride, *Church for the World*, pp. 16-17.

Repentance is first enacted in the Eleuthero Community through renewed thinking, a process that the apostle Paul says is central to repentance (Greek *metanoia*): "Be transformed into a new form by the renewing of your minds," he writes to the Roman churches (Rom 12:2).[5] A common concern drawing the members of Eleuthero together is the felt need to unlearn and learn anew the central messages of Scripture. This entails deliberately reexamining their embedded theology and rearticulating the gospel in relation to a renewed understanding of the person and work of Jesus, the identity and mission of the church, and the relationship between the church and world. For the church's view of its role in social and political life is rooted in its articulation of these basic Christian understandings. The members of Eleuthero are attracted to Tim's ability to articulate the failures of Christian public engagement and to craft an alternative understanding of the church's witness—one that avoids triumphalism, moralism and taking an oppositional stance toward the world. As David Stankiewicz, an adjunct professor and founding member of Eleuthero, says, "One of the first things Tim said to me is that we are not here to be culture warriors in the sense of fighting the surrounding society, and I liked that the second he said it." Raised in evangelical congregations and educated in an evangelical college, Dave says he was no longer "interested in the knee-jerk conservatism of a lot of the evangelical church." Likewise, Sarrah Stankiewicz, who works for the environmental organization Maine Audubon, describes the deep need she has for renewed biblical and theological understanding. With painful honesty, she says that she felt "jaded," "disgusted" and "disillusioned" by the faith modeled in her home church in Massachusetts. As a result, she went through a "period of change where [she] felt very distant from the faith" as she tried "to figure out" Christianity's "core emphasis." She says she needed to see "that the way many evangelicals feel politically is not really built into Christian faith." Echoing the concerns of a new generation of evangelicals, she was turned off not only by a triumphal Christian presence in partisan politics but also by Christians who market faith as if Jesus were a commodity to be bought and sold and who fill themselves with "easy answers that [make] them feel secure." Sarrah now feels "comfortable" with her faith

---

[5] As translated in Dietrich Bonhoeffer, *Discipleship*, ed. Geffrey B. Kelly and John D. Godsey, trans. Barbara Green and Reinhard Krauss, vol. 4 of Dietrich Bonhoeffer Works (Minneapolis: Fortress Press, 2003), p. 247.

not only because she has found "common ground" with other committed Christians but also because their very faith compels them to seek common ground with people outside the Christian tradition, especially with those whose work aligns with the vision of the kingdom of God.[6]

The Eleuthero Community seeks common ground with others through confession and repentance. Tim says, "Whenever I contact an environmental organization I make the point somewhere relatively subtly but pretty early [on] that we [Christians] have not paid enough attention [to ecological care] but that we would like . . . to learn." When he is slow to confess Christians' lack of concern for the environment it "always comes up." He describes how this dynamic played out with a biologist at the US Fish and Wildlife Service with whom he met to talk about an island property that Eleuthero was hoping to buy and preserve. He says,

> So I called her up out of the blue and gave her my one-sentence spiel about how we are trying to start this Christian community that looks at the inter-action between Christianity and the earth. . . . There is this long silence on the other end. You can hear that she is irritated and she said, "Well, it's about time you Christians did something about this."
>
> So I went to meet her and sat down at the table and the next thing she said was, "Okay, I'll talk to you but don't you dare talk to me about the Bible." And you know, my sense that we need to confess is very useful, because I just kind of laughed and smiled and said, "You are absolutely right. I'm not hurt . . . be-cause what you say is true."

Tim says that although confession and repentance is "the most basic aspect of being a Christian," it surprises those with whom he speaks. The exchange above led to productive conversation, demonstrating that confession and re-pentance open up new possibilities for reconciliation and redemption. This is due to the fact, Tim says, that confession and repentance are "very disarming in the way that Christianity should be disarming."[7]

A primary goal of the Eleuthero Community is to create space for environ-mental professionals and Christians who have no ecological expertise to come together in order, in Tim's words, "to get people who love Jesus to care about

---

[6]Sarrah Stankiewicz, interview with author, September 9, 2006; Dave Stankiewicz, interview with author, September 10, 2006.

[7]McBride, Church for the World, pp. 168-69.

the earth and to ask those who love the earth to take an honest look at Jesus" and at the resources within Christian faith. Eleuthero's contribution to the ecological work is then "doing the biblical witness justice." The community facilitates public discussions about spirituality and ecology that allow them to both "confess where we haven't been and learn from other people . . . but without pitching our conviction about the uniqueness of Jesus out the window," Tim says. As a community trying to build bridges between Portland's environmental experts and Christians, though, Eleuthero raises suspicions from people both inside and outside North American evangelicalism. Tim says, "I have to be careful when [environmental activists] define me as friend and then assume that I must be the only kind of friendly Christian they have ever met—the kind that assumes that all stories wash out to the same thing. I don't believe that at all, and so it is very challenging to keep the uniqueness of Jesus piece and learn how to steward that conviction in these conversations . . . when there hasn't been time for much relational depth to unfold between us." When Tim talks to evangelicals about Eleuthero's mission, the common response is, "Aren't you trying to convert people?" while environmentalists who do not self-describe as Christian are afraid he *is* trying to convert them—to which Tim proclaims, "I am trying to convert everybody, including myself!"[8]

Central to Eleuthero's mission is "reaching out to *convert Christians*" to a way of life based on repentance, as the members undergo continuous conversion themselves. Evan Pillsbury, a musician and staff member of Inter-Varsity Christian Fellowship, says that when he joined Eleuthero, care for the environment was not an active concern for him and his family; rather, he simply wanted "to engage culture in a positive way" and was drawn to the community because of its "local sense of mission." He says, "My family has been in Maine for generations and in my lifetime I have never seen an effective engagement with the culture in any church or para-church ministry." Still, he was open to growing in ecological understanding and is now undergoing what he explicitly calls a "conversion." "I am seeing new aspects of myself," he says. "[Being a part of Eleuthero] has changed the way we eat, shop. . . . We are going through a lot of turnover as a family. What this community has provided me

---

[8]Ibid., pp. 170-72.

is not necessarily all the answers but it has helped me to start to see what the questions are. I don't think I was expecting that sort of change." Eleuthero's public witness is grounded in this continuous conversion—in a recognition that Christians should not present themselves before the world as models of righteousness but as a people in need of constant conversion. This, I argue, is the witness that is transformative for both the church and the world.[9]

CHRIST'S SOLIDARITY WITH SINNERS: DIETRICH BONHOEFFER

I present Eleuthero not as a blueprint all churches should follow but as one compelling model of a community witnessing to the lordship of Christ through confession and repentance. Because each congregation has the resources to enact public repentance (which may be embodied communally in various ways) and must discern for itself what this looks like in its particular setting, I want to provide a theological—or better, a christological—foundation on which confession and repentance makes sense as public witness. To do so I turn to German pastor-theologian Dietrich Bonhoeffer.[10] In prison, Bonhoeffer asked a question arising out of his own historical moment that nevertheless cuts to the core of our driving concern: how US Christians may offer a witness at once bold and humble, a non-triumphal witness to the lordship of Christ.[11] Bonhoeffer writes, "How do we go about being 'religionless-worldly' Christians? How can we be the [ekklesia], those who are called out, without understanding ourselves religiously as privileged, but instead seeing ourselves as belonging wholly to the world? Christ would no longer be the object of religion, but something else entirely, truly lord of the world."[12]

Bonhoeffer views the church as called out—*chosen* for a particular mission—but not specially favored, be it morally or religiously. As we will see, US Protestants tend to communicate a sense of special favor when they in-

---

[9]McBride, *Church for the World*, pp. 156-57.

[10]Bonhoeffer is an appropriate dialogue partner in North American conversations about political witness given the honored place he holds in the imaginations of many US evangelicals and the deep admiration many have for him because of the integrity of his life and thought and his clear devotion to Jesus Christ. When taken as a whole, though, Bonhoeffer's work challenges commonly held theological assumptions, ones that I argue need to be disrupted in order for Protestants to offer a non-triumphal public witness.

[11]McBride, *Church for the World*, pp. 23-24

[12]Dietrich Bonhoeffer, *Letters and Papers from Prison*, ed. John W. de Gruchy, trans. Isabel Best et al., vol. 8 of Dietrich Bonhoeffer Works (Minneapolis: Fortress, 2010), p. 364.

terpret Christian faith as the possession of morality or religious righteousness.[13] In prison, Bonhoeffer draws a sharp distinction between presuming one's group is specially favored and being in solidarity with others, that is, "belonging wholly to the world." In doing so, he suggests that Christians rethink the nature of their chosen status. If Christians are chosen but not specially favored then what does it mean to be chosen? What are Christians chosen *for*? Bonhoeffer interprets quite literally Paul's claim that the church is "the body of Christ" (1 Cor 12:27)—the continued physical manifestation of Christ in the world—and so his answer is this: The church is chosen to carry on the work of the incarnate and crucified God. The church's election is not for itself, as if the reach of redemption ends there, but like Christ the church is chosen to exist for others—for the world—and it does so by taking the form, or the shape, of Jesus in public life. For Bonhoeffer, in order to witness faithfully to Christ, the church must mirror Jesus' own public presence. When we examine Jesus' public presence we see that he belonged wholly to the world— he was in solidarity with real human beings—by taking the form of a sinner, culminating on the cross where he directed God's judgment away from others and to himself. As the body of Christ, the church is called to do the same—to be present in public life as sinners who direct God's judgment away from others by taking responsibility for sin through repentance. In doing so, the church faithfully witnesses to the lordship of Christ and participates in Christ's transformation of this world.

Jesus was in solidarity with sinners—he took the form of a sinner—in three ways that define his person and work: (1) He assumed sinful flesh (as Paul says in Rom 8:3); he was fully human and so took on the intrinsically damaged state of human nature as it is. (2) He was baptized with sinners in response to John's call to repent. (3) And, refusing to be called good, he accepted responsibility for sin as a convicted criminal on the cross. In the form of a sinner, Jesus redeems the world.

Before examining these in more detail, I want to further ground this line of thinking in Bonhoeffer's prison theology. In prison, Bonhoeffer speaks of the possibility of a "religionless Christianity" and asks what it might mean to reinterpret central concepts of Christian faith in a "non-religious" manner. Although

---

[13]McBride, *Church for the World*, p. 25.

"religionless Christianity" and a "non-religious interpretation" have been contested notions in Bonhoeffer scholarship, there is consensus now that whatever else he meant by these terms, his concern was a renewed practice and proclamation of the faith based on the incarnation—that central event through which God "belongs wholly to the world." He asks how concepts like repentance, faith, justification, rebirth and sanctification gain greater meaning when interpreted in a "'worldly' way . . . in the sense of John 1:14," the Word become flesh.[14] When Bonhoeffer asks how repentance (along with other central concepts of Christian faith) may be interpreted christologically, he is suggesting that Jesus' work may, in some intriguing way, be understood as repentance—but he does so without suggesting that the problem of sin has its origin in God. Jesus' person and work may be an expression or embodiment of repentance, albeit one that directly challenges common understandings of the term. While most Christians tend to make repentance a private end in itself—a preoccupation with individual sin and need—repentance rooted in the Christ event is definitively social and political. It entails existing for others by taking responsibility for the sin that harms fellow human beings.[15] If Jesus' public work may be understood as repentance, then it follows that the church's repentance may imitate God's presence in public life and participate in Christ's redemptive work.

Mentioning Jesus and repentance in the same sentence has likely and appropriately set off theological alarm bells. With Bonhoeffer, I affirm the orthodox claim that Jesus is sinless. Jesus is sinless in the sense that he obeys the will of God at every turn. He is not controlled by death-dealing powers and principalities that seek to humiliate, destroy and oppress human beings. Bonhoeffer, following Paul, affirms the sinlessness of Jesus through the notion of perfect obedience, but he guards against putting too much distance between Jesus and sin because such a move would lessen the central meaning of the incarnation—that Jesus is in solidarity with human beings in our sin and in our redemption. God wills Jesus to be in solidarity with real human beings, and God's will, as seen through the cross, can be scandalous.[16] Furthermore, the unusual and scandalous claim that Jesus' work may be understood as re-

---

[14]Bonhoeffer, *Letters and Papers*, pp. 364, 373. Cf. McBride, *Church for the World*, p. 59.
[15]McBride, *Church for the World*, p. 66. See also pp. 62-67 for further analysis of the social and political character of repentance, especially as seen in the Synoptic Gospels.
[16]Ibid., pp. 73-74.

pentance finds a home within the paradoxes of Christian faith, especially in a Lutheran view, that characterize God's revelation through Christ as hidden. Christological repentance may be understood as one mode of the hidden God, as one of the startling ways that God reveals God's self to the world—a way that confounds our human, religious expectations: God is visible in the world and present in public life in the form of a sinner. Describing God's righteousness in Christ as repentance mirrors the move Luther makes when he says that Jesus is both guilty and sinless. Christ exists as a "sinner among sinners," even as the *peccator pessimus*, Luther's term for "the worst sinner," and yet as "sinless among sinners." "He is himself thief, murder, adulterer, as we are, because he bears our sin," contends Luther.[17] Or, in Bonhoeffer's words, his "genuine guiltlessness" is demonstrated precisely by him "enter[ing] into community with the guilt of other human beings."[18]

At stake in the claim linking Jesus and repentance is the redemptive power of the church's political witness, which has no lasting effect unless it participates in the transformative power of the Christ event. For we can do nothing for God that God has not already done for us. Karl Barth, Bonhoeffer's colleague in the Church Struggle, says it poignantly.

> What are we with our little conversion, our little repentance and revising, our little ending and beginning, our changed lives? . . . It is in His conversion that we are engaged. . . . It is in His baptism in Jordan that we are baptized. . . . It is in His death on the cross that we are dead . . . and in His resurrection . . . that we are risen. . . . It is because this is the case . . . that the awakening to repentance is the power of the Gospel, and that it has the force and depth . . . which are proper to it. . . . It remains for us to know that . . . we are [upheld] by the great movement which He has fulfilled.[19]

Repentance is central to Christian political witness, then, not only because it manifests a proper humility—it acknowledges before the world that (unlike the sinless Jesus) Christians *are* complicit in the structural sin of our society, especially those of us who effortlessly benefit from and uphold an unjust

---

[17]Dietrich Bonhoeffer, *Christ the Center*, trans. Edwin H. Robertson (New York: HarperCollins, 1978), p. 107. Cf. McBride, *Church for the World*, p. 73.

[18]Dietrich Bonhoeffer, *Ethics*, trans. Reinhold Krauss et al., vol. 6 of Dietrich Bonhoeffer Works (Minneapolis: Fortress, 2005), p. 276.

[19]Karl Barth, *Church Dogmatics IV/2: The Doctrine of Reconciliation*, ed. G. W. Bromiley and T. F. Torrance, trans. G. W. Bromiley (Edinburgh: T & T Clark, 1978), pp. 583-84.

status quo—but also because it participates in the transformative work of Christ in the world. Jesus' repentance is what gives the church's repentance its meaning and power. This unusual claim—that the category of repentance offers a renewed understanding of the work of Christ—is rooted in the reality that Jesus takes the form of a sinner in public life.

Jesus takes the form of a sinner first through the incarnation itself. He becomes intimately involved with sin through his bodily immersion in fallen existence. In Romans 8:3, Paul claims that in the incarnation God took "the likeness of sinful flesh" in order to "deal with sin" (NRSV). While the term *likeness* may seem at first to distance Christ from humanity's fallen condition, in his 1933 Christology lectures Bonhoeffer argues that Christ not only appears to take sinful flesh, he actually takes the very flesh of fallen humanity, the intrinsically damaged state of human nature as it is. Bonhoeffer's interpretation is in line with the majority of contemporary biblical scholarship that argues that Paul is affirming Jesus' "true likeness" (to use the language of Phil 2:7), not distinguishing him from other human beings. Jesus' flesh was our fallen flesh, Bonhoeffer says, with its tendency to sin and self-will, and to this extent he differed not at all. He was tempted in the same way, only the stakes were higher. As a result of bearing sinful flesh and living in a fallen world, "he was not the perfect good," Bonhoeffer argues, meaning that he did things that looked like sin. "He became angry, he was harsh to his mother, . . . he broke the law of his people, he stirred up revolt against the rulers and religious men of his country." In the public realm, Jesus is clearly regarded as a sinner. "Beyond recognition he stepped into [humanity's] sinful way of existence," and in doing so, "robs sin of its power." The astounding reality of the incarnation is that God freely chose to be visible in the world through sinful flesh. This reality enables a renewed reflection on Christ's redemptive work, rooted in the notion of repentance.[20]

Not only does Jesus take the form of a sinner by assuming sinful flesh, but his first public appearance is as a penitent in solidarity with other penitents. The opening act of the story of Jesus' public ministry begins at the Desert of Judea with John the Baptist preaching, "Repent, for the kingdom of God is near." Jesus responds to John's call directed at sinners, and by being baptized appropriates the practice of repentance to his own work as redeemer. Being

---

[20]Bonhoeffer, *Christ the Center*, p. 108. Cf. McBride, *Church for the World*, pp. 73-75.

baptized by John was not an arbitrary act of humility for the sinless Christ. The public ministry of Jesus is inaugurated precisely through baptism—through the act of human beings responding to the call to repent. By being baptized by John, Jesus numbers himself with the transgressors (to use Isaiah's language about the suffering servant; Is 53:12) and is present to humanity as such.[21]

Finally, throughout his ministry Jesus avoids identifying himself as God, referring to himself instead as the "Son of Man"—the human one—and repudiates any claim about his own moral righteousness. "Why do you call me good?" Jesus says to the rich young man. "No one is good but God alone" (Mk 10:18 NRSV).[22] Jesus not only refuses to acknowledge his righteousness during his public ministry, he actively accepts responsibility for the world's sin and suffering on the cross. In *Ethics* Bonhoeffer writes,

> In an incomprehensible reversal of all righteous and pious thought, God . . . declares [God's self] as guilty toward the world, and thereby extinguishes the [world's] guilt. God treads the humble way of reconciliation and thereby sets the world free. God wills to be guilty of our guilt. God takes on the punishment and suffering that guilt has brought on us. God takes responsibility for godlessness. . . . Now there is no longer any reality, any world, that is not reconciled with God and at peace.[23]

Jesus glorifies God by taking responsibility for sin, in turn letting divine judgment fall on God's very self. "Jesus Christ is . . . God's judgment on himself," writes Bonhoeffer.[24] Jesus' acceptance of guilt is not the result of a burdened conscience but is an active determination that the guilty verdict falls on him instead of others. Bonhoeffer continues,

> Jesus does not want to be considered the only perfect one at the expense of human beings, nor, the only guiltless one, to look down on humanity perishing under its guilt. . . . Because he loves them, he does not acquit himself of the guilt in which human beings live. A love that abandons human beings to their guilt would not be a love for real human beings. . . . It is God's love that lets Jesus become guilty.[25]

---

[21]McBride, *Church for the World*, pp. 65-66.
[22]Ibid., p. 43.
[23]Bonhoeffer, *Ethics*, DBWE 6, p. 83.
[24]Bonhoeffer, *Christ the Center*, p. 103.
[25]Bonhoeffer, *Ethics*, DBWE 6, p. 233. Cf. McBride, *Church for the World*, pp. 82-83.

In a fallen world, acceptance of guilt is the definitive expression of God's goodness and love.

The church-community that faithfully witness to Christ must act out of the same divine love for the world. This means that the church will not wish to distinguish itself from others—to lift itself up as a model of moral righteousness and thus exonerate itself from present complicity in sin—but rather will want to be in solidarity with sinners through confession and repentance. And yet, Protestants ranging from fundamentalists to evangelicals to mainline Christians all tend to do the opposite—to base our witness on the presumption that we are called to be exemplars of morality and to shape society into the image we have of ourselves.

We have seen this tendency for over thirty years, most notoriously in the political witness of the Religious Right, Christians who deemed themselves morally elite citizens called by God to combat the immoral "godless elite," who advocate such things as gender equality and teaching evolution in public schools. In a 1997 interview celebrating Focus on the Family's twentieth anniversary, James Dobson summarized the Religious Right's sense of mission in society: "As Christians, I believe we are obligated to defend the principles of morality and righteousness in this representative form of government."[26] We see this tendency in those whom sociologist Christian Smith calls "ordinary evangelicals," Christians who disavow the Religious Right's desire for political dominance yet believe Jesus calls them to be "salt and light" to the world—which translates politically into the nondescript task of being a "moral presence" and advocating "better morality" in society, with issues espoused by the Religious Right often animating their moral vision.[27] We observe this tendency at times among progressive evangelicals, who, exasperated by the Religious Right's direct and indirect influence over evangelicals, have been gaining a more unified voice through the ongoing leadership of Jim Wallis and his magazine *Sojourners*. Although the progressive evangelical movement is rooted in the 1973 "Chicago Declaration of Evangelical Social Concern," which calls

---

[26]Quoted in Joshua Yates, "11/9/1989 to 9/11/2001 and Beyond: The Return of Jeremiad and the Specter of Secularization," in *Prophesies of Godlessness: Predictions of America's Imminent Secularization from the Puritans to the Present Day*, ed. Charles Mathewes and Christopher McKnight Nichols (New York: Oxford University Press, 2008), p. 219. Cf. McBride, *Church for the World*, pp. 43-45.

[27]Christian Smith, *Christian America? What Evangelicals Really Want* (Berkeley: University of California Press, 2000), pp. 18, 99, 109, 158-59. Cf. McBride, *Church for the World*, pp. 45-46.

Christians to repent by transforming unjust social structures, Wallis's most successful book, *God's Politics*, veers from this central focus on repentance. In this text Wallis succumbs to the dominant political discourse, offering a "new moral politics," one that advocates "consistent moral ground" and a "return to the moral center." While Wallis's commendable intent in *God's Politics* is to call Christians to a prophetic faith that cares about all matters of justice and proposes solutions that go beyond false dichotomies, when he utilizes the dominant rhetoric, as he continues to do in media sound-bites, he positions progressive evangelicals as one more side in the battle over morality.[28]

The problem with a political witness based on morality is that it presumes the church is specially positioned as judge over society, which not only ignores the clear command of Jesus in the Sermon on the Mount, "Do not judge" (Mt 7:1), but also denies the form of Christ. Bonhoeffer contrasts the human being as judge with Christ's form. The former directs God's judgment away from oneself or one's group and toward others, and the latter directs God's judgment not to others but to oneself. Christ takes humanity's "true form" as judged, Bonhoeffer says, enabling the church to then take the form of Christ, which is characterized by an exclusive acceptance of guilt.[29] The church witnesses to God's judgment on the sin and injustice that harms human beings when—as the continued incarnation of Christ in the world—it also exclusively accepts responsibility for the sin and injustice that plagues our society. The church plays a central role in exposing sin in the world by acknowledging it in itself. Bonhoeffer says,

> Should a few super-righteous people . . . try to prove that not the church but all others are guilty? Would a few churchmen . . . presuming to be called on as judges of the world, proceed to weigh the mass of guilt . . . and distribute it accordingly? . . . Free confession of guilt is not something [the church] can take or leave; it is the form of Jesus Christ breaking through in the church. The church can let this happen to itself or it will cease to be the church of Christ."[30]

By exclusively accepting guilt, the church lives "beyond the knowledge of

---

[28]Jim Wallis, *God's Politics: Why the Right Gets It Wrong and the Left Doesn't Get It* (New York: Harper-Collins, 2005), pp. 18-19. Cf. McBride, *Church for the World*, pp. 46-48. See McBride, pp. 49-51, for an analysis of how mainline Protestants also reduce the church's public witness to claims about morality or to ethical acts.

[29]Bonhoeffer, *Ethics*, DBWE 6, p. 91. Cf. McBride, *Church for the World*, p. 106.

[30]Bonhoeffer, *Ethics*, DBWE 6, pp. 141-42. Cf. McBride, *Church for the World*, p. 133.

good and evil" as God intended before the fall. Bonhoeffer interprets the fall—
Adam and Eve's original sin—as religious desire, wanting to "be for God" by
possessing the knowledge of good and evil. Seeking after such knowledge,
presuming it is God's will we possess such knowledge, is precisely what led to
the fall—to broken relationship with God and one another. This sinful, religious desire finds expression today when the church tries to "be for God" by
modeling and marketing its own pious devotion to moral principles and religious standards that it demands the world adopt. Ironically, the religious attempt "be for God" readily leads to "being against God," because it denies the
way of the crucified Christ. This religious desire to possess moral knowledge
is, according to Bonhoeffer, "disobedience" disguised as obedience, "the will
to power" disguised as "service."[31]

CONCLUSION

So what then of our political witness? Are Christians never to take a stand on
any issue of political consequence because we cannot presume to know good
from evil? I contend that there is indeed an ethic by which Christians are to
live, but it is not an ethic of moral or religious righteousness. It is an opposing
ethic, a totally new mode of being and doing good based on repentance. An
ethic of repentance is not an attempt to be more moral; it is not the correction
of morality but the opposite of morality, an expression that God alone is
righteous. An ethic of repentance mirrors Jesus' words to the rich young man
and reflects that core Reformation truth: No one is good but God alone.[32] It
is, then, an ironic ethic, an ethic that proclaims that we Christians are the
greatest of all sinners. Bonhoeffer says,

> Confession of guilt happens without a sidelong glance at others who are also
> guilty. This confession is strictly exclusive in that it takes all guilt upon itself.
> When one calculates and weighs things, an unfruitful self-righteous morality
> takes the place of confessing guilt face-to-face with the figure of Christ. . . .
> Looking on this grace of Christ frees us completely from looking on the guilt
> of others and brings Christians to fall on their knees before Christ with the
> confession: *mea culpa, mea culpa, mea maxima culpa*. With this confession the

---

[31]Dietrich Bonhoeffer, *Creation and Fall* and *Temptation*, trans. John C. Fletcher (New York: Touchstone,
    1997), pp. 71, 73-74, 81. Cf. McBride, *Church for the World*, pp. 133-37.
[32]See Mark 10:18 and Romans 3:10-11.

whole guilt of the world falls on the church, on Christians, and because here it is confessed and not denied, the possibility of forgiveness [and redemption] is opened.[33]

Because a political witness rooted in repentance arises from the church acknowledging and exposing its own sin, public engagement characterized by confession and repentance resists triumphalism. Instead of a witness that is divisive, positioning the church as morally superior to the world, the church that takes the shape of Jesus is in solidarity with sinners and becomes a secondary form of his own reconciling life.

Furthermore, this non-triumphal witness is constructive. Repentance has the power to guide a church, like the Eleuthero Community, into social and political activity based on the conviction that Christians have been complicit in some form of social/structural sin that stands in opposition to the kingdom of God.[34] For, at its core, repentance is socially and politically significant, a fact that the Synoptic Gospels make clear when John the Baptist links repentance with God's new social order: "Repent, for the kingdom of God is at hand!" he proclaims (see Mt 3:1). Political witness faithful to Christ necessitates that the church mirror Jesus' public presence first by immersing itself in situations of struggle and distress and then by accepting responsibility for the sin and suffering found there. The content of the church's confession and its repentant activity together become the church-community's political witness. A witness based on repentance necessitates that Christians first be people who have ears to hear God convict us of our present complicity in sin and injustice, and have the courage and honesty to face and name that sin. May such a confession ground Christian political witness, as it leads church-communities into social practices full of the transformative power of Christ.

---

[33]Bonhoeffer, *Ethics*, DBWE 6, p. 136. Cf. McBride, *Church for the World*, p. 129.

[34]This vocation may arise from conviction over a particular sin it has committed as a local body, such as racism, which may lead the community not only to repentant activity in relation to its own sin but also to a wider engagement with issues surrounding race and white privilege. Or, individual members within a church body may become convicted of a social/structural sin on a local or global level that they bring before the church body to help bear, as together they learn to live within their local, national or global context in a manner that resists these larger powers through redemptive, constructive repentance. For more on discernment, see McBride, *Church for the World*, pp. 137-46.

11

Toward an Evangelical Social Tradition

Key Current Debates

David P. Gushee

On an Evangelical Social Teaching Tradition or the Lack Thereof

I have been assigned in this paper the task of "discuss[ing] some specific social-political cases in current debate," based on my "'hands-on' experience with these issues." It seems that I am the "nitty-gritty" speaker asked to bring the broader historical, theoretical and theological reflections of the conference thus far "right into the present context, and to point the way forward for evangelicals."[1]

I very much appreciate this assignment, however daunting. But I do feel the need to offer, at least briefly, a few preliminary comments at the theoretical and historical levels.

I begin with the claim that evangelicals suffer greatly from lack of the kind of "social teaching tradition" that one can find both in Roman Catholicism and in ecumenical Protestantism. In Catholicism, this social teaching tradition, though it has deep historical roots, really begins with a series of papal social encyclicals that launched in 1891 with the essay *Rerum novarum*. That first papal essay concerned the unhappy condition of labor in essentially unregulated capitalist economies. Contemporary presentations of modern Catholic

---

[1]Letter from Jeffrey Greenman to David Gushee, January 26, 2012.

social teaching analyze the encyclicals one by one;[2] distill the themes of Catholic social teaching into broad categories, such as human rights, the common good and solidarity; or present Catholic positions on key issues such as abortion, war and immigration.[3]

Ecumenical (mainline) Protestantism has also developed a body of social teaching. This is especially visible in the documents emerging from the World Council of Churches, and, in the United States, the documents of first the Federal and then the National Council of Churches. Also just over one hundred years old, this ecumenical body of social teaching does still function as a tradition, accessible both in terms of a body of documents and a series of themes and concrete issue declarations related to major social problems in the modern world.[4] Ecumenical Protestantism also was blessed by a series of authoritative and widely recognized theologians and social ethicists in the twentieth century, such as Dietrich Bonhoeffer, Reinhold Niebuhr and Martin Luther King Jr., whose writings themselves can be seen as constitutive of the ecumenical Protestant social teaching tradition that lives on to this day.

By contrast, evangelical Christianity lacks a similar authoritative body of social teaching. Certainly evangelicals can and sometimes do look back to leading thinkers or documents of their particular denominational or ecclesial traditions, perhaps tracing their ethics as far back as Luther, Calvin, Wesley or the early Anabaptists. Some American evangelicals claim, and study, thinkers and movements that emerged in the United States as far back as the nineteenth century, such as the evangelical abolitionists or early women's suffragists. If our understanding of evangelicalism fixes on the World War II era and the birth of neo-fundamentalism through the work of Carl F. H. Henry and others, the story can be told beginning there. Perhaps the writings of people like Carl Henry and Francis Schaeffer, or the social statements of the National Association of Evangelicals, will be featured. But, in all honesty, there is not an evangelical social teaching tradition to be found in these texts that

---

[2]As in Kenneth R. Himes, ed., *Modern Catholic Social Teaching* (Washington: Georgetown University Press, 2005).

[3]As in Pontifical Council for Justice and Peace, *Compendium of the Social Doctrine of the Church* (Washington: US Council of Catholic Bishops, 2005).

[4]See J. Philip Wogaman, *Christian Ethics: A Historical Introduction* (Louisville: Westminster John Knox, 1993), chap. 21, and the associated readings in *Readings in Christian Ethics*, ed. J. Philip Wogaman and Douglas M. Strong (Louisville: Westminster John Knox, 1996).

can match the others I have profiled in terms of depth or breadth.

We could continue to push forward. We might suggest that the Christian Right has offered an evangelical social teaching tradition. But who would really suggest that the scattered speeches, pamphlets and popular books of Jerry Falwell, Pat Robertson, James Dobson and their ilk offer a usable, substantive social teaching tradition with twenty-first-century staying power? Or the resolutions passed by the National Association of Evangelicals and the articles published in *Christianity Today*—do these constitute a social teaching tradition for evangelicals? To some extent, perhaps; dissertation writers even today pore over the resolutions of the NAE and the articles in *CT*, but these are not enough to constitute an evangelical social teaching tradition.

Or perhaps we look to the evangelical left, as David Swartz did in his excellent book *Moral Minority*,[5] and suggest that a social teaching tradition can be found in the works of people like Mark Hatfield, Jim Wallis and Ron Sider. The latter has gone the furthest in attempting to develop and broker a body of documents that might help form an evangelical social teaching tradition, but his personal and edited works cannot and do not amount to such a tradition.[6]

In my own work over the last twenty years, I have been aware of the absence of a coherent evangelical social teaching tradition, and have in some ways been attempting to offer elements of one and to cooperate with others whose work can also contribute constructively to it. In my dissertation, *Righteous Gentiles of the Holocaust*, I work inductively from the example of Christians who rescued Jews during the Holocaust to propose what amounts to a "social ethics of costly practical solidarity with the oppressed."[7] In our textbook *Kingdom Ethics*, Glen Stassen and I propose a social ethic rooted in the teachings of Jesus and seeking to participate in a Kingdom ethic which we identify with seven marks: deliverance, justice, peace, healing, restored community, God's presence and joy.[8] In *The Future of Faith in American Politics*, I suggest that evangelical public engagement now falls into conservative, liberal and moderate camps, and argue for an "'emerging evangelical center' with a

---

[5]David R. Swartz, *Moral Minority* (Philadelphia: University of Pennsylvania Press, 2012).

[6]After forty years in the spotlight, Ron Sider retired in July 2013. His organization, Evangelicals for Social Action, lives on. See www.evangelicalsforsocialaction.org (accessed March 20, 2013).

[7]David P. Gushee, *Righteous Gentiles of the Holocaust* (Minneapolis: Fortress, 1994).

[8]Glen Stassen and David P. Gushee, *Kingdom Ethics* (Downers Grove, IL: InterVarsity Press, 2003).

broad issue range and fierce political-ideological independence."[9] And in my new *Sacredness of Human Life*, I claim that the best rendering of the central norm of the biblical and Christian social ethical tradition is a "comprehensive sacredness of life ethic."[10] This latter book breaks out of the evangelical sub-culture more than my other books since *Righteous Gentiles*, and links my version of Christian ethics *both* to the sanctity-of-life ethic of the Catholic moral teaching tradition and the social-justice/liberationist ethic more often identified with ecumenical Protestant tradition.

I continue to hope for the emergence of a coherent, robust evangelical Christian social teaching tradition. I fear that evangelical biblicism, anti-institutionalism and ideological fragmentation will continue to make the de-velopment of such a tradition a very difficult achievement indeed. Lacking such a tradition, I will present my issue-specific reflections based on the rudi-ments of the Christian social ethic I have outlined above. I want to offer an ethic that stands in costly practical solidarity with the oppressed, that reflects plausible participation in the coming reign of God, that engages a broad range of issues and remains fiercely politically and ideologically independent, and that treats each and every human life as ineffably sacred.

I have decided to spice things up a bit by trying to treat as many important contemporary policy issues as I can in the space permitted. I will therefore have to be brief in relation to each of the ten issues I will address, and will trust that further dialogue can deepen the discussion of any particular issue. I will move alphabetically. I have four hundred words for each issue. I have been invited by our hosts to "don the mantle of prophet." Well, we'll see about that. But I will tell you exactly what I think, avoiding equivocations and hedges.

TEN CONTEMPORARY ISSUES

Abortion. Though the precise moral status of embryonic and fetal life is not clearly established in Scripture,[11] the Christian movement in the first three centuries treated both abortion and infanticide as child-murder and as such utterly incompatible with Christian discipleship. But the church also taught a sexual ethic that restricted sex to marriage, an ethic of hospitality for and

---

[9]David P. Gushee, *The Future of Faith in American Politics* (Waco, TX: Baylor University Press, 2008).
[10]David P. Gushee, *The Sacredness of Human Life* (Grand Rapids: Eerdmans, 2013).
[11]For discussion of this claim, see *Kingdom Ethics*, chap. 10.

solidarity with unwanted people of all types, and an ethic of economic sharing.[12] Those who practice such an ethic today do not need abortion, because they have sexual relations only in contexts in which children can be welcomed; or, if they do face crisis pregnancies, they can find Christian communities that will lovingly travel the journey through pregnancy with them; and they never have to abort due to lack of access to the economic resources necessary to sustain a pregnancy or raise a child.

The ethos I am describing is a fair rendering, sadly, of only a minority of our churches. And it certainly does not describe modern Western cultures, especially the United States. Here we do not restrict sex to marriage, we do not stand in solidarity with unwanted people, and we do not participate in adequate economic sharing. And because it is women rather than men who get pregnant, legal access to abortion became a non-negotiable demand of the organized women's movement in the 1960s. For forty years abortion on demand has been our cultural practice despite nods in the law toward a more restrictive stance. Despite ever-stricter symbolic antiabortion legislation passed recently by states such as Arkansas,[13] it is hard to imagine that the basic structure of federal abortion law will be changed any time soon.

My efforts on this issue have been based on the observation that our society has become dependent on abortion to underwrite our libertine sexual practices and individualist-libertarian social and economic practices. While consistently defending the position that the sacredness of human life extends into the womb, and that our abortion laws do not adequately protect fetal life, I have focused on addressing the cultural sources of our dependence on abortion, and on practical abortion-reduction measures that can be pursued by individuals, churches, civil society and policymakers. These include emphasizing sexual responsibility, including the responsibility to use contraception properly if one intends to have sex but not make a baby, strengthening the permanence of male-female relationships, and providing social supports for those facing crisis pregnancies. Rolling back *Roe v. Wade* is not enough. The goal here is less and less and finally no more killing of the unborn. The

---

[12]See *Sacredness of Life*, chap. 4.
[13]See Susie Parker, "Arkansas Abortion Law Likely to Face Legal Challenges," *The Huffington Post*, March 7, 2013, www.huffingtonpost.com/2013/03/07/arkansas-abortion-law_n_2833244.html.

best means to get there is a practical question requiring careful and realistic analysis in each cultural context.

Creation care. I have had the privilege of being a part of evangelical creation care efforts since I began working with Ron Sider in 1990. It has been exciting to watch these efforts go mainstream during these two decades. Well before there was any discussion of climate change, the essentials of evangelical creation care were well established: a combination of the retrieval and recasting of biblical theology and ethics related to caring for God's creation, and serious attention to contemporary environmental science.[14] Together these essentials teach both that this is God's glorious, resilient and life-sustaining creation, and that God's creation is indeed vulnerable to the damaging human mistreatment we mete out to it.

To get there, evangelicals have had to do some important theological and ethical work. We first had to retrieve a theology of creation and integrate it into our salvation-heavy, often other-worldly theology. Then we began to see that it is not just a theology of creation that we need, but a more cosmic theology of creation, fall, redemption and eschatology. In other words, it isn't just that God created the world and we need to care for it, but also that God's project on the planet has never been just about human beings but has always involved relating to and acting to redeem the entire cosmic order. This has integrated nicely into biblical work, for example, retrieving the ecologically rich shalom teachings of the Old Testament, as well as a broad kingdom ethic in the New Testament leading to an eschatology of renewal rather than destruction of creation.[15]

And evangelicals have had to begin to come to terms with contemporary science. If the global scientific community tells us that we are altering or damaging creation, whether in terms of species losses or fishery depletion or, yes, climate change, then we must take those claims seriously—never uncritically, as if science were infallible, but always seriously, as if science has a particular role to play in monitoring and theorizing the health of creation. My encounters with great scientists like E. O. Wilson[16] and climatologists like Judy Curry[17]—

---

[14]See the work of the Evangelical Environmental Network, including the 1993 statement on the care of creation: http://creationcare.org/blank.php?id=39.

[15]See, for example, N. T. Wright, *Surprised by Hope* (New York: HarperOne, 2008).

[16]Every Christian really must read Wilson's *The Creation* (New York: Norton, 2007).

[17]Curry's blog on climate change science is fair and authoritative: http://judithcurry.com.

and being raised by a rigorous environmental scientist, my own father—have given me a deep and informed appreciation of the gifts and limits of the scientific method. Certainly evangelicals need to listen closely to the research of the scientific community and not stop up our ears on the basis of an outmoded theology of dominion or oddly ahistorical belief in the supposed imperviousness of creation to human maltreatment.[18]

Death penalty. The US retention of the death penalty places us at odds with our peers in the modern Western world, and probably reflects both our relative innocence of massive unjust governmental killing and the continued influence of Old Testament death-penalty law (unfiltered either by the Talmudic tradition or a Christ-centered kingdom ethic). It is certainly instructive to note that any map of US states retaining, and especially those broadly employing, the death penalty tracks rather closely with high levels of religiosity, and especially southern religiosity.[19]

I have become convinced that a Christian social ethic that leans into the inaugurated reign of God cannot ultimately abide the state practice of killing a small, select number of criminals, even murderers, from among the universe of murderers we unfortunately produce every year in this country.[20] My position is informed by the early church's revulsion against violence, including state violence; by the massive misuse of the state power to kill, especially in the twentieth century; by the manifest and obvious injustices in the US application of the death penalty, which remains essentially arbitrary, though tied to systemic racial and economic injustices; and by the near-total rejection of the death penalty in contemporary Catholic and ecumenical social ethics.

I do understand that a sacredness of life argument can be made in favor of the death penalty, and that this is precisely what appears to be happening in Genesis 9:6 and in Old Testament death-penalty law.[21] I also can see how practical solidarity with the oppressed can lead one to sympathy not just with people on death row but also with cruelly murdered people and their bereaved

---

[18]A signal example of the theology I am rejecting is found in the work of Calvin Beisner.

[19]The most authoritative source of updated information is found at www.deathpenaltyinfo.org/docu ments/FactSheet.pdf.

[20]There were 16,259 homicides in the US in 2010. See Centers for Disease Control and Prevention, "Assault or Homicide," www.cdc.gov/nchs/fastats/homicide.htm (accessed March 20, 2013). Only 104 convicted murderers were sentenced to death. That is a rate of 0.63 percent.

[21]We deal with this text and the biblical evidence generally in *Kingdom Ethics*, chap. 9.

families. And I know that Christian ethics, even an ethics of the inaugurated kingdom, must come to terms with the extent to which the world is not yet redeemed, and the extent to which evil must still be restrained by the hand of the state. But a robust theology of sin extends to include the sins of the state in its bungling of, and misuse of, its ultimate power, the power to kill. This ultimately shapes my opposition to the use of that power when there is any available alternative, as there is in our criminal justice system. I also believe that those who enter into concern about the anachronistic survival of the death penalty also need to engage other abuses in our criminal justice system, including the overuse of solitary confinement, the continued role of racism, the fearful powerlessness of those lacking adequate legal representation, and the way that those who have been imprisoned are so often disenfranchised for life, both in terms of civic rights and economic opportunity.[22]

Economic justice. Probably the central theme of both ecumenical and Catholic social teaching in the past century has been economic justice. The context has been the paradox of modern capitalism, which over its four-century run has proven to be both an engine of unimagined economic growth and prosperity (for its individual, corporate and national winners) and an engine of economic injustice and poverty (for its individual, corporate and national losers). Modern Christian social ethics was born in response to modern capitalism, especially in response to the manifest cruelties that inspired the Marxist critique that by the late nineteenth and early twentieth centuries threatened to delegitimize capitalism altogether.

Of course, we know what happened. The Russian and Chinese empires eventually chose communism, which turned out to produce regimes of mass poverty, a wealthy governing class and unimaginable mass killing. The fascist regime in Germany rejected communism and also produced unimaginable mass killing. Western Europe and the United States ultimately chose to retain some form of free-market capitalism embedded within liberal democratic political regimes that imposed regulatory schemes, progressive taxation, and a social safety net to care for those who could not, or could no longer, earn a living in a capitalist economy. Nearly every political or public-policy argument in the United States today seems to revolve around these questions of how

---

[22]See justicefellowship.org for one version of justice reform efforts.

much government regulation is best, how much taxation and how progressive
a taxation scheme is right, and what kind of and how expensive a social safety
net is appropriate.

There has essentially been a convergence of Catholic, ecumenical and
much evangelical social ethics in this arena around such principles as human
dignity, solidarity, the common good, worries over consumerism and com-
modification, concern for capitalism's losers, global economic injustice and so
on. Ron Sider has been a leader here.[23] Most everyone agrees that there is
little alternative today to some form of capitalism but also that a morally blind
and rapacious capitalism that loses a vision for anything other than profit ultimately devours itself. Evangelicals have contributed little of theoretical significance here but have been effective in expressing biblically resonant concern
for the domestic and global poor, in offering innovations in poverty relief and
economic development, and in attempting to protect social-safety-net programs for children, the poor and the aged.[24] The goal of a full-employment
economy offering everyone the opportunity to do dignified work at a living
wage, reducing income inequality, feeding everyone and preventing easily preventable diseases, offering decent and affordable health care to all, regulating
and taxing just enough but not too much, continues to elude most countries,
including our own. But, apart from ideological libertarians and a few surviving
Christian Marxists, contemporary Christian social teaching at least offers
these shared goals as well as significant programs that ameliorate some of the
worst effects of global capitalism.

Gay rights. Evangelical Christians have treated homosexuality as an issue
of sexual ethics, and have almost unanimously ruled out the moral legitimacy
of any same-sex acts and relationships as part and parcel of our heterosexual-
marital sexual ethic.

Today "the gay issue," in society at least, is no longer an issue in sexual
ethics. It has become a civil rights issue, an issue of social equality. Gays and
lesbians have successfully made the transition from a hidden minority viewed
as sexually deviant to a public minority viewed as civilly oppressed and

---

[23]His work began, of course, with *Rich Christians in an Age of Hunger*, 1st ed. (Downers Grove, IL: Inter-
Varsity Press, 1977).
[24]The ministries of countless organizations such as World Vision, Compassion International and Bread for
the World come to mind.

making deeply American demands for access to equal civil rights along with other minority groups in areas such as military service, employment non-discrimination and legal recognition of their intimate relationships.

Evangelicals, together with Mormons, and far more vocally than Catholics (even though all share a similar sexual ethic), have invested both dollars and political capital in increasingly unsuccessful efforts to block advances in gay rights. The tide is clearly turning in public opinion and politics in favor of gay rights, including gay marriage, though patterns differ regionally.[25] Those opposed to such advances are increasingly seen as retrograde, and are sometimes compared to those who opposed civil rights for black Americans in the 1960s. It is not at all unthinkable that the tide will turn to such an extent that evangelical institutions that continue to discriminate against gays will face our own *Bob Jones* moment, in which our posture on these issues will lead to our social and legal delegitimation and loss of access to federal tax-exempt status, with all of the associated symbolic and practical ramifications.[26] Meanwhile, as Gabe Lyons and David Kinnaman have shown, evangelical antigay rhetoric has increasingly cost us missionally and in the transmission of our faith to the next generation of our own children.[27]

Regardless of whether one is open to a reconsideration of Christian sexual ethics per se, many of the most important themes in Christian social ethics argue for evangelicals to reconsider our posture toward gay rights in society. Practical solidarity with the oppressed; radically inclusive kingdom community in Christ; a broad, holistic sacredness-of-life vision—these are among the reasons why I personally have never been willing to join antigay public policy efforts. We need to remember that everything we say and do about "gay issues" is heard by a national gay community; by gay Christians, hidden or out, in our churches and schools; by family members and friends who love gay people; and by impressionable straight Christians who sometimes have found authorization for hatred in our antigay rhetoric, even when we are not shouting. I personally recommend taking this issue off the agenda of evangelical

---

[25]See for example, Pew Research Center, "Changing Attitudes on Gay Marriage," Pew Forum on Religion and Public Life, June 2013, http://features.pewforum.org/same-sex-marriage-attitudes (accessed March 20, 2013).

[26]For *Bob Jones* case (1983), see "Bob Jones University v. U.S.," The Oyez Project at IIT Chicago-Kent College of Law, www.oyez.org/cases/1980-1989/1982/1982_81_3.

[27]David Kinnaman and Gabe Lyons, *unChristian* (Grand Rapids: Baker, 2007).

Christian social ethics, or even better, looking for areas in which we can stand in friendly solidarity with the efforts of the gay community, as in, for example, antibullying initiatives.[28]

Guns. Bullets pierce the fragile human bodies that God so fearfully and wonderfully made, wounding and killing those who are sacred in God's sight at a rate of nearly one thousand per month each year in our bloodstained country.[29]

There are at least two kinds of gun incidents that afflict US society in a profound and disproportionate way as compared to other parts of the world. There are first the handgun killings that take one or two lives daily in cities such as Chicago. The victims of these killings are mainly poor, urban, racial and ethnic minority citizens whose neighborhoods are deeply blighted by drugs, gangs, unemployment and violence. And then there are the mass shootings that have become so terribly ubiquitous, usually involving an alienated young white man with an assault weapon killing large numbers of innocent people in some supposedly safe public place like a school, mall or movie theater. And this is not to mention the daily suicides and domestic violence incidents and accidents that take so many lives among us.[30]

The only possible legitimate use of violent force is defensive. The Bible certainly offers grounds for suggesting that the responsibility for such legitimate defensive force belongs to the state rather than individuals (see Rom 13:1-7). The Second Amendment right to bear arms is not in the Bible, not even in Leviticus. Most people in the 34 percent of US households that possess firearms intend them for defensive and recreational purposes.[31] But so often these purposes are shattered: when a depressed person kills herself; when an angry person kills his perhaps estranged lover; when a homicidal-suicidal young man decides to make some sick kind of social statement at a school or church.

We are afflicted by a gun culture, perhaps traceable to our Revolutionary War roots and our Wild West heritage. We love our guns and we associate

---

[28]See www.itgetsbetter.org. It has swept the nation. Do evangelicals really want to oppose antibullying initiatives?

[29]For documentation of this and other terrifying statistics, see "Statistics on Gun Deaths & Injuries," Law Center to Prevent Gun Violence, November 16, 2012, http://smartgunlaws.org/gun-deaths-and-injuries -statistics.

[30]One authoritative organization is the Coalition to Stop Gun Violence. See www.csgv.org.

[31]Sabrina Tavernise and Robert Gebeloff, "Share of Homes With Guns Shows 4-Decade Decline," *The New York Times,* March 9, 2013, www.nytimes.com/2013/03/10/us/rate-of-gun-ownership-is-down -survey-shows.html?pagewanted=all&_r=0.

them with self-defense, justice and virility. The more we kill each other with guns the more guns we buy to secure ourselves,[32] and thus the more guns we make available for further suicides, murders, accidents and rages.

Christians surely can do better than this. Surely the sacredness of life, basic social justice and the demands of peace lead us away from rather than toward an adoration of guns or trust in guns for our security. Surely we can stand in solidarity with the thousands of victims of gun violence and against the gun makers and their lobby in Washington and state capitals. There is a deep cultural sickness here that we must address as Christians. Surely Christians should stand in support both of cultural change and of commonsense gun-control measures such as stricter background checks examining both criminal and mental-health records, banning straw purchasing, mandating smaller gun magazines, and limiting military-style weapons in private hands.

Immigration. Approximately 11 million human beings, primarily but not exclusively from Latin America, live illegally in the shadows of American society because they came here without documents or stayed here beyond the time permitted or perhaps were brought here as children by their parents. Many serve in the underground economy, doing jobs that Americans do not want to do. They have no legal rights and live in fear of arrest and deportations that shatter their families. Most came here because they simply wanted a better life.

For at least a decade policymakers have been attempting to solve the illegal immigration problem, with solutions ranging from a proposed mass deportation to various legalization plans. Currently the winds are blowing in a favorable direction for a relatively humane solution. A comprehensive plan involving a path to citizenship for illegal immigrants, together with efforts to block further illegal immigration and assimilate undocumented immigrants into US economic and political life, is gaining bipartisan steam. Evangelicals are to be commended, across the left-center-right political spectrum to a very large extent, for supporting comprehensive immigration reform.[33] Perhaps this is the year that such a law will be passed, and if so, evangelicals will have

---

[32]The more gun killings in America, the more we buy guns. See Nick Carey, "Background Checks for Gun Purchases Up Since Newtown Massacre: FBI Data," Reuters, January 28, 2013, www.reuters.com/article/2013/01/29/us-usa-guns-fbi-checks-idUSBRE90S01J20130129.

[33]See the astonishing breadth of the coalition assembled at the Evangelical Immigration Table, which I support, http://evangelicalimmigrationtable.com.

played a significant role, as part of a broader coalition of religious, civic, human rights, business and law enforcement officials.

This is an issue where Christian insights genuinely make a difference. We know that this world's classification of nation-states and their borders is not ultimate. We know that earthly citizenship matters greatly to nation-states but really very little in the context of the reign of God. We know that we are called to stand with the oppressed, with those in the shadows, with those hungry, afraid and powerless, and we find that illegal immigrants quite often dwell exactly there. We know that each and every human life is sacred, and so we are not easily persuaded by language crudely differentiating "illegals" from the rest of us good regular-citizen types. We are moved by the experience of inclusive, border-crossing community, as when illegal immigrants worship with native Christians in worship services directed toward the God of the Hebrew refugees and our refugee Savior Jesus and his parents. Let us continue to fight the good fight on this issue, making use of electoral realities and leverage where needed but Christian principles always.

Torture. In March 2013 a blue-ribbon panel called the Detainee Treatment Taskforce, organized out of the Constitution Project in Washington, reported to the nation the results of our three-year inquiry into the US treatment of suspected terrorist detainees since the Clinton years.[34] I am on this panel, perhaps culminating my efforts to oppose detainee abuse by the United States, which began with a cover story in *Christianity Today* in February 2006 called "Five Reasons Why Torture Is Always Wrong."[35]

After much further study, the facts remain clear: The United States was threatened by non-state terrorists who targeted civilians. These terrorists did real and terrible damage, of course, most horribly in the 9/11 attacks. Policymakers were rightly aware of their responsibility for preventing and deterring future attacks. In wars in Iraq and Afghanistan, and in global antiterror operations, the US Government detained tens of thousands of suspected terrorists. In contravention of US law, international law and our treaty obligations, we abused many of these suspected terrorists and crossed the line to torture in a number of cases. This happened sometimes when soldiers and

---

[34]See detaineetaskforce.org.
[35]David P. Gushee, "Five Reasons Torture Is Always Wrong," *Christianity Today*, February 1, 2006, www .christianitytoday.com/ct/2006/february/23.32.html.

intelligence officers went beyond policy, but also when they attempted to follow interrogation policy as revised by the White House. The bulk of the abuses occurred at the hands of the CIA and its contractors, but responsibility for the revised policies goes to the top of the US government. A primary way in which abuses and torture were justified was by a strategy of euphemism, in which a combination of abusive and torturous techniques was authorized under the term "enhanced interrogation."

Most Christians accept the defensive role of government as authorized in a text like Romans 13. But too many Christians uncritically believed government and popular arguments that the demands of national defense in this "new kind of war"[36] justified extreme and abusive measures that most international and many fair-minded domestic observers would classify as torture. Evangelicals polled as more open to the legitimation of torture than people of other faiths or no faith.[37] I consider this the most distressing polling result that I have ever seen in my thirty-four years as a Christian and the most compelling reason I have ever encountered to renounce my connection to the American evangelical community. I continue to urge us to resist in the strongest possible manner any resort to torture or any moral legitimation of torture from anyone, even if they call it "enhanced interrogation." This debate continues in public life. Surely it should have been conclusively decided among us long ago.

US war making. We are coming near the end of twelve years of war in Afghanistan. We have just passed the ten-year anniversary of our invasion and former occupation of Iraq. The public debate about US war making is shifting away from ground invasions to the propriety of technologically advanced drone warfare. Defense spending cuts in the context of a massive budget deficit may constrain the freedom of US policymakers to pursue aggressive military engagement around the world, though we still have 1.4 million US troops in over 150 nations,[38] we patrol the seas, and we have a $700 billion

---

[36]A phrase commonly used to describe the post–9/11 situation, as in this speech by then Defense Secretary Donald Rumsfeld: "A New Kind of War," U.S. Department of Defense, September 27, 2001, www.defense .gov/speeches/speech.aspx?speechid=440.

[37]Pew Research Center Analysis, "Religious Dimensions of the Torture Debate," Pew Forum for Religion and Public Life, May 7, 2009, www.pewforum.org/Politics-and-Elections/The-Religious-Dimensions-of -the-Torture-Debate.aspx.

[38]"US Troops Around the World," Associated Press, February 22, 2013, http://bigstory.ap.org/article/ us-troops-around-world.

military budget, larger than the next ten nations combined.[39] It can hardly be said that as of now the United States has rolled back its massive military presence terribly far.

In retrospect, the twentieth century created the conditions for the United States to become an expansive military power and to create a bloated national security apparatus. We entered World War I very late and contributed to Allied victory with relatively minimal losses. We entered World War II late, and contributed again to Allied victory, with much larger losses. We entered immediately into a global ideological-geopolitical battle with the Soviet Union in which proxy wars and covert operations played a very large part. We built the Pentagon, the CIA, the National Security Agency and undoubtedly a dozen clandestine services whose names we don't yet know. The power to wage war became increasingly centered in the executive branch, the Constitution notwithstanding. A volunteer (i.e., paid) military after Vietnam localized the human costs of war to a tiny sliver of our population, now significantly traumatized after the wars of this past decade. The near-seamless transition from a war on communism to a war on Islamist terror reinforced in us the habit of permanent war, open or clandestine. Our vast size and economic prosperity enabled us to afford a global military presence and massive national security bureaucracy with little difficulty. And we were convinced that all our operations were good and just.

Christians have the theological and ethical resources to question all of this, but most evangelicals were generally rather uncritical, the evangelical left excluded. If our leaders told us it was time to fight, we fought. We provided and still provide a disproportionate number of US foot soldiers and chaplains.[40] With notable exceptions, especially in leaders such as Glen Stassen, we did not strongly protest the nuclear arms race, with its threat of mass global death. The Christian Right identified the US cause with God's cause and saw no problem with supporting constant US military engagements. Perhaps we lacked the critical distance to see the United States the way others did; international evangelicals provided dissonant observations, but we were not always receptive.

---

[39]"The U.S. spent more on defense in 2012 than did the countries with the next 10 highest defense budgets," Peter G. Peterson Foundation, April 12, 2013, www.pgpf.org/Chart-Archive/0053_defense-comparison.
[40]See www.instituteforscienceandhumanvalues.net/articles/religious%20discrimination%20military.htm (accessed March 20, 2013).

The challenge today is for evangelical Americans to lead the way in helping wean our nation off of its global pride and hegemony; in gradually unraveling the national security bureaucracy and shrinking the size of the military; in restoring greater democratic accountability to national decision making about war, including questioning the use of drones; and in denormalizing the permanent war footing that has come to characterize our way of life.

Women's rights. I applaud the discovery of human trafficking issues by evangelicals and the strong role groups such as International Justice Mission have played in fighting child and sex slavery here and around the world.[41] Our newfound passion on trafficking provides an entrée into broader global women's rights issues if we will follow the thread of our own commitments.

While we evangelicals were (are) fighting over whether women could be youth pastors, or maybe non-ordained youth directors doing everything youth pastors do without the title, we were mainly missing global women's rights concerns such as honor killings, bride burnings, sex-selective abortions, neglect and infanticide of female babies and children, lack of access to basic health care for women, easily preventable maternal mortality, gender-based violence against women, and lack of women's control over decisions such as whether and with whom to have sex, to marry and to have children. Our more recent discovery of sex slavery ought to lead us into an engagement with the wider range of human rights violations against women and the very many ways in which women continue to be treated as less than fully human in many places in the world.[42]

This in turn should lead to a reconsideration of what still remains a common cause of disdain from women's rights or feminist movements among many evangelicals, and a turn toward appreciation for those who have flown the flag of a genuinely evangelical feminism over the past three decades.[43] When we learn about women who are routinely raped during war, or married against their will, or sold into sex slavery, or are unable to get their AIDS-infected husband to wear a condom during sex, or are denied access to an education or the ability to own property, or cannot get decent medical

---

[41]See ijm.org.

[42]One indispensable source is Nicholas D. Kristof and Sheryl WuDunn, *Half the Sky* (New York: Vintage Books, 2009).

[43]Congratulations to Christians for Biblical Equality for their leadership: www.cbeinternational.org.

care while delivering babies, perhaps we will be motivated to reconsider the gains that the feminist movement has won for women here—our mothers, sisters, wives and daughters.

Clearly, it is difficult to simultaneously oppose abortion on demand and support a global women's rights movement that often supports legal abortion, but it is possible, and I understand that when I attend the Women Deliver conference in Kuala Lumpur in May 2013 I will meet many women's rights activists who take precisely this position.[44] I call on evangelicals to become informed about the broad range of women's rights issues around the world and to engage these in the name of the sacred worth of every person in God's sight.

CHRISTIAN HOPE AND PUBLIC WITNESS

I believe in a Christian public witness that stands in costly practical solidarity with those who are marginalized and trampled on, whatever their gender, skin color, nationality, citizenship status or sexual orientation. I seek a Christian public witness that seeks to participate in Christ's kingdom of deliverance, justice, peace, healing, reconciled community, joy and divine presence. I hope for a winsome and holistic Christian public witness of broad range and political and ideological independence. I yearn for Christians to advance a comprehensive vision of the sacred worth of each and every human being in God's sight.

In advancing such Christian public witness we will partner with others of good will and similar goals, whether evangelical or not, Christian or not. We will work for the common good and a renewed world and not for Christian privilege or cultural hegemony. We will demonstrate love for our nation but always a critical patriotism. We will be grateful for democracy but aware of its vulnerability and its particular problems in any given moment and context. We will know that our public words have little credibility apart from our ecclesial practices and integral discipleship. We will pay attention to voices from outside our land in order to help us see our context more clearly and live more faithfully. And we will remain calm, steadily pursuing our public witness, trusting in God's sovereignty and the certainty that the kingdoms of this world will one day become the kingdom of our God and of his Christ.

---

[44]See womendeliver.org.

For after all:

Then I saw a new heaven and a new earth; for the first heaven and the first earth had passed away, and the sea was no more. And I saw the holy city, the new Jerusalem, coming down out of heaven from God, prepared as a bride adorned for her husband. And I heard a loud voice from the throne saying,

> "See, the home of God is among mortals.
> He will dwell with them;
> they will be his peoples,
> and God himself will be with them;
> he will wipe every tear from their eyes.
> Death will be no more;
> mourning and crying and pain will be no more,
> for the first things have passed away." (Rev 21:1-4 NRSV)

12

"You Are in the World but Not of It"

David Gitari†

In the Gospel of John chapter 17, which contains Jesus' High Priestly Prayer for his disciples, Jesus says, "I do not ask that you take them out of the world, but that you keep them from the evil one. They are not of the world, just as I am not of the world. Sanctify them in the truth; your word is truth. As you sent me into the world, so I have sent them into the world" (Jn 17:15-18).[1] These verses may be summarized by the statement that Christians are "in the world but not of it." This provides a good starting point for the general theme of this twenty-second Wheaton Theology Conference. Following the example of our Lord Jesus Christ, the Christian is called *to live for the kingdom of God and at the same time to be involved in the affairs of this world in which we live.*

Yet this formulation hardly resolves all practical questions. As John Gladwin has argued, Christians throughout the centuries have wrestled with discerning the level of political commitment that faithfulness demands.[2] Even in the early church, the Thessalonian Christians' expectation of Christ's imminent return prompted such a detached posture toward the world that they gave up working. The Corinthians, on the other hand, took their freedom in Christ as permission for all manner of indulgence. Paul rejected both extremes.

Martin Luther struggled with this issue, and he thought he resolved the problem by his concept of two kingdoms. The kingdom of heaven, the church,

---

[1]Unless otherwise noted, Scripture quotations in this chapter are from the ESV.
[2]In what follows, I depend heavily on John Gladwin, *God's People in God's World: Biblical Motives for Social Involvement* (Downers Grove, IL: InterVarsity Press, 1980), pp. 11-15.

is to proclaim the good news of Jesus Christ. The kingdom of the world pro-vides social and political stability by instituting laws and restraining evil. The distinction between these two kingdoms and their tasks is fundamental. In Gladwin's words, "If the church interferes in the political order it goes beyond its role of providing the community's preacher. Its sole business is the Good News. In like manner the state has no responsibility for preaching. It is there to make laws and, thereby, to restrain evil in the community. It is essential that these two roles be kept separate."[3]

John Calvin did not distinguish as clearly between church and state. Calvin defended the church's authority to discipline and punish its members, and thus play a role in enacting and enforcing laws. Calvin's concern was the question of how Christians must view and relate to the state. He rejected the view of Ana-baptists that the state is unclean and therefore Christians must abstain from any contact with lawmakers. As Justo Gonzalez has described Calvin's position, "The state is created by God and it is he that has called its magistrates to their function, which is to serve divine justice. As a result, the state has the legitimate right to impose the penalty of death, to raise taxes, and to wage just and nec-essary wars."[4] The Reformed tradition extends the lordship of Christ over the state, and thus calls the community to act for Christ's kingdom. In contrast, Lutherans do not consider the state to bear such responsibilities.

In the English Reformation, the state came to govern the church. Acts of Parliament could initiate reforms and establish doctrines with only reluctant affirmation by church convocations. According to Hooker's *Laws of Ecclesias-tical Polity*, the convocations represented the clergy and Parliament repre-sented the laity. Society was both political and ecclesiastical, it was thought, and both elements should be ruled by a common authority. This perspective even resulted in the dissolution of the convocations for more than a hundred years in the eighteenth century. The Church of England has thus conferred on laity considerable power through civil political arrangements. Despite a good number of reforms, the state has significant control over the church. The Church of England is nationally established and Her Majesty the Queen ap-points bishops after consultation with the Church. The twenty-five most senior bishops by consecration are Members of Parliament.

---

[3]Ibid., p. 13.
[4]Justo L. Gonzalez, *A History of Christian Thought*, vol. 3 (Nashville: Abington Press, 1975), p. 158.

THE BOSSEY STATEMENT OF CHURCH AND STATE RELATIONS

In August 1976 a conference on church-state relations was organized by the World Council of Churches and the Ecumenical Institute of Bossey, Switzerland. The conference provided a useful outline of four possible attitudes of churches toward political powers.

1. The churches adapt themselves actively when they identify themselves with the goals and intentions of the powers of the state.

2. The churches adapt themselves passively when they withdraw into a sphere of purely religious rigidity and abstain from any political involvement.

3. The churches engage in critical and constructive collaboration with the powers of the state by evaluating, on the basis of their understanding of the gospel, political decisions and proposed programs.

4. The churches may be led to resist the power of the state. The obligation to resist that may arise under certain circumstances has no destructive intentions. The attitude of resistance will be adopted to serve society and even the state because the state as well is called to be the servant of God and the people.[5]

The first category of churches, which adapt themselves actively by identifying themselves with the goals and intentions of the state, take a very dangerous position. When the government is overthrown by military coups d'état the church suffers together with the state it supported. The best example I have is that of Ethiopia. The Coptic Church of Ethiopia worked very closely with the government of Emperor Haile Salassie. The closeness of the church and state was symbolized by the fact that the throne of the emperor and that of the head of the Coptic Church were placed side by side in St. George's Cathedral in Addis Ababa. When the communists came to power they killed both the emperor and the head of the Coptic Church.

Second, there are those churches that adapt themselves passively when they withdraw into the sphere of the purely religious and abstain from any political involvement. That is also a very dangerous position for the church to

---

[5]John S. Mbiti, ed., *African and Asian Contributions to Contemporary Theology: Report of Consultation Held at the World Council of Churches Ecumenical Institute Bossey* (Céligny, Switzerland: Ecumenical Institute, 1977).

take. Such churches should be reminded that even silence is a political decision. Members of the East Africa Revival Movement adopted this passive attitude in Uganda and other East African countries and were totally uninterested in politics. So when Idi Amin took power, he overthrew the government of Milton Obote in the early 1970s. The Christians were so naive that they even offered prayers at Navuiremve Cathedral to thank God for the coming of Idi Amin. Before long, Idi Amin, a Muslim, started persecuting Christians, which culminated in the assassination of Jenani Luxum, the Anglican archbishop of Uganda. In a country where 80 percent of the population considered itself Christian, the majority was not interested in politics. So this 80 percent allowed itself to have a Muslim dictator. The consequences of this were bad for the state and for the church.

Third, the Bossey conference stated that some churches engage in a critical and constructive relationship with the state by evaluating political decisions and proposed programs on the basis of their understanding of the gospel. In this case the church can praise and support the government when its activities are in accordance with the gospel of Christ. When the state makes decisions that contradict the gospel, the church can directly and courageously criticize the government. The government is likely to listen to those criticisms because the church has been working with the state in the programs that are not contrary to the gospel.

Finally, the churches may be led to resist the power of the state. If the *powers that be* become autocratic and ignore universal human rights, the church may do all it can to resist such a state. During the struggle against apartheid in South Africa it was mainly the church, led by Bishop Desmond Tutu, that opposed apartheid. It led the struggle for liberation, and eventually South Africa became free from apartheid. Taking arms to fight autocratic regimes should only be done when all other means of bringing the desired political change have failed. A good example of disobeying authorities is when the disciples Peter and John, were ordered by the Sanhedrin not to preach in the name of Jesus. They answered, "Shall we obey God or you?" (see Acts 4:19). This may be called holy defiance.

A CALL TO SOCIAL-POLITICAL INVOLVEMENT

This gives me the opportunity to share with you my own experience in seeking to understand the church-state relationship. I was brought up in a conservative evangelical tradition, shaped by missionaries that the Church Missionary Society (CMS) of England sent to my part of Kenya. The missionaries came from a conservative evangelical tradition in the Anglican Church. CMS discouraged Christians from being involved in politics. This discouragement was enhanced by the East African Revival, which began in Rwanda in the early 1930s and quickly spread to Uganda, Kenya, Tanzania and Burundi. The movement has for the last eight decades challenged sinners to accept Jesus Christ as their personal Savior in preparation for his coming again.

However, the East African Revival has been an inward-looking spiritual movement concerned more about the kingdom to come than about participating in the kingdom that Jesus Christ came to inaugurate here on earth. Christians are so concerned with their own individual souls that they show no concern for the corrupt and sinful world around them, except to invite sinners to come out of "the sinking ship" and join "the lifeboat" of the brethren. They have discouraged those who are born again from getting involved in politics. The movement fits well in the second position of the Bossey conference.

These are the two backgrounds I have come from. I went to study theology at Tyndale Hall in Bristol, England, a college committed to the conservative evangelical position. The syllabus did not include instruction on church and politics. When I was ordained a priest and consecrated a bishop, I struggled to understand my ministry as a priest and bishop in a country ruled by an imperial and autocratic president who cared little about justice.

Just before I became a bishop I was privileged to attend and participate in the International Congress on World Evangelization held at Lausanne, Switzerland, in July 1974. The congress, whose theme was, "Let the Earth Hear His Voice," was sponsored by Dr. Billy Graham and was attended by 2,700 participants from various parts of the world. At the end of the congress we agreed on a Lausanne Covenant, which was edited by John Stott. The covenant has a clause on Christian social responsibility that reads:

> We affirm that God is both the Creator and the Judge of all men. We therefore should share his concern for justice and reconciliation throughout human society and for the liberation of men and women from every kind of oppression. Because men and women are made in the image of God, every person, regardless of race, religion, color, culture, class, sex or age, has an intrinsic dignity

because of which he or she should be respected and served, not exploited. Here too we express penitence both for our neglect and for having sometimes regarded evangelism and social concern as mutually exclusive. Although reconciliation with other people is not reconciliation with God, nor is social action evangelism, nor is political liberation salvation, nevertheless we affirm that evangelism and socio-political involvement are both part of our Christian duty. . . . The message of salvation implies also a message of judgment upon every form of alienation, oppression and discrimination, and we should not be afraid to denounce evil and injustice wherever they exist.[6]

I left Lausanne with much joy that evangelicals all over the world had at last repented for having put a wedge between evangelism and social responsibility. After the Lausanne Congress, it became necessary for conservative evangelicals to define the relationship between evangelism and social responsibility. Again, I was privileged to attend a consultation held in June 1982 at Reformed Bible College in Grand Rapids, Michigan, and attended by fifty theologians. The consultation concluded that there are three relationships between evangelism and social responsibility that are equally valid.

1. Christian social concern is a consequence of evangelism.

2. Christian social concern can be a bridge to evangelism.

3. Christian social concern should be a partner of evangelism.

Soon after becoming a bishop of the church, I found it necessary to study the biblical foundation and justification for Christians to be involved not only in evangelism but also in social-political issues. My conviction is that the church should be involved in social-political activities. My position is based on five doctrines: the doctrine of creation, the doctrine of humanity, the doctrine of the incarnation, the doctrine of the kingdom of God, and the ministry of the Old Testament prophets. I unfortunately cannot go into great detail of my study on these five doctrines, but they are the ones that give me the encouragement to feel that it was quite an honor for a conservative evangelical to be involved in the politics and political demonstrations of Kenya. I would then like to give some concrete examples of our involvement in political activities in our country.

---

[6]"The Lausanne Covenant," The Lausanne Movement, accessed December 4, 2013, www.lausanne.org/en/documents/lausanne-covenant.html.

DOCTRINES FOR SOCIAL-POLITICAL INVOLVEMENT

The doctrine of creation. The story of creation in the book of Genesis portrays God as the one who "lets be." "And God said, 'Let there be light,' and there was light" (Gen 1:3). God is the one who says, "Let there be," and whatever he wishes comes in existence. God the creator can therefore be called "He who lets be." As John Macquarrie has put it, this "letting-be" is God's conferral of being on what he creates, and it is an expression of both his creativity and his love. God did not create the universe and then abandon it. He continues to sustain his creation by letting be. The creatures that God has made are in turn called to participate in God's creativity. "Thus the fullest imitation of or participation in God comes about when the creature in turn 'lets be.' . . . Living beings which produce themselves participate in 'letting-be' more than do inanimate things; but on a far higher level is man who, with his capacity—however limited—for creativity and love brings the 'imitation' of God to an altogether new level, that of free co-operation in letting-be."[7]

The climax of God's creation was the creation of human beings. "Then God said, 'Let us make man in our image . . . and let them have dominion over the fish of the sea and over the birds of the heavens and over the livestock and over all the earth and over every creeping thing that creeps on the earth'" (Gen 1:26). As Alan Richardson has noted, the doctrine of the *imago Dei* taught in this passage shows that humanity is created in the image of God and that humanity is supposed to have dominion over all creation. "When the image is obscured, then the dominion is impaired; when the image is restored, the dominion is fulfilled."[8] Humankind was created in God's image so that they could cooperate with God not only in "letting be" but also in caring for what God has created.

It should be noted that God did not say the dominion over all creation was reserved only to certain sections of humanity. It was not the male who was told to have dominion over the earth—it was both male and female. It was not politicians alone who were given dominion over creation—this dominion belongs to all human beings. Politicians left on their own have sometimes made decisions that have devastated creation, and their actions have demonstrated the reality of the doctrine of the fall. Politicians and those who rule

[7]John Macquarrie, *Principles of Christian Theology*, 2nd ed. (New York City: Scribner, 1977), p. 225.
[8]Alan Richardson, *Genesis 1-11*, Torch Bible Commentaries (London: SCM Press, 1953), p. 56.

must be reminded that though humanity is the Lord's creation and ruler of nature, this must not be taken as a personal right. Rather they should see themselves as God's vicegerents, responsible to God in their stewardship. Otherwise, as Richardson says, "[humans'] science and industry will bring not a blessing but a curse; they will make of the earth not a paradise but a dust-bowl or a Hiroshima. When we survey human history and review the sad spectacle of man's age-long effort to subdue the earth to his own ends and not to God's glory, we understand that the divine image in man is indeed defaced."[9] With this understanding church leaders have every right to remind decision makers that the earth belongs to God (Ps 24:1). God has appointed human beings (not politicians only) to be the stewards of creation and to exercise proper accountability in their stewardship.

The doctrine of humanity. The creation story clearly shows that God's purpose in creating man was not to leave him as a lonely creature, but to make him a social being. Thus God says, "I will make him a helper fit for him" (Gen 2:18). This is because God himself is social and the decision to create humans in Genesis 1:26 is introduced with plural words, "Let us make man in our image, after our likeness." As Christopher Wright puts it, "The first fact about this 'image of God' that the text immediately notes is our sexuality, that complementary duality in unity, from which flows the rest of our social nature: marriage, parenthood, family, kinship and outwards in widening circles."[10]

> God, therefore, in the mystery of the Trinity, lives in the harmonious relationship of equal Persons, each of whom possesses his proper function, authority and relatedness to each of the others. Human beings, therefore, made in God's image, were created to live in the harmony of personal equality but with social organization that required functional structures and patterns of relationship. The ordering of social relationships and structures, locally, nationally and globally, is of direct concern to our Creator God, then. But such ordering is precisely the stuff of politics. The Bible, therefore, makes no unnatural separation between "politics" and "religion," though neither does it identify them. Both are essential dimensions of what it is to be human.[11]

---

[9]Ibid., p. 55.
[10]Christopher J. H. Wright, *Old Testament Ethics for the People of God* (Downers Grove, IL: InterVarsity Press, 2004), p. 214.
[11]Ibid., p. 215.

Humans are worshipers and at the same time political animals, for God made
us so.

The doctrine of the incarnation. The third justification for our involvement
in social-political activities is the example of our Lord Jesus Christ, "who,
though he was in the form of God, did not count equality with God a thing to
be grasped, but emptied himself, by taking the form of a servant, being born
in the likeness of men. And being found in human form, he humbled himself
by becoming obedient to the point of death, even death on a cross" (Phil
2:6-8). The prologue to the Gospel of John declares: "And the Word became
flesh and dwelt among us, full of grace and truth; we have beheld his glory,
glory as of the only Son from the Father" (Jn 1:14 RSV). The Logos that had
existed before the world was created and that participated with God the Father
in the creation of all things now became flesh without losing the qualities of
the Logos in any way. The Word does not only become human but also dwells
among human beings. The phrase "and dwelt among us" emphasizes that he
really shared our human lot by taking residence in our midst. The writer of
Hebrews also begins his letter by introducing his own form of incarnational
theology. "In many and various ways God spoke of old to our fathers by the
prophets; but in these last days he has spoken to us by a Son, whom he
appointed the heir of all things, through whom also he created the world"
(Heb 1:1-2 RSV).

In the days gone by, God spoke to people in many and various ways—
visions, angels, prophets and so forth. The prophets spoke with God's authority against injustice and other evils and were often mistreated as a result.
As Donald Guthrie says, "Their stories make heroic reading but what they said
was incomplete. The writer knows that it needed a better method of commu-
nication, and he recognizes that this has come in Jesus Christ."[12] The essence
of Christian revelation is that God himself has now spoken in his Son because
Jesus Christ perfectly shows all that is knowable about the Father. In days gone
by God was speaking by the mouth of agents. But in these last days God has
spoken in a much superior way—by his own Son. To see the Son and to hear
him is to see God and to hear God: "Whoever has seen me has seen the Father"
(Jn 14:9). By the coming of Jesus to this world, God himself has come on the

---

[12]Donald Guthrie, *Hebrews*, Tyndale New Testament Commentaries (Grand Rapids: Eerdmans, 1983),
p. 62.

stage of human history, not to be a spectator but to be deeply involved in the affairs of men and women. Jesus has come on the stage of human history to confront men and women with the very message of God himself and with a challenge to accept or reject it.

Jesus assumed human form and took up residence in this world, prepared to take part as a perfect being in every sphere of life, with the hope of bringing salvation to the world. In his earthly life Jesus did not live in the ivory tower of meditative asceticism like the Qumran community or the early Christian monks. He went out into every city and every village, as Matthew tells us: "And Jesus went throughout all the cities and villages, teaching in their synagogues and proclaiming the gospel of the kingdom and healing every disease and every affliction" (Mt 9:35).

By going where people were, Jesus was able to see with his own eyes the plight of the people and to make statements that the politicians of the day would have considered highly political and provocative. "When he saw the crowds, he had compassion for them, because they were harassed and helpless, like sheep without a shepherd" (Mt 9:36). The crowds he saw were harassed politically as they were under Roman colonialism, they were harassed economically as the rich were making themselves richer at the expense of the poor, and they were harassed religiously as the Pharisees were putting unbearable burdens on the people. "They tie up heavy burdens, hard to bear, and lay them on people's shoulders, but they themselves are not willing to move them with their finger" (Mt 23:4).

The incarnate Lord seeing all this harassment could not help being moved by compassionate pity—the kind of pity that touches the core of one's being. He could not be moved by such compassion and remain the same. He had to take the necessary action to help the helpless—to feed the hungry, heal the sick, cast out demons and challenge the status quo. "Woe to you, scribes and Pharisees, hypocrites! For you tithe mint and dill and cumin, and have neglected the weightier matters of the law: justice and mercy and faithfulness. These you ought to have done, without neglecting the others. You blind guides, straining out a gnat and swallowing a camel!" (Mt 23:23-24). The Pharisees and Sadducees of the day had been "so concerned to apply the tithing law in respect of every garden herb that justice, mercy and faith were ignored."[13]

The doctrine of the incarnation expresses the reality that Jesus "'emptied himself' and chose to 'become flesh' and 'to live among us,'" thus identifying himself with humanity.[14] This demands our Christian presence in the world so that we may be able not only to evangelize but also to be involved in every aspect of human life. "The Incarnational Model . . . invites us to proclaim the Gospel not from a distance but rather by penetrating communities and cultures," cities and villages, so that we can see for ourselves the harassment and helplessness of God's people and stand in solidarity with them, even if that means taking a political stand to bring hope to humanity.[15]

The doctrine of the kingdom of God. The doctrine of the kingdom of God demonstrates how the incarnate son of God got deeply involved in the affairs of the world, be they economic, political, social or spiritual. The Synoptic Gospels are all agreed that the main theme of the preaching of Jesus was the kingdom of God. The Gospel of Mark tells us that after the arrest of John the Baptist, Jesus went into Galilee preaching the gospel of God and saying "the time is fulfilled, and the kingdom of God is at hand; repent and believe in the gospel" (Mk 1:15). Jesus was convinced that he had an obligation to preach the kingdom of God because it was for that purpose that he came to this world (see Lk 4:43). As Ron Sider has put it:

> There is a growing consensus that, in striking contrast to contemporary Jewish thought, Jesus viewed the kingdom as both present and future. Jewish eschatology . . . looked forward to a supernatural convulsion when the Messiah would come to destroy Israel's national enemies in a bloody battle and initiate the new age of messianic peace. In Jewish expectation, there was a radical, almost total break, between the old age and the new messianic age. Jesus, on the other hand, taught that the messianic age had actually broken into the old age. Its powers were already at work in this old age in his person and work, even though the kingdom would come in its fullness only at the end of history.[16]

---

[13]R. T. France, *Matthew*, Tyndale New Testament Commentaries (Grand Rapids: Eerdmans, 1985), p. 328.

[14]David Gitari, "Evangelism and Culture," in *Proclaiming Christ in Christ's Way: Studies in Integral Mission*, ed. Vinay Samuel and Albrecht Hauser (Oxford: Regnum Books, 1989), p. 118.

[15]Ibid.

[16]Ronald F. Sider, "Christian Ethics and the Good News of the Kingdom," in *Proclaiming Christ in Christ's Way: Studies in Integral Mission*, ed. Vinay Samuel and Albrecht Hauser (Oxford: Regnum Books, 1989), pp. 127-28.

René Padilla goes further to emphasize that the central theme of the preaching of Jesus

> is not the hope of the coming of the kingdom at some predictable date in the future but the fact that in his own person and work the Kingdom is already present among men and women in great power.... The kingdom is God's dynamic power made visible through concrete signs pointing to him as the Messiah: "The blind receive sight, the lame walk, those who have leprosy are cured, and the good news is preached to the poor" (Luke 7:22). In other words, God in Christ is showing his passionate concern for the poor; a new eschatological reality is present in human history affecting human life not only morally and spiritually but also physically and psychologically, materially and socially.... The completion of God's purpose still lies in the future, but a foretaste of the eschaton is already possible.[17]

The ministry of the prophets. The fifth example of why we should be involved in politics is the ministry of prophets in the Old Testament. They were called by God to tell the rulers of Israel and other nations the message they had received from God. Some prophets such as Jeremiah were reluctant because they were young and did not know how to speak. But the Lord said to Jeremiah, "Do not say, 'I am only a youth'; for to all to whom I send you, you shall go" (Jer 1:7). He was sent "to pluck up and to break down, to destroy and to overthrow, to build and to plant" (Jer 1:10). Micah says,

> Woe to those who devise wickedness
>> and work evil on their beds!
> When the morning dawns, they perform it....
> They covet fields and seize them,
>> and houses, and take them away;
> they oppress a man and his house,
>> a man and his inheritance.
> Therefore thus says the LORD:
> behold, against this family I am devising disaster,
>> from which you cannot remove your necks. (Mic 2:1-3)

Of course the Old Testament prophets are a great inspiration, especially because of the courage that they had. They always begin by quoting what God

---

[17]C. René Padilla, "Politics of the Kingdom of God," in *Proclaiming Christ in Christ's Way: Studies in Integral Mission*, ed. Vinay Samuel and Albrecht Hauser (Oxford: Regnum Books, 1989), pp. 185-86.

has said. Once a prophet is sent to prophesy, he has no alternative but to go and say what God tells him. You cannot be a prophet if you are a coward, just as you cannot be a bishop who is a coward. A cowardly bishop is a contradiction in terms. So armed with this encouraging understanding of the Scriptures, and coming from the tradition of conservative evangelicals, I found sufficient courage to be able to prophesy in my own nation, Kenya.

"YOUR KINGDOM COME"

In Matthew 25, Jesus says that at the end of time those who will possess the kingdom of God are those who on this earth feed the hungry, give a drink to the thirsty, give hospitality to strangers, clothe the naked, care for the sick and visit those in prison. When God's will is done in response to the needs of the poor, the poor themselves have a taste of the kingdom, and those who respond to their needs qualify to be received into the kingdom to come. But note the cries of the present-day poor:

"I was hungry and you appointed a commission to inquire into my hunger."
"I was thirsty and you made Coca Cola to exploit my thirst."
"I was a stranger and you put a sign 'Mbwa Kali' ('beware fierce dog') at the
    entrance to your home."
"I was naked and you seemed to enjoy my nakedness and even took a
    photograph."
"I was sick with AIDS and you said you cannot visit a sinner."
"I was in detention without trial and you feared to visit me in case you'd lose
    your political position."

Because of your failure to respond to the needy around you, the Lord will say to you:

Depart from me, you cursed, into the eternal fire prepared for the devil and his angels. For I was hungry and you gave me no food, I was thirsty and you gave me no drink, I was a stranger and you did not welcome me, naked and you did not clothe me, sick and in prison and you did not visit me. (Mt 25:41-43)

The church has a vital role to play in the politics of a nation. To this end I have tried as much as possible to be actively involved in the politics of my country; though I have often been warned by politicians to "leave politics to politicians." I have never personally called a political rally in order to give a political address. Rather I have always confined myself to the Word of God, expounding it faithfully and systematically and applying the same to the prevailing political situation. As is commonly said, "truth hurts"—indeed it should because the word of God is like a double-edged sword. For this reason, in spite of hard times my diocese and I have undergone, we have not stopped declaring God's will for our nation. The struggle to uphold and to work for justice and peace must continue. I have challenged the authorities over the assassination of some of our powerful politicians. Tom Mboya, J. M. Kariuki, Robert Ouko—they were assassinated because they were very popular with the people of Kenya. In nearly every case the president feared that the people wanted to take power and change the status quo. The government said every stone will be turned to find the killers. I said some stones are too heavy to be turned. Though the government knew the killers, who were probably sent by the top authorities, and appointed commissions to investigate these crimes, the recommendations of the investigators have never been made public. I have every year challenged the government to make reports, but they have still never been public. When there is a crisis in Kenya the government appoints investigators to make people cool down and eventually forget the crime.

ASSASSINATIONS AND ELECTIONS

When I became a bishop, there were issues that were of great concern. I became a bishop in 1975 in one of the largest dioceses in Kenya. Two political assassinations had taken place. Tom Mboya, a very talented politician, was murdered in 1969. J. M. Kariuki was murdered in 1975. Robert Ouko was murdered later in 1990. In each of these political assassinations it was clear that the people behind the killing were very close to the current president.

I was asked by the Christian Council of Kenya to preach about the sanctity of human life based on our own national anthem: "Oh God of all creation bless this our land and nation, justice be our shield and defender and sword." And so I preached on national radio live sermons for six days, five minutes before the main news at seven o'clock in the morning. I touched on what I meant by the sanctity of human life. On the fourth day I was invited to meet with the officials of broadcasting in Kenya. When I went there I found a committee of seven people waiting for me. They kept me waiting for one hour.

When they called me in I said, "Good afternoon," and only one person answered me. Then the chairman said, "Your sermons this week are so disturbing to the whole nation." And I answered him, "If they are disturbing they have served their purpose, because the gospel of Christ is very disturbing, especially to sinners." Then I asked him, "What in particular is disturbing?" They had taken my script from earlier and read a phrase where I said "the cries of the blood of Abel have reached the heaven." This is what disturbed the Kenyans. "This is what I'm saying, Mr. Chairman," I replied. "Every human being is created in God's image and nobody should kill him or her. Mr. Chairman, you are created in God's image and no one should kill you. Mr. Vice Chairman, you are created in God's image and no one should kill you." And I went on down the line. And when I came to the end they said, "We have heard what you are saying, continue."

After these assassinations took place, commissions were appointed to investigate who the murderers were, but I'm sure those who appointed the commissions already knew who the murderers were. A lot of money was spent appointing commissions, and we have never been told the results of these commissions—the height of impunity in our country.

When Daniel arap Moi became president, he had a philosophy that he called in Swahili the *Nyayo* philosophy, or following the footsteps of his predecessor. It was given the meaning of peace, love and unity. These are three very important biblical desires. I studied the biblical meaning of those desires and wrote a book together with Enasis Kay for the National Christian Council of Kenya. Our conclusion was that Kenya was neither peaceful nor loving, and there was no unity. And when we published the book I sent a copy to President Daniel arap Moi in his statehouse.

Then in 1982 the constitution was changed so that Kenya became a *de jure* one-party state. Before that it was one party *de facto*. The constitution allowed for multiple parties, but after the first election the other parties dissolved themselves and joined the ruling party. Any attempt to start another party would have been quite legal, until June 1982 when Parliament passed a law to say there would be only one legal party, KANU (Kenya African National Union). And so we had to fight a battle to return to a multiparty democracy. The battle took ten years, but eventually we won. But President Moi was also very clever, especially in rigging elections. He discovered that the best way of rigging is voting with queues behind the candidate you want. No records were kept; you would simply go to see who had the longest queue. One candidate would have five, and another five thousand people. Then the radio would say that the one who had five won the election, and the one who had five thousand lost. This became the best way of rigging the election because you cannot check any records. The people who won the elections are the ones the president wanted, not the ones the people wanted. That is why my brother Bishop Henry Okullu says, "In the sixth parliament, 70 percent of parliamentarians were selected, not elected."

During this period I was chairman of the National Christian Council, and we fought against the queuing system. For more than ten years I was preaching against this every Sunday, and some people did not seem to be very happy with what I was doing. So one night in April 1989 my house was raided by thugs, and they had come with a mission to kill me. But my family and I climbed to the roof of my house and called neighbors, and these political thugs were chased away. The matter received national and international media attention. Moi was not happy with that, so he appointed a commission of inquiry into my problems. Within two hours of his announcing that he was appointing a commission, four policemen showed up. They started an investigation into my problem, and they must have given Moi a report. I was waiting for my report so that I could tell the whole world the truth. Eventually Moi retired the same year that I did, in 2002. I had told the nation the exact date that I would retire. Moi retired without telling me who it was that had come to kill me. But I'm still asking him, because he is still alive, to let me know who they were.

And so during this time, especially in the '80s, when everyone was silenced, only a few church leaders were willing to stand and challenge the government concerning the injustices that were going on. Some of the churches of course followed the other methods stated by Bossey: either they became passive, or they became supportive of the government whether it was doing what was right or not.

I advised the Anglican Church bishops not to identify themselves with any political party or to be too close to the president and politicians. Our relationship with powers that be should be like our relationship with fire. If you go too close to the fire you get burnt, and if you go too far away you will freeze.

Hence, stay in a strategic place so that you can be of help. You can support the authority, but when they become corrupt you can criticize fearlessly.

However, any Christian layman who wishes to join politics we should encourage and support. We should remind Christians in politics that they are the salt of the earth and light of the world. They should also encourage other Christian politicians to share the message of the good news of Jesus Christ. The laity are called to share this good news wherever they happen to be. It is also my view that church leaders who want to vie for elected political positions should first resign their leadership in the church.

SOCIAL WORK AND SOCIAL TRANSFORMATION

Now before I conclude my discussion, I would like to say that there is a big difference between social activity and social-political action. In Kenya when the churches do work in the core humanitarian activities, such as building hospitals and schools and feeding the hungry and refugees, the government is very happy and even congratulates us. But when churches ask the question, "Why is there hunger when there is enough food to feed every hungry stomach?" the government tells us that this is a political question that should not be the concern of the church. Whether they call it politics or not, we must continue asking, "Why is there hunger?" even if they say there is not enough food for everybody. Maybe food is not equally distributed and so on. So we must go beyond just humanitarian activities. We need to go to transformation, to the root cause of the problem.

There was a factory where many accidents were occurring every day. A well-intended humanitarian committee got very concerned about the many accidents. The committee discussed the matter and came to the conclusion that they could raise money to buy an ambulance and employ two nurses. The ambulance was placed outside the factory, and every time someone was injured he was rushed to the ambulance, given first aid and rushed to the hospital for further treatment. The ambulance would then come back for the next victim. This went on for a long time until a member of the committee asked why there were so many accidents in this factory. They resolved to enter the factory. Going in was taking political action. They were shocked to find that the factory was overcrowded and the machinery was very old. They decided to take political action. They reported the state of the factory to the authorities.

The authorities came and the factory was inspected and orders were made to provide for more space and new machinery. When the factory authorities took these steps, the accidents became minimal and the ambulance committee could be relocated to pursue more worthy humanitarian activities.

Providing an ambulance is a worthy endeavor, but seeking to find the real cause of the suffering is far more important. Those in authority welcome our humanitarian activities, but they do not like to hear the question "why," because that is a political question. So sometimes we need to go beyond social activities to transformation of societies to find where the root cause of the problem is—and this is taking political action. We cannot avoid social-political action when there is something that must be done.

CONCLUSION

Let me close by quoting Martin Niemöller, a prominent Lutheran pastor in Germany during the regime of Hitler. He said this:

> In Germany the Nazis came for communists,
> and I did not speak up
> because I was not a communist.
>
> They came for Jews,
> and I did not speak
> because I was not a Jew.
>
> Then they came for Labor Unionists,
> and I did not speak up
> because I was not a Labor Unionist.
>
> Then they came for the Catholics.
> And I was a Protestant,
> so I did not speak up.
>
> Then they came for me.
> By that time there was no one left
> to speak for anyone.[18]

In the name of the Father, the Son and the Holy Spirit, amen.

---

[18]Adapted from a speech delivered by Martin Niemöller on January 6, 1946.

Contributors

Daniel M. Bell Jr. is professor of theology and ethics at Lutheran Theological Southern Seminary.

Jana Marguerite Bennett is associate professor of theological ethics at the University of Dayton.

William T. Cavanaugh is professor of Catholic studies at DePaul University.

David Gitari† (1937-2013) was the third Primate and Archbishop of the Anglican Church of Kenya and Bishop of the Diocese of Nairobi.

Timothy G. Gombis is associate professor of New Testament at Grand Rapids Theological Seminary.

David P. Gushee is the Distinguished University Professor of Christian Ethics and director of the Center for Theology and Public Life at Mercer University.

Stanley Hauerwas is the Gilbert T. Rowe Professor Emeritus of Divinity and Law at Duke Divinity School.

George Kalantzis is associate professor of theology and director of the Wheaton Center for Early Christian Studies at Wheaton College.

Peter J. Leithart is pastor of Trinity Reformed Church in Moscow, Idaho, and senior fellow of theology at New Saint Andrews College.

Jennifer M. McBride is assistant professor of religion and Regents Chair of Ethics at Wartburg College.

Scot McKnight is professor of New Testament at Northern Seminary.

Mark A. Noll is the Francis A. McAnaney Professor of History at the University of Notre Dame.

Subject Index

Name Index

Scripture Index

Finding the Texbook You Need

The IVP Academic Textbook Selector
is an online tool for instantly finding the IVP books
suitable for over 250 courses across 24 disciplines.

www.ivpress.com/academic/textbookselector